Learning OpenCV 4
Vision with Python 3
Third Edition

Get to grips with tools, techniques, and algorithms for computer vision and machine learning

Joseph Howse
Joe Minichino

Packt>

BIRMINGHAM - MUMBAI

Learning OpenCV 4 Computer Vision with Python 3
Third Edition

Commissioning Editor: Richa Tripathi
Acquisition Editor: Alok Dhuri
Content Development Editor: Digvijay Bagul
Senior Editor: Rohit Singh
Technical Editor: Ketan Kamble
Copy Editor: Safis Editing
Project Coordinator: Francy Puthiry
Proofreader: Safis Editing
Indexer: Pratik Shirodkar
Production Coordinator: Shraddha Falebhai

First published: April 2013
Second edition: September 2015
Third edition: February 2020

Production reference: 1190220

Published by Packt Publishing Ltd.
Livery Place
35 Livery Street
Birmingham
B3 2PB, UK.

ISBN 978-1-78953-161-9

www.packt.com

I dedicate my work to Sam, Jan, Bob, Bunny, and the cats, who have been my lifelong guides and companions.

– Joseph Howse

Packt.com

Subscribe to our online digital library for full access to over 7,000 books and videos, as well as industry leading tools to help you plan your personal development and advance your career. For more information, please visit our website.

Why subscribe?

- Spend less time learning and more time coding with practical eBooks and Videos from over 4,000 industry professionals

- Improve your learning with Skill Plans built especially for you

- Get a free eBook or video every month

- Fully searchable for easy access to vital information

- Copy and paste, print, and bookmark content

Did you know that Packt offers eBook versions of every book published, with PDF and ePub files available? You can upgrade to the eBook version at www.packt.com and as a print book customer, you are entitled to a discount on the eBook copy. Get in touch with us at customercare@packtpub.com for more details.

At www.packt.com, you can also read a collection of free technical articles, sign up for a range of free newsletters, and receive exclusive discounts and offers on Packt books and eBooks.

Contributors

About the authors

Joseph Howse lives in a Canadian fishing village with four cats; the cats like fish, but they prefer chicken.

Joseph provides computer vision expertise through his company, Nummist Media. His books include *OpenCV 4 for Secret Agents, Learning OpenCV 4 Computer Vision with Python 3, OpenCV 3 Blueprints, Android Application Programming with OpenCV 3, iOS Application Development with OpenCV 3,* and *Python Game Programming by Example,* published by Packt.

> *I want to thank all the people who have shaped this book's three editions: the readers, my coauthor Joe Minichino, and the teams of editors, technical reviewers, and marketers. Above all, my family makes my work possible and I dedicate this book to them.*

Joe Minichino is an R&D labs engineer at Teamwork. He is a passionate programmer who is immensely curious about programming languages and technologies and constantly experimenting with them. Born and raised in Varese, Lombardy, Italy, and coming from a humanistic background in philosophy (at Milan's Università Statale), Joe has lived in Cork, Ireland, since 2004. There, he became a computer science graduate at the Cork Institute of Technology.

About the reviewer

Sri Manikanta Palakollu is an undergraduate student pursuing his bachelor's degree in computer science and engineering at SICET under JNTUH. He is a founder of the Open Stack Developer Community in his college. He started his journey as a competitive programmer. He loves to solve problems related to the data science field. His interests include data science, app development, web development, cyber security, and technical writing. He has published many articles on data science, machine learning, programming, and cyber security with publications such as Hacker Noon, freeCodeCamp, Towards Data Science, and DDI.

I would like to thank God Almighty for giving me the strength, knowledge, ability, and opportunity to review this book. I would like to express my deepest gratitude to my father, Basaveswara Rao, and mother, Vijaya Lakshmi, for everything that they have done for me. Special thanks to my friends and well-wishers for supporting me and to Packt Publishing for giving me the opportunity to review this book.

Packt is searching for authors like you

If you're interested in becoming an author for Packt, please visit `authors.packtpub.com` and apply today. We have worked with thousands of developers and tech professionals, just like you, to help them share their insight with the global tech community. You can make a general application, apply for a specific hot topic that we are recruiting an author for, or submit your own idea.

Table of Contents

Preface   1

Chapter 1: Setting Up OpenCV   7
  Technical requirements   8
  What's new in OpenCV 4   9
  Choosing and using the right setup tools   9
    Installation on Windows   10
      Using a ready-made OpenCV package   11
      Building OpenCV from source   11
    Installation on macOS   15
      Using Homebrew with ready-made packages   15
      Using Homebrew with your own custom packages   17
    Installation on Debian, Ubuntu, Linux Mint, and similar systems   17
      Using a ready-made OpenCV package   18
      Building OpenCV from source   19
    Installation on other Unix-like systems   21
  Running samples   22
  Finding documentation, help, and updates   23
  Summary   24

Chapter 2: Handling Files, Cameras, and GUIs   25
  Technical requirements   26
  Basic I/O scripts   26
    Reading/writing an image file   26
    Converting between an image and raw bytes   29
    Accessing image data with numpy.array   32
    Reading/writing a video file   34
    Capturing camera frames   36
    Displaying an image in a window   38
    Displaying camera frames in a window   39
  Project Cameo (face tracking and image manipulation)   41
  Cameo – an object-oriented design   42
    Abstracting a video stream with managers.CaptureManager   42
    Abstracting a window and keyboard with managers.WindowManager   48
    Applying everything with cameo.Cameo   49
  Summary   52

Chapter 3: Processing Images with OpenCV   53
  Technical requirements   53
  Converting images between different color models   54
    Light is not paint   55

Exploring the Fourier transform 55
HPFs and LPFs 56
Creating modules 60
Edge detection 60
Custom kernels – getting convoluted 62
Modifying the application 64
Edge detection with Canny 66
Contour detection 68
Bounding box, minimum area rectangle, and minimum enclosing circle 69
Convex contours and the Douglas-Peucker algorithm 73
Detecting lines, circles, and other shapes 75
Detecting lines 76
Detecting circles 77
Detecting other shapes 78
Summary 79

Chapter 4: Depth Estimation and Segmentation 81
Technical requirements 82
Creating modules 82
Capturing frames from a depth camera 83
Converting 10-bit images to 8-bit 85
Creating a mask from a disparity map 88
Modifying the application 89
Depth estimation with a normal camera 92
Foreground detection with the GrabCut algorithm 99
Image segmentation with the Watershed algorithm 103
Summary 106

Chapter 5: Detecting and Recognizing Faces 107
Technical requirements 108
Conceptualizing Haar cascades 108
Getting Haar cascade data 109
Using OpenCV to perform face detection 110
Performing face detection on a still image 111
Performing face detection on a video 113
Performing face recognition 117
Generating the data for face recognition 117
Recognizing faces 119
Loading the training data for face recognition 120
Performing face recognition with Eigenfaces 122
Performing face recognition with Fisherfaces 124
Performing face recognition with LBPH 125
Discarding results based on the confidence score 125
Swapping faces in the infrared 126
Modifying the application's loop 127

Masking a copy operation	130
Summary	133
Chapter 6: Retrieving Images and Searching Using Image Descriptors	135
Technical requirements	136
Understanding types of feature detection and matching	136
Defining features	137
Detecting Harris corners	137
Detecting DoG features and extracting SIFT descriptors	140
Anatomy of a keypoint	143
Detecting Fast Hessian features and extracting SURF descriptors	143
Using ORB with FAST features and BRIEF descriptors	145
FAST	146
BRIEF	147
Brute-force matching	147
Matching a logo in two images	148
Filtering matches using K-Nearest Neighbors and the ratio test	151
Matching with FLANN	155
Performing homography with FLANN-based matches	160
A sample application – tattoo forensics	164
Saving image descriptors to file	164
Scanning for matches	166
Summary	169
Chapter 7: Building Custom Object Detectors	171
Technical requirements	172
Understanding HOG descriptors	172
Visualizing HOG	173
Using HOG to describe regions of an image	175
Understanding NMS	176
Understanding SVMs	177
Detecting people with HOG descriptors	178
Creating and training an object detector	181
Understanding BoW	182
Applying BoW to computer vision	183
k-means clustering	184
Detecting cars	184
Combining an SVM with a sliding window	193
Detecting a car in a scene	194
Saving and loading a trained SVM	202
Summary	203
Chapter 8: Tracking Objects	205
Technical requirements	206
Detecting moving objects with background subtraction	206

Implementing a basic background subtractor	208
Using a MOG background subtractor	211
Using a KNN background subtractor	216
Using GMG and other background subtractors	218
Tracking colorful objects using MeanShift and CamShift	221
Planning our MeanShift sample	222
Calculating and back-projecting color histograms	223
Understanding the parameters of cv2.calcHist	226
Understanding the parameters of cv2.calcBackProject	227
Implementing the MeanShift example	228
Using CamShift	231
Finding trends in motion using the Kalman filter	232
Understanding the predict and update phases	233
Tracking a mouse cursor	234
Tracking pedestrians	237
Planning the flow of the application	237
Comparing the object-oriented and functional paradigms	238
Implementing the Pedestrian class	240
Implementing the main function	242
Considering the next steps	246
Summary	247
Chapter 9: Camera Models and Augmented Reality	249
Technical requirements	250
Understanding 3D image tracking and augmented reality	250
Understanding camera and lens parameters	253
Understanding cv2.solvePnPRansac	258
Implementing the demo application	261
Importing modules	261
Performing grayscale conversion	262
Performing 2D-to-3D spatial conversions	263
Implementing the application class	265
Initializing the tracker	266
Implementing the main loop	274
Tracking the image in 3D	275
Initializing and applying the Kalman filter	279
Drawing the tracking results and masking the tracked object	283
Running and testing the application	286
Improving the 3D tracking algorithm	291
Summary	292
Chapter 10: Introduction to Neural Networks with OpenCV	293
Technical requirements	294
Understanding ANNs	295
Understanding neurons and perceptrons	297
Understanding the layers of a neural network	298

Choosing the size of the input layer 299
Choosing the size of the output layer 299
Choosing the size of the hidden layer 299
Training a basic ANN in OpenCV 300
Training an ANN classifier in multiple epochs 303
Recognizing handwritten digits with an ANN 308
Understanding the MNIST database of handwritten digits 308
Choosing training parameters for the MNIST database 310
Implementing a module to train the ANN 310
Implementing a minimal test module 315
Implementing the main module 315
Trying to improve the ANN's training 321
Finding other potential applications 323
Using DNNs from other frameworks in OpenCV 324
Detecting and classifying objects with third-party DNNs 325
Detecting and classifying faces with third-party DNNs 329
Summary 336

Appendix A: Bending Color Space with the Curves Filter 339

Other Book You May Enjoy 349

Index 351

Preface

Now in its third edition, this is the original book on OpenCV's Python bindings. Readers will learn a great range of techniques and algorithms, from the classics to the state-of-the-art, and from geometry to machine learning. All of this is in aid of solving practical computer vision problems in well-built applications. Using OpenCV 4 and Python 3, we adopt an approach that is accessible to computer vision novices, yet also informative for experts who want to expand and update their skills.

We start with an introduction to OpenCV 4 and explain how to set it up with Python 3 on various platforms. Next, you'll learn how to perform basic operations such as reading, writing, manipulating, and displaying still images, videos, and camera feeds. You'll learn about image processing and video analysis, along with depth estimation and segmentation, and you'll gain practice by building a simple GUI application. Next, you'll tackle two popular problems: face detection and face recognition.

As we advance, we'll explore concepts of object classification and machine learning, enabling you to create and use object detectors and classifiers, and even track objects in movies or video camera feeds. Then, we'll extend our work into 3D tracking and augmented reality. Finally, we'll learn about **artificial neural networks (ANNs)** and **deep neural networks (DNNs)** as we develop applications to recognize handwritten digits, and to classify a person's gender and age.

By the end of this book, you will have acquired the right knowledge and skills to embark on your own real-world computer vision projects.

Who this book is for

This book is intended for people interested in learning computer vision, machine learning, and OpenCV in the context of practical real-world applications. The book will appeal to computer vision novices as well as experts who want to get up to date with OpenCV 4 and Python 3. Readers should be familiar with basic Python programming, but no prior knowledge of image processing, computer vision, or machine learning is required.

What this book covers

Chapter 1, *Setting Up OpenCV*, explains how to set up OpenCV 4 with Python 3 on various platforms. It also provides troubleshooting steps for common problems.

Chapter 2, *Handling Files, Cameras, and GUIs*, introduces OpenCV's I/O functionalities. It also discusses an object-oriented design for a GUI project that we will develop further in other chapters.

Chapter 3, *Processing Images with OpenCV*, presents some techniques required to alter images, such as manipulating colors, sharpening an image, marking contours of objects, and detecting geometric shapes.

Chapter 4, *Depth Estimation and Segmentation*, shows you how to use data from a depth camera to identify foreground and background regions, such that we can limit an effect to only the foreground or background.

Chapter 5, *Detecting and Recognizing Faces*, introduces some of OpenCV's functionality for face detection and recognition, along with the data files that define particular types of detectable objects.

Chapter 6, *Retrieving Images and Searching Using Image Descriptors*, shows how to describe the features of an image with the help of OpenCV, and how to make use of features to match and search for images.

Chapter 7, *Building Custom Object Detectors*, applies a combination of computer vision and machine learning algorithms to locate and classify objects in an image. It shows how to implement this combination of algorithms with OpenCV.

Chapter 8, *Tracking Objects*, demonstrates ways to track and predict the motion of people and objects in a video or live camera feed.

Chapter 9, *Camera Models and Augmented Reality*, enables you to build an augmented reality application that uses information about cameras, objects, and motion to superimpose 3D graphics atop tracked objects in real time.

Chapter 10, *Introduction to Neural Networks with OpenCV*, introduces you to **artificial neural networks (ANNs)** and **deep neural networks (DNNs)** in OpenCV, and illustrates their usage in real-world applications.

Appendix A, *Bending Color Space with a Curves Filter*, describes the concept of color curves and our implementation of them using SciPy.

To get the most out of this book

The reader is expected to have at least basic proficiency in the Python programming language.

A Windows, macOS, or Linux development machine is recommended. You can refer to Chapter 1, *Setting Up OpenCV*, for instructions about setting up OpenCV 4, Python 3, and other dependencies.

This book takes a hands-on approach to learning and includes 77 sample scripts, along with sample data. Working through these examples as you read the book will help enforce the concepts.

The code for this book is released under the BSD 3-Clause open source license, which is the same as the license used by OpenCV itself. The reader is encouraged to use, modify, improve, and even publish their changes to these example programs.

Download the example code files

You can download the example code files for this book from your account at www.packt.com. If you purchased this book elsewhere, you can visit www.packtpub.com/support and register to have the files emailed directly to you.

You can download the code files by following these steps:

1. Log in or register at www.packt.com.
2. Select the **Support** tab.
3. Click on **Code Downloads**.
4. Enter the name of the book in the **Search** box and follow the onscreen instructions.

Once the file is downloaded, please make sure that you unzip or extract the folder using the latest version of:

- WinRAR/7-Zip for Windows
- Zipeg/iZip/UnRarX for Mac
- 7-Zip/PeaZip for Linux

The code bundle for the book is also hosted on GitHub at https://github.com/PacktPublishing/Learning-OpenCV-4-Computer-Vision-with-Python-Third-Edition. In case there's an update to the code, it will be updated on the existing GitHub repository.

We also have other code bundles from our rich catalog of books and videos available at https://github.com/PacktPublishing/. Check them out!

Code in Action

Code in Action videos for this book can be viewed at http://bit.ly/2STXnRN.

Download the color images

We also provide a PDF file that has color images of the screenshots/diagrams used in this book. You can download it here: https://static.packt-cdn.com/downloads/9781789531619_ColorImages.pdf.

Conventions used

There are a number of text conventions used throughout this book.

CodeInText: Indicates code words in text, database table names, folder names, filenames, file extensions, pathnames, dummy URLs, user input, and Twitter handles. Here is an example: "OpenCV provides the VideoCapture and VideoWriter classes, which support various video file formats."

A block of code is set as follows:

```
import cv2

grayImage = cv2.imread('MyPic.png', cv2.IMREAD_GRAYSCALE)
cv2.imwrite('MyPicGray.png', grayImage)
```

When we wish to draw your attention to a particular part of a code block, the relevant lines or items are set in bold:

```
import cv2

cameraCapture = cv2.VideoCapture(0)
fps = 30  # An assumption
size = (int(cameraCapture.get(cv2.CAP_PROP_FRAME_WIDTH)),
        int(cameraCapture.get(cv2.CAP_PROP_FRAME_HEIGHT)))
videoWriter = cv2.VideoWriter(
    'MyOutputVid.avi', cv2.VideoWriter_fourcc('M','J','P','G'), fps, size)
```

In general, command-line input or output is written as follows:

```
$ pip install opencv-contrib-python
```

Alternatively, for Windows, command-line input or output may be written as follows:

```
> pip install opencv-contrib-python
```

Bold: Indicates a new term, an important word, or words that you see onscreen. For example, words in menus or dialog boxes appear in the text like this. Here is an example: "Now, under **System variables**, select **Path** and click on the **Edit...** button."

 Warnings or important notes appear like this.

 Tips and tricks appear like this.

Get in touch

Feedback from our readers is always welcome.

General feedback: If you have questions about any aspect of this book, mention the book title in the subject of your message and email us at customercare@packtpub.com.

Errata: Although we have taken every care to ensure the accuracy of our content, mistakes do happen. If you have found a mistake in this book, we would be grateful if you would report this to us. Please visit www.packtpub.com/support, selecting your book, clicking on the Errata Submission Form link, and entering the details. Also, if you encounter a problem with the code from the book's GitHub repository, you can file an issue report at https://github.com/PacktPublishing/Learning-OpenCV-4-Computer-Vision-with-Python-Third-Edition/issues.

Piracy: If you come across any illegal copies of our works in any form on the Internet, we would be grateful if you would provide us with the location address or website name. Please contact us at copyright@packt.com with a link to the material.

If you are interested in becoming an author: If there is a topic that you have expertise in and you are interested in either writing or contributing to a book, please visit authors.packtpub.com.

Reviews

Please leave a review. Once you have read and used this book, why not leave a review on the site that you purchased it from? Potential readers can then see and use your unbiased opinion to make purchase decisions, we at Packt can understand what you think about our products, and our authors can see your feedback on their book. Thank you!

For more information about Packt, please visit `packt.com`.

Setting Up OpenCV

1

You've picked up this book, so you may already have an idea of what OpenCV is. Maybe you heard of capabilities that seem to come straight out of science fiction, such as training an artificial intelligence model to recognize anything that it sees through a camera. If this is your interest, you will not be disappointed! **OpenCV** stands for **Open Source Computer Vision**. It is a free computer vision library that allows you to manipulate images and videos to accomplish a variety of tasks, from displaying frames from a webcam to teaching a robot to recognize real-life objects.

In this book, you will learn to leverage the immense potential of OpenCV with the Python programming language. Python is an elegant language with a relatively shallow learning curve and very powerful features. This chapter is a quick guide to setting up Python 3, OpenCV 4, and other dependencies. As part of OpenCV, we will set up the opencv_contrib modules, which offer additional functionality that is maintained by the OpenCV community rather than the core development team. After setup, we will also look at OpenCV's Python sample scripts and documentation.

The following related libraries are covered in this chapter:

- **NumPy**: This library is a dependency of OpenCV's Python bindings. It provides numeric computing functionality, including efficient arrays.
- **SciPy**: This library is a scientific computing library that is closely related to NumPy. It is not required by OpenCV, but it is useful if you wish to manipulate data in OpenCV images.
- **OpenNI 2**: This library is an optional dependency of OpenCV. It adds support for certain depth cameras, such as the Asus Xtion PRO.

OpenCV 4 has dropped support for OpenNI 1 along with all OpenNI 1 modules, such as SensorKinect. This change means that some old depth cameras, such as the Xbox version of Microsoft Kinect, might not be supported in OpenCV 4.

For this book's purposes, OpenNI 2 can be considered optional. It is used throughout Chapter 4, *Depth Estimation and Segmentation*, but is not used in the other chapters or appendices.

 This book focuses on OpenCV 4, the new major release of the OpenCV library. Additional information about OpenCV is available at http://opencv.org, and the official documentation is available at http://docs.opencv.org/master.

We will cover the following topics in this chapter:

- What's new in OpenCV 4
- Choosing and using the right setup tools
- Running samples
- Finding documentation, help, and updates

Technical requirements

This chapter assumes that you are using one of the following operating systems:

- Windows 7 SP1 or a later version
- macOS 10.7 (Lion) or a later version
- Debian Jessie or a later version, or a derivative such as the following:
    - Ubuntu 14.04 or a later version
    - Linux Mint 17 or a later version

For editing Python scripts and other text files, this book's authors simply recommend that you should have a good text editor. Examples include the following:

- Notepad++ for Windows
- BBEdit (free version) for macOS
- GEdit for the GNOME desktop environment on Linux
- Kate for the KDE Plasma desktop environment on Linux

Besides the operating system, there are no other prerequisites for this setup chapter.

What's new in OpenCV 4

If you are an OpenCV veteran, you might want to know more about OpenCV 4's changes before you decide to install it. Here are some of the highlights:

- The C++ implementation of OpenCV has been updated to C++11. OpenCV's Python bindings wrap the C++ implementation, so as Python users, we may gain some performance advantages from this update, even though we are not using C++ directly.
- The deprecated C implementation of OpenCV and the deprecated Python bindings for the C implementation have been removed.
- Many new optimizations have been implemented. Existing OpenCV 3 projects can take advantage of many of these optimizations without further changes beyond updating the OpenCV version. For OpenCV C++ projects, an entirely new optimization pipeline named G-API is available; however, OpenCV's Python bindings currently do not support this optimization pipeline.
- Many new machine learning models are available in OpenCV's DNN module.
- The tools to train Haar cascades and LBP cascades (to detect custom objects) have been removed. There is a proposal to reimplement these tools, along with support for additional models, in a future update for OpenCV 4.
- The KinectFusion algorithm (for three-dimensional reconstruction using a Microsoft Kinect 2 camera) is now supported.
- The DIS algorithm for dense optical flow has been added.
- A new module has been added for detecting and decoding QR codes.

Whether or not you have used a previous version of OpenCV, this book will serve you as a general guide to OpenCV 4, and some of the new features will receive special attention in subsequent chapters.

Choosing and using the right setup tools

We are free to choose various setup tools, depending on our operating system and how much configuration we want to do.

Regardless of the choice of operating system, Python offers some built-in tools that are useful for setting up a development environment. These tools include a package manager called `pip` and a virtual environment manager called `venv`. Some of this chapter's instructions will cover `pip` specifically, but if you would like to learn about `venv`, please refer to the official Python documentation at `https://docs.python.org/3/library/venv.html`.

You should consider using `venv` if you plan to maintain a variety of Python projects that might have conflicting dependencies – for example, projects that depend on different versions of OpenCV. Each of `venv`'s virtual environments has its own set of installed libraries, and we can switch between these environments without reinstalling anything. Within a given virtual environment, libraries can be installed using `pip` or, in some cases, other tools.

Let's take an overview of the setup tools available for Windows, macOS, Ubuntu, and other Unix-like systems.

Installation on Windows

Windows does not come with Python preinstalled. However, an installation wizard is available for Python, and Python provides a package manager called `pip`, which lets us easily install ready-made builds of NumPy, SciPy, and OpenCV. Alternatively, we can build OpenCV from source in order to enable nonstandard features, such as support for depth cameras via OpenNI 2. OpenCV's build system uses CMake for configuring the system and Visual Studio for compilation.

Before anything else, let's install Python. Go to `https://www.python.org/getit/` and download and run the most recent installer for Python 3.8. You probably want an installer for 64-bit Python, though OpenCV can work with 32-bit Python too.

Once Python has been installed, we can use `pip` to install NumPy and SciPy. Open the Command Prompt and run the following command:

```
> pip install numpy scipy
```

Now, we must decide whether we want a ready-made build of OpenCV (without support for depth cameras) or a custom build (with support for depth cameras). The next two subsections cover these alternatives.

Using a ready-made OpenCV package

OpenCV, including the `opencv_contrib` modules, can be installed as a `pip` package. This is as simple as running the following command:

```
> pip install opencv-contrib-python
```

If you want your OpenCV installation to include *non-free* content, such as patented algorithms, then you can run the following command instead:

```
> pip install opencv-contrib-python-nonfree
```

 If you intend to distribute software that depends on OpenCV's non-free content, you should do your own investigation of how the patent and licensing issues might apply in specific countries and to specific use cases. OpenCV's non-free content includes implementations of the patented SIFT and SURF algorithms, which we will introduce in Chapter 6, *Retrieving Images and Searching Using Image Descriptors*.

You might find that one of these `pip` packages offers all the OpenCV features you currently want. On the other hand, if you intend to use depth cameras, or if you want to learn about the general process of making a custom build of OpenCV, you should *not* install the OpenCV `pip` package; you should proceed to the next subsection instead.

Building OpenCV from source

If you want support for depth cameras, you should also install OpenNI 2, which is available as a set of precompiled binaries with an installation wizard. Then, we must build OpenCV from source using CMake and Visual Studio.

To obtain OpenNI 2, go to `https://structure.io/openni` and download the latest ZIP for Windows and for your system's architecture (x64 or x86). Unzip it to get an installer file, such as `OpenNI-Windows-x64-2.2.msi`. Run the installer.

Now, let's set up Visual Studio. To build OpenCV 4, we need Visual Studio 2015 or a later version. If you do not already have a suitable version, go to `https://visualstudio.microsoft.com/downloads/` and download and run one of the installers for one of the following:

- The free Visual Studio 2019 Community edition
- Any of the paid Visual Studio 2019 editions, which have a 30-day trial period

During installation, ensure that any optional C++ components are selected. After the installation finishes, reboot.

For OpenCV 4, the build configuration process requires CMake 3 or a later version. Go to https://cmake.org/download/, download the installer for the latest version of CMake for your architecture (x64 or x86), and run it. During installation, select either **Add CMake to the system PATH for all users** or **Add CMake to the system PATH for current user**.

At this stage, we have set up the dependencies and build environment for our custom build of OpenCV. Now, we need to obtain the OpenCV source code and configure and build it. We can do this by following these steps:

1. Go to https://opencv.org/releases/ and get the latest OpenCV download for Windows. It is a self-extracting ZIP. Run it and, when prompted, enter any destination folder, which we will refer to as <opencv_unzip_destination>. During extraction, a subfolder is created at <opencv_unzip_destination>\opencv.

2. Go to https://github.com/opencv/opencv_contrib/releases and download the latest ZIP of the opencv_contrib modules. Unzip this file to any destination folder, which we will refer to as <opencv_contrib_unzip_destination>.

3. Open the Command Prompt and run the following command to make another folder where our build will go:

   ```
   > mkdir <build_folder>
   ```

   Change the directory to the build folder:

   ```
   > cd <build_folder>
   ```

4. Now, we are ready to configure our build with CMake's command-line interface. To understand all the options, we can read the code in <opencv_unzip_destination>\opencv\CMakeLists.txt. However, for this book's purposes, we only need to use the options that will give us a release build with Python bindings, opencv_contrib modules, non-free content, and depth camera support via OpenNI 2. Some options differ slightly, depending on the Visual Studio version and target architecture (x64 or x86). To create a 64-bit (x64) solution for Visual Studio 2019, run the following command (but replace <opencv_contrib_unzip_destination> and <opencv_unzip_destination> with the actual paths):

   ```
   > cmake -DCMAKE_BUILD_TYPE=RELEASE -DOPENCV_SKIP_PYTHON_LOADER=ON
   -DPYTHON3_LIBRARY=C:/Python37/libs/python37.lib
   -DPYTHON3_INCLUDE_DIR=C:/Python37/include -DWITH_OPENNI2=ON
   ```

```
-DOPENCV_EXTRA_MODULES_PATH="<opencv_contrib_unzip_destination>
/modules" -DOPENCV_ENABLE_NONFREE=ON -G "Visual Studio 16 2019" -A
x64 "<opencv_unzip_destination>/opencv/sources"
```

Alternatively, to create a 32-bit (x86) solution for Visual Studio 2019, run the following command (but replace `<opencv_contrib_unzip_destination>` and `<opencv_unzip_destination>` with the actual paths):

```
> cmake -DCMAKE_BUILD_TYPE=RELEASE -DOPENCV_SKIP_PYTHON_LOADER=ON
-DPYTHON3_LIBRARY=C:/Python37/libs/python37.lib
-DPYTHON3_INCLUDE_DIR=C:/Python37/include -DWITH_OPENNI2=ON
-DOPENCV_EXTRA_MODULES_PATH="<opencv_contrib_unzip_destination>
/modules" -DOPENCV_ENABLE_NONFREE=ON -G "Visual Studio 16 2019" -A
Win32 "<opencv_unzip_destination>/opencv/sources"
```

As the preceding command runs, it prints information about dependencies that are either found or missing. OpenCV has many optional dependencies, so do not panic (yet) about missing dependencies. However, if the build does not finish successfully, try installing missing dependencies. (Many are available as prebuilt binaries.) Then, repeat this step.

5. CMake will have generated a Visual Studio solution file at `<opencv_build_folder>/OpenCV.sln`. Open it in Visual Studio. Ensure that the **Release** configuration (not the **Debug** configuration) is selected in the drop-down list in the toolbar near the top of the Visual Studio window. (OpenCV's Python bindings will probably not build in Debug configuration, because most Python distributions do not contain debug libraries.) Go to the **BUILD** menu and select **Build Solution**. Watch the build messages in the **Output** pane at the bottom of the window, and wait for the build to finish.

6. By this stage, OpenCV has been built, but it hasn't been installed at a location where Python can find it. Before proceeding further, let's ensure that our Python environment does not already contain a conflicting build of OpenCV. Find and delete any OpenCV files in Python's DLLs folder and `site_packages` folder. For example, these files might match the following patterns:
`C:\Python37\DLLs\opencv_*.dll`, `C:\Python37\Lib\site-packages\opencv`, and `C:\Python37\Lib\site-packages\cv2.pyd`.

7. Finally, let's install our custom build of OpenCV. CMake has generated an INSTALL project as part of the OpenCV.sln Visual Studio solution. Look in the **Solution Explorer** pane on the right-hand side of the Visual Studio window, find the **CMakeTargets | INSTALL** project, right-click on it, and select **Build** from the context menu. Again, watch the build messages in the **Output** pane at the bottom of the window and wait for the build to finish. Then, quit Visual Studio. Edit the system's Path variable and append either ;<build_folder>\install\x64\vc15\bin (for a 64-bit build) or ;<build_folder>\install\x86\vc15\bin (for a 32-bit build). This folder is where the INSTALL project put the OpenCV DLL files, which are library files that Python will load dynamically at runtime. The OpenCV Python module is located at a path such as C:\Python37\Lib\site-packages\cv2.pyd. Python will find it there, so you do not need to add it to the Path. Log out and log back in (or reboot).

> The preceding instructions refer to editing the system's Path variable. This task can be done in the **Environment Variables** window of **Control Panel**, as described in the following steps:
>
>
>
> 1. Click on the Start menu and launch **Control Panel**. Now, navigate to **System and Security | System | Advanced system settings**. Click on the **Environment Variables...** button.
>
> 2. Now, under **System variables**, select **Path** and click on the **Edit...** button.
>
> 3. Make changes as directed.
>
> 4. To apply the changes, click on all the **OK** buttons (until we are back in the main window of the **Control Panel**).
>
> 5. Then, log out and log back in. (Alternatively, reboot.)

Now, we have completed the OpenCV build process on Windows, and we have a custom build that is suitable for all of this book's Python projects.

> In the future, if you want to update to a new version of the OpenCV source code, repeat all the preceding steps, starting from downloading OpenCV.

Installation on macOS

macOS comes with a preinstalled Python distribution that has been customized by Apple for the system's internal needs. To develop our own projects, we should make a separate Python installation to ensure that we do not conflict with the system's Python needs.

For macOS, there are several possible approaches for obtaining standard versions of Python 3, NumPy, SciPy, and OpenCV. All approaches ultimately require OpenCV to be compiled from source using the Xcode command-line tools. However, depending on the approach, this task is automated for us in various ways by third-party tools. We will look at this kind of approach using a package manager called Homebrew. A package manager can potentially do everything that CMake can, plus it helps us resolve dependencies and separate our development libraries from system libraries.

 MacPorts is another popular package manager for macOS. However, at the time of writing, MacPorts does not offer packages for OpenCV 4 or OpenNI 2, so we will not use it in this book.

Before proceeding, let's make sure that the Xcode command line tools are set up properly. Open a Terminal and run the following command:

```
$ xcode-select --install
```

Agree to the license agreement and any other prompts. The installation should run to completion. Now, we have the compilers that Homebrew requires.

Using Homebrew with ready-made packages

Starting on a system where Xcode and its command-line tools are already set up, the following steps will give us an OpenCV installation via Homebrew:

1. Open a Terminal and run the following command to install Homebrew:

   ```
   $ /usr/bin/ruby -e "$(curl -fsSL https://raw.github
   usercontent.com/Homebrew/install/master/install)"
   ```

2. Homebrew does not automatically put its executables in PATH. To do so, create or edit the ~/.profile file and add the following line at the top of the code:

   ```
   export PATH=/usr/local/bin:/usr/local/sbin:$PATH
   ```

Save the file and run this command to refresh `PATH`:

```
$ source ~/.profile
```

Note that executables installed by Homebrew now take precedence over executables installed by the system.

3. For Homebrew's self-diagnostic report, run the following command:

```
$ brew doctor
```

Follow any troubleshooting advice it gives.

4. Now, update Homebrew:

```
$ brew update
```

5. Run the following command to install Python 3.7:

```
$ brew install python
```

6. Now, we want to install OpenCV with the `opencv_contrib` modules. At the same time, we want to install dependencies such as NumPy. To accomplish this, run the following command:

```
$ brew install opencv
```

Homebrew does not provide an option to install OpenCV with OpenNI 2 support. Homebrew always installs OpenCV with the `opencv_contrib` modules, including non-free content such as the patented SIFT and SURF algorithms, which we will cover in `Chapter 6`, *Retrieving Images and Searching Using Image Descriptors*. If you intend to distribute software that depends on OpenCV's non-free content, you should do your own investigation of how the patent and licensing issues might apply in specific countries and to specific use cases.

7. Similarly, run the following command to install SciPy:

```
$ brew install scipy
```

Now, we have all we need to develop OpenCV projects with Python on macOS.

Using Homebrew with your own custom packages

Just in case you ever need to customize a package, Homebrew makes it easy to edit existing package definitions:

```
$ brew edit opencv
```

The package definitions are actually scripts in the Ruby programming language. Tips on editing them can be found on the Homebrew wiki page at `https://github.com/Homebrew/brew/blob/master/docs/Formula-Cookbook.md`. A script may specify Make or CMake configuration flags, among other things.

 To see which CMake configuration flags are relevant to OpenCV, refer to `https://github.com/opencv/opencv/blob/master/CMakeLists.txt` in the official OpenCV repository on GitHub.

After making edits to the Ruby script, save it.

The customized package can be treated as normal. For example, it can be installed as follows:

```
$ brew install opencv
```

Installation on Debian, Ubuntu, Linux Mint, and similar systems

Debian, Ubuntu, Linux Mint, and related Linux distributions use the `apt` package manager. On these systems, it is easy to install packages for Python 3 and many Python modules, including NumPy and SciPy. An OpenCV package is also available via `apt`, but at the time of writing, this package has not been updated to OpenCV 4. Instead, we can obtain OpenCV 4 (without support for depth cameras) from Python's standard package manager, `pip`. Alternatively, we can build OpenCV 4 from source. When built from source, OpenCV can support depth cameras via OpenNI 2, which is available as a set of precompiled binaries with an installation script.

Regardless of our approach to obtaining OpenCV, let's begin by updating `apt` so that we can obtain the latest packages. Open a Terminal and run the following command:

```
$ sudo apt-get update
```

Having updated `apt`, let's run the following command to install NumPy and SciPy for Python 3:

```
$ sudo apt-get install python3-numpy python3-scipy
```

 Equivalently, we could have used the Ubuntu Software Center, which is the `apt` package manager's graphical frontend.

Now, we must decide whether we want a ready-made build of OpenCV (without support for depth cameras) or a custom build (with support for depth cameras). The next two subsections cover these alternatives.

Using a ready-made OpenCV package

OpenCV, including the `opencv_contrib` modules, can be installed as a `pip` package. This is as simple as running the following command:

```
$ pip3 install opencv-contrib-python
```

If you want your OpenCV installation to include *non-free* content, such as patented algorithms, then you can run the following command instead:

```
$ pip install opencv-contrib-python-nonfree
```

 If you intend to distribute software that depends on OpenCV's non-free content, you should do your own investigation of how the patent and licensing issues might apply in specific countries and to specific use cases. OpenCV's non-free content includes implementations of the patented SIFT and SURF algorithms, which we will introduce in `Chapter 6`, *Retrieving Images and Searching Using Image Descriptors*.

You might find that one of these `pip` packages offers all the OpenCV features you currently want. On the other hand, if you intend to use depth cameras, or if you want to learn about the general process of making a custom build of OpenCV, you should *not* install the OpenCV `pip` package; you should proceed to the next subsection instead.

Building OpenCV from source

To build OpenCV from source, we need a C++ build environment and the CMake build configuration system. Specifically, we need CMake 3. On Ubuntu 14.04, Linux Mint 17, and related systems, the `cmake` package is CMake 2, but a more up-to-date `cmake3` package is also available. On these systems, run the following commands to ensure that the necessary versions of CMake and other build tools are installed:

```
$ sudo apt-get remove cmake
$ sudo apt-get install build-essential cmake3 pkg-config
```

On the other hand, on more recent operating systems, the `cmake` package is CMake 3, and we can simply run the following command:

```
$ sudo apt-get install build-essential cmake pkg-config
```

As part of the build process for OpenCV, CMake will need to access the internet to download additional dependencies. If your system uses a proxy server, ensure that your environment variables for the proxy server have been configured properly. Specifically, CMake relies on the `http_proxy` and `https_proxy` environment variables. To define these, you can edit your `~/.bash_profile` script and add lines such as the following (but modify them so that they match your own proxy URLs and port numbers):

```
export http_proxy=http://myproxy.com:8080
export https_proxy=http://myproxy.com:8081
```

If you are unsure whether your system uses a proxy server, it probably doesn't, so you can ignore this step.

To build OpenCV's Python bindings, we need an installation of the Python 3 development headers. To install these, run the following command:

```
$ sudo apt-get install python3-dev
```

To capture frames from typical USB webcams, OpenCV depends on **Video for Linux** (**V4L**). On most systems, V4L comes preinstalled, but just in case it is missing, run the following command:

```
$ sudo apt-get install libv4l-dev
```

As we mentioned previously, to support depth cameras, OpenCV depends on OpenNI 2. Go to `https://structure.io/openni` and download the latest ZIP of OpenNI 2 for Linux and for your system's architecture (x64, x86, or ARM). Unzip it to any destination, which we will refer to as `<openni2_unzip_destination>`. Run the following commands:

```
$ cd <openni2_unzip_destination>
$ sudo ./install.sh
```

The preceding installation script configures the system so that it supports depth cameras as USB devices. Moreover, the script creates environment variables that refer to library files inside `<openni2_unzip_destination>`. Therefore, if you move `<openni2_unzip_destination>` at a later date, you will need to run `install.sh` again.

Now that we have the build environment and dependencies installed, we can obtain and build the OpenCV source code. To do so, follow these steps:

1. Go to `https://opencv.org/releases/` and download the latest source package. Unzip it to any destination folder, which we will refer to as `<opencv_unzip_destination>`.

2. Go to `https://github.com/opencv/opencv_contrib/releases` and download the latest source package for the `opencv_contrib` modules. Unzip it to any destination folder, which we will refer to as `<opencv_contrib_unzip_destination>`.

3. Open a Terminal. Run the following commands to create a directory where we will put our OpenCV build:

   ```
   $ mkdir <build_folder>
   ```

   Change into the newly created directory:

   ```
   $ cd <build_folder>
   ```

4. Now, we can use CMake to generate a build configuration for OpenCV. The output of this configuration process will be a set of Makefiles, which are scripts we can use to build and install OpenCV. A complete set of CMake configuration options for OpenCV is defined in the `<opencv_unzip_destination>/opencv/sources/CMakeLists.txt` file. For our purposes, we care about the options that relate to OpenNI 2 support, Python bindings, `opencv_contrib` modules, and non-free content. Configure OpenCV by running the following command:

   ```
   $ cmake -D CMAKE_BUILD_TYPE=RELEASE -D BUILD_EXAMPLES=ON -D
   WITH_OPENNI2=ON -D BUILD_opencv_python2=OFF -D
   BUILD_opencv_python3=ON -D PYTHON3_EXECUTABLE=/usr/bin/python3.6 -D
   ```

```
PYTHON3_INCLUDE_DIR=/usr/include/python3.6 -D
PYTHON3_LIBRARY=/usr/lib/python3.6/config-3.6m-x86_64-linux-
gnu/libpython3.6.so -D
OPENCV_EXTRA_MODULES_PATH=<opencv_contrib_unzip_destination> -D
OPENCV_ENABLE_NONFREE=ON <opencv_unzip_destination>
```

5. Finally, run the following commands to interpret our newly generated makefiles, and thereby build and install OpenCV:

```
$ make -j8
$ sudo make install
```

So far, we have completed the OpenCV build process on Debian, Ubuntu, or a similar system, and we have a custom build that is suitable for all of this book's Python projects.

Installation on other Unix-like systems

On other Unix-like systems, the package manager and available packages may differ. Consult your package manager's documentation and search for packages with opencv in their names. Remember that OpenCV and its Python bindings might be split into multiple packages.

Also, look for any installation notes that have been published by the system provider, the repository maintainer, or the community. Since OpenCV uses camera drivers and media codecs, getting all of its functionality to work can be tricky on systems with poor multimedia support. Under some circumstances, system packages might need to be reconfigured or reinstalled for compatibility.

If packages are available for OpenCV, check their version number. OpenCV 4 is recommended for this book's purposes. Also, check whether the packages offer Python bindings and depth camera support via OpenNI 2. Finally, check whether anyone in the developer community has reported success or failure in using the packages.

If, instead, you want to do a custom build of OpenCV from source, it might be helpful to refer to the previous section's steps for Debian, Ubuntu, and similar systems, and adapt these steps to the package manager and packages that are present on another system.

Running samples

Running a few sample scripts is a good way to test whether OpenCV has been set up correctly. Some samples are included in OpenCV's source code archive. If you have not already obtained the source code, go to `https://opencv.org/releases/` and download one of the following archives:

- For Windows, download the latest archive, labeled **Windows**. It is a self-extracting ZIP. Run it and, when prompted, enter any destination folder, which we will refer to as `<opencv_unzip_destination>`. Find the Python samples in `<opencv_unzip_destination>/opencv/samples/python`.
- For other systems, download the latest archive, labeled **Sources**. It is a ZIP file. Unzip it to any destination folder, which we will refer to as `<opencv_unzip_destination>`. Find the Python samples in `<opencv_unzip_destination>/samples/python`.

Some of the sample scripts require command-line arguments. However, the following scripts (among others) should work without any arguments:

- `hist.py`: This script displays a photo. Press *A*, *B*, *C*, *D*, or *E* to see the variations of the photo, along with a corresponding histogram of color or grayscale values.
- `opt_flow.py`: This script displays a webcam feed with a superimposed visualization of the optical flow, or in other words, the direction of motion. Slowly wave your hand at the webcam to see the effect. Press *1* or *2* for alternative visualizations.

To exit a script, press *Esc* (not the Windows close button).

If we encounter the `ImportError: No module named cv2` message, then this means that we are running the script from a Python installation that does not know anything about OpenCV. There are two possible explanations for this:

- Some steps in the OpenCV installation might have failed or been missed. Go back and review the steps.

- If we have multiple Python installations on the machine, we might be using the wrong version of Python to launch the script. For example, on macOS, it might be the case that OpenCV has been installed for Homebrew Python, but we are running the script with the system's version of Python. Go back and review the installation steps about editing the system's PATH variable. Also, try launching the script manually from the command line using commands such as the following:

```
$ python hist.py
```

You can also try the following command:

```
$ python3.8 python/camera.py
```

As another possible means of selecting a different Python installation, try editing the sample script to remove the #! lines. These lines might explicitly associate the script with the wrong Python installation (for our particular setup).

Finding documentation, help, and updates

OpenCV's documentation can be found at http://docs.opencv.org/, where you can either read it online or download it for offline reading. If you write code on airplanes or other places without internet access, you will definitely want to keep offline copies of the documentation.

The documentation includes a combined API reference for OpenCV's C++ API and its Python API. When you look up a class or function, be sure to read the section under the heading **Python**.

 OpenCV's Python module is named cv2. The **2** in cv2 has nothing to do with the version number of OpenCV; we really are using OpenCV 4. Historically, there was a cv Python module that wrapped a now-obsolete C version of OpenCV. The cv module does not exist anymore in OpenCV 4. However, the OpenCV documentation sometimes erroneously refers to the module name as cv instead of cv2. Just remember that in OpenCV 4, the correct Python module name is always cv2.

If the documentation does not seem to answer your questions, try talking to the OpenCV community. Here are some sites where you will find helpful people:

- The OpenCV forum: https://answers.opencv.org/questions/
- Adrian Rosebrock's website: http://www.pyimagesearch.com/
- Joseph Howse's website for his books and presentations:
  http://nummist.com/opencv/

Lastly, if you are an advanced user who wants to try new features, bug fixes, and sample scripts from the latest (unstable) OpenCV source code, have a look at the project's repository at https://github.com/opencv/opencv/.

Summary

By now, we should have an OpenCV installation that will serve our needs for the diverse projects described in this book. Depending on which approach we took, we may also have a set of tools and scripts that can be used to reconfigure and rebuild OpenCV for our future needs.

Now, we also know where to find OpenCV's Python samples. These samples covered a different range of functionalities outside this book's scope, but they are useful as additional learning aids.

In the next chapter, we will familiarize ourselves with the most basic functions of the OpenCV API, namely, displaying images and videos, capturing videos through a webcam, and handling basic keyboard and mouse inputs.

Handling Files, Cameras, and GUIs

2

Installing OpenCV and running samples is fun, but at this stage, we want to try things out in our own way. This chapter introduces OpenCV's I/O functionality. We also discuss the concept of a project and the beginnings of an object-oriented design for this project, which we will flesh out in subsequent chapters.

By starting with a look at I/O capabilities and design patterns, we will build our project in the same way we would make a sandwich: from the outside in. Bread slices and spread, or endpoints and glue, come before fillings or algorithms. We choose this approach because computer vision is mostly extroverted—it contemplates the real world outside our computer—and we want to apply all of our subsequent algorithmic work to the real world through a common interface.

Specifically, in this chapter, our code samples and discussions will cover the following tasks:

- Reading images from image files, video files, camera devices, or raw bytes of data in memory
- Writing images to image files or video files
- Manipulating image data in NumPy arrays
- Displaying images in windows
- Handling keyboard and mouse input
- Implementing an application with an object-oriented design

Technical requirements

This chapter uses Python, OpenCV, and NumPy. Please refer back to `Chapter 1`, *Setting Up OpenCV*, for installation instructions.

The complete code for this chapter can be found in this book's GitHub repository, `https://github.com/PacktPublishing/Learning-OpenCV-4-Computer-Vision-with-Python-Third-Edition`, in the `Chapter02` folder.

Basic I/O scripts

Most CV applications need to get images as input. Most also produce images as output. An interactive CV application might require a camera as an input source and a window as an output destination. However, other possible sources and destinations include image files, video files, and raw bytes. For example, raw bytes might be transmitted via a network connection, or they might be generated by an algorithm if we incorporate procedural graphics into our application. Let's look at each of these possibilities.

Reading/writing an image file

OpenCV provides the `imread` function to load an image from a file and the `imwrite` function to write an image to a file. These functions support various file formats for still images (not videos). The supported formats vary—as formats can be added or removed in a custom build of OpenCV—but normally BMP, PNG, JPEG, and TIFF are among the supported formats.

Let's explore the anatomy of the representation of an image in OpenCV and NumPy. An image is a multidimensional array; it has columns and rows of pixels, and each pixel has a value. For different kinds of image data, the pixel value may be formatted in different ways. For example, we can create a 3x3 square black image from scratch by simply creating a 2D NumPy array:

```
img = numpy.zeros((3, 3), dtype=numpy.uint8)
```

If we print this image to a console, we obtain the following result:

```
array([[0, 0, 0],
       [0, 0, 0],
       [0, 0, 0]], dtype=uint8)
```

Here, each pixel is represented by a single 8-bit integer, which means that the values for each pixel are in the 0-255 range, where 0 is black, 255 is white, and the in-between values are shades of gray. This is a grayscale image.

Let's now convert this image into **blue-green-red (BGR)** format using the `cv2.cvtColor` function:

```
img = cv2.cvtColor(img, cv2.COLOR_GRAY2BGR)
```

Let's observe how the image has changed:

```
array([[[0, 0, 0],
        [0, 0, 0],
        [0, 0, 0]],

       [[0, 0, 0],
        [0, 0, 0],
        [0, 0, 0]],

       [[0, 0, 0],
        [0, 0, 0],
        [0, 0, 0]]], dtype=uint8)
```

As you can see, each pixel is now represented by a three-element array, with each integer representing one of the three color channels: B, G, and R, respectively. Other common color models, such as HSV, will be represented in the same way, albeit with different value ranges. For example, the hue value of the HSV color model has a range of 0-180.

> For more information about color models, refer to Chapter 3, *Processing Images with OpenCV*, specifically the *Converting between different color models* section.

You can check the structure of an image by inspecting the `shape` property, which returns rows, columns, and the number of channels (if there is more than one).

Consider this example:

```
img = numpy.zeros((5, 3), dtype=numpy.uint8)
print(img.shape)
```

The preceding code will print `(5, 3)`; in other words, we have a grayscale image with 5 rows and 3 columns. If you then converted the image into BGR, the shape would be `(5, 3, 3)`, which indicates the presence of three channels per pixel.

Images can be loaded from one file format and saved to another. For example, let's convert an image from PNG into JPEG:

```
import cv2

image = cv2.imread('MyPic.png')
cv2.imwrite('MyPic.jpg', image)
```

 OpenCV's Python module is called `cv2` even though we are using OpenCV 4.x and not OpenCV 2.x. Historically, OpenCV had two Python modules: `cv2` and `cv`. The latter wrapped a legacy version of OpenCV implemented in C. Nowadays, OpenCV has only the `cv2` Python module, which wraps the current version of OpenCV implemented in C++.

By default, `imread` returns an image in the BGR color format even if the file uses a grayscale format. BGR represents the same color model as **red-green-blue (RGB)**, but the byte order is reversed.

Optionally, we may specify the mode of `imread`. The supported options include the following:

- `cv2.IMREAD_COLOR`: This is the default option, providing a 3-channel BGR image with an 8-bit value (0-255) for each channel.
- `cv2.IMREAD_GRAYSCALE`: This provides an 8-bit grayscale image.
- `cv2.IMREAD_ANYCOLOR`: This provides either an 8-bit-per-channel BGR image or an 8-bit grayscale image, depending on the metadata in the file.
- `cv2.IMREAD_UNCHANGED`: This reads all of the image data, including the alpha or transparency channel (if there is one) as a fourth channel.
- `cv2.IMREAD_ANYDEPTH`: This loads an image in grayscale at its original bit depth. For example, it provides a 16-bit-per-channel grayscale image if the file represents an image in this format.
- `cv2.IMREAD_ANYDEPTH | cv2.IMREAD_COLOR`: This combination loads an image in BGR color at its original bit depth.
- `cv2.IMREAD_REDUCED_GRAYSCALE_2`: This loads an image in grayscale at half its original resolution. For example, if the file contains a 640 x 480 image, it is loaded as a 320 x 240 image.
- `cv2.IMREAD_REDUCED_COLOR_2`: This loads an image in 8-bit-per-channel BGR color at half its original resolution.

- `cv2.IMREAD_REDUCED_GRAYSCALE_4`: This loads an image in grayscale at one-quarter of its original resolution.
- `cv2.IMREAD_REDUCED_COLOR_4`: This loads an image in 8-bit-per-channel color at one-quarter of its original resolution.
- `cv2.IMREAD_REDUCED_GRAYSCALE_8`: This loads an image in grayscale at one-eighth of its original resolution.
- `cv2.IMREAD_REDUCED_COLOR_8`: This loads an image in 8-bit-per-channel color at one-eighth of its original resolution.

As an example, let's load a PNG file as a grayscale image (losing any color information in the process), and then save it as a grayscale PNG image:

```
import cv2

grayImage = cv2.imread('MyPic.png', cv2.IMREAD_GRAYSCALE)
cv2.imwrite('MyPicGray.png', grayImage)
```

The path of an image, unless absolute, is relative to the working directory (the path from which the Python script is run), so, in the preceding example, `MyPic.png` would have to be in the working directory or the image would not be found. If you prefer to avoid assumptions about the working directory, you can use absolute paths, such as `C:\Users\Joe\Pictures\MyPic.png` on Windows, `/Users/Joe/Pictures/MyPic.png` on Mac, or `/home/joe/pictures/MyPic.png` on Linux.

The `imwrite()` function requires an image to be in the BGR or grayscale format with a certain number of bits per channel that the output format can support. For example, the BMP file format requires 8 bits per channel, while PNG allows either 8 or 16 bits per channel.

Converting between an image and raw bytes

Conceptually, a byte is an integer ranging from 0 to 255. Throughout real-time graphic applications today, a pixel is typically represented by one byte per channel, though other representations are also possible.

An OpenCV image is a 2D or 3D array of the `numpy.array` type. An 8-bit grayscale image is a 2D array containing byte values. A 24-bit BGR image is a 3D array, which also contains byte values. We may access these values by using an expression such as `image[0, 0]` or `image[0, 0, 0]`. The first index is the pixel's *y* coordinate or row, 0 being the top. The second index is the pixel's *x* coordinate or column, 0 being the leftmost. The third index (if applicable) represents a color channel. The array's three dimensions can be visualized in the following Cartesian coordinate system:

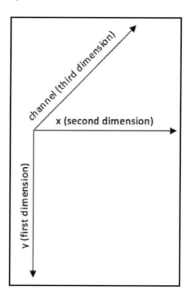

For example, in an 8-bit grayscale image with a white pixel in the upper-left corner, `image[0, 0]` is 255. For a 24-bit (8-bit-per-channel) BGR image with a blue pixel in the upper-left corner, `image[0, 0]` is `[255, 0, 0]`.

Provided that an image has 8 bits per channel, we can cast it to a standard Python `bytearray` object, which is one-dimensional:

```
byteArray = bytearray(image)
```

Conversely, provided that `bytearray` contains bytes in an appropriate order, we can cast and then reshape it to get a `numpy.array` type that is an image:

```
grayImage = numpy.array(grayByteArray).reshape(height, width)
bgrImage = numpy.array(bgrByteArray).reshape(height, width, 3)
```

As a more complete example, let's convert `bytearray` that contains random bytes into a grayscale image and a BGR image:

```
import cv2
import numpy
import os

# Make an array of 120,000 random bytes.
randomByteArray = bytearray(os.urandom(120000))
flatNumpyArray = numpy.array(randomByteArray)

# Convert the array to make a 400x300 grayscale image.
grayImage = flatNumpyArray.reshape(300, 400)
cv2.imwrite('RandomGray.png', grayImage)

# Convert the array to make a 400x100 color image.
bgrImage = flatNumpyArray.reshape(100, 400, 3)
cv2.imwrite('RandomColor.png', bgrImage)
```

 Here, we use Python's standard `os.urandom` function to generate random raw bytes, which we then convert into a NumPy array. Note that it is also possible to generate a random NumPy array directly (and more efficiently) using a statement such as `numpy.random.randint(0, 256, 120000).reshape(300, 400)`. The only reason we use `os.urandom` is to help to demonstrate conversion from raw bytes.

After running this script, we should have a pair of randomly generated images, `RandomGray.png` and `RandomColor.png`, in the script's directory.

Here is an example of `RandomGray.png` (though yours will almost certainly differ since it is random):

Similarly, here is an example of `RandomColor.png`:

Now that we have a better understanding of how an image is formed from data, we can start performing basic operations on it.

Accessing image data with numpy.array

We already know that the easiest (and most common) way to load an image in OpenCV is to use the `imread` function. We also know that this will return an image, which is really an array (either a 2D or 3D one, depending on the parameters you passed to `imread`).

The `numpy.array` class is greatly optimized for array operations, and it allows certain kinds of bulk manipulations that are not available in a plain Python list. These kinds of `numpy.array` type-specific operations come in handy for image manipulations in OpenCV. However, let's explore image manipulations step by step, starting with a basic example. Say you want to manipulate a pixel at coordinates (0, 0) in a BGR image and turn it into a white pixel:

```
import cv2

img = cv2.imread('MyPic.png')
img[0, 0] = [255, 255, 255]
```

If you then save the modified image to file and view it, you will see a white dot in the top-left corner of the image. Naturally, this modification is not very useful, but it begins to show the possibilities. Now, let's leverage the capabilities of `numpy.array` to perform transformations on an array much faster than we could do with a plain Python list.

Let's say that you want to change the blue value of a particular pixel, say, the pixel at coordinates, (150, 120). The `numpy.array` type provides a handy method, `item`, which takes three parameters: the x (or left) position, the y (or top) position, and the index within the array at the (x, y) position (remember that in a BGR image, the data at a certain position is a three-element array containing the B, G, and R values in this order) and returns the value at the index position. Another method, `itemset`, sets the value of a particular channel of a particular pixel to a specified value. `itemset` takes two arguments: a three-element tuple (x, y, and index) and the new value.

In the following example, we change the value of the blue channel at (150, 120) from its current value to an arbitrary `255`:

```
import cv2

img = cv2.imread('MyPic.png')
img.itemset((150, 120, 0), 255)   # Sets the value of a pixel's blue channel
print(img.item(150, 120, 0))  # Prints the value of a pixel's blue channel
```

For modifying a single element in an array, the `itemset` method is somewhat faster than the indexing syntax that we saw in the first example in this section.

Again, modifying an element of an array does not do much in itself, but it does open a world of possibilities. However, for performance reasons, this is only suitable for small regions of interest. When you need to manipulate an entire image or a large region of interest, it is advisable that you utilize either OpenCV's functions or NumPy's **array slicing**. The latter allows you to specify a range of indices. Let's consider an example of using array slicing to manipulate color channels. Setting all G (green) values of an image to `0` is as simple as the following code:

```
import cv2

img = cv2.imread('MyPic.png')
img[:, :, 1] = 0
```

This piece of code performs a fairly significant operation and is easy to understand. The relevant line is the last one, which basically instructs the program to take all pixels from all rows and columns and set the green value (at index one of the three-element BGR array) to `0`. If you display this image, you will notice a complete absence of green.

There are several interesting things we can do by accessing raw pixels with NumPy's array slicing; one of them is defining **regions of interests** (**ROI**). Once the region is defined, we can perform a number of operations. For example, we can bind this region to a variable, define a second region, and assign the value of the first region to the second (hence, copying a portion of the image over to another position in the image):

```
import cv2

img = cv2.imread('MyPic.png')
my_roi = img[0:100, 0:100]
img[300:400, 300:400] = my_roi
```

It is important to make sure that the two regions correspond in terms of size. If not, NumPy will (rightly) complain that the two shapes are mismatched.

Finally, we can access the properties of `numpy.array`, as shown in the following code:

```
import cv2

img = cv2.imread('MyPic.png')
print(img.shape)
print(img.size)
print(img.dtype)
```

These three properties are defined as follows:

- `shape`: This is a tuple describing the shape of the array. For an image, it contains (in order) the height, width, and—if the image is in color—the number of channels. The length of the `shape` tuple is a useful way to determine whether an image is grayscale or color. For a grayscale image, we have `len(shape) == 2`, and for a color image, `len(shape) == 3`.
- `size`: This is the number of elements in the array. In the case of a grayscale image, this is the same as the number of pixels. In the case of a BGR image, it is three times the number of pixels because each pixel is represented by three elements (B, G, and R).
- `dtype`: This is the datatype of the array's elements. For an 8-bit-per-channel image, the datatype is `numpy.uint8`.

All in all, it is strongly advised that you familiarize yourself with NumPy in general, and `numpy.array` in particular, when working with OpenCV. This class is the foundation of any image processing done with OpenCV in Python.

Reading/writing a video file

OpenCV provides the `VideoCapture` and `VideoWriter` classes, which support various video file formats. The supported formats vary depending on the operating system and the build configuration of OpenCV, but normally it is safe to assume that the AVI format is supported. Via its `read` method, a `VideoCapture` object may be polled for new frames until it reaches the end of its video file. Each frame is an image in a BGR format.

Conversely, an image may be passed to the `write` method of the `VideoWriter` class, which appends the image to a file in `VideoWriter`. Let's look at an example that reads frames from one AVI file and writes them to another with a YUV encoding:

```
import cv2

videoCapture = cv2.VideoCapture('MyInputVid.avi')
fps = videoCapture.get(cv2.CAP_PROP_FPS)
size = (int(videoCapture.get(cv2.CAP_PROP_FRAME_WIDTH)),
        int(videoCapture.get(cv2.CAP_PROP_FRAME_HEIGHT)))
videoWriter = cv2.VideoWriter(
    'MyOutputVid.avi', cv2.VideoWriter_fourcc('I','4','2','0'),
    fps, size)

success, frame = videoCapture.read()
while success:  # Loop until there are no more frames.
    videoWriter.write(frame)
    success, frame = videoCapture.read()
```

The arguments to the constructor of the `VideoWriter` class deserve special attention. A video's filename must be specified. Any preexisting file with this name is overwritten. A video codec must also be specified. The available codecs may vary from system to system. The supported options may include the following:

- 0: This option is an uncompressed raw video file. The file extension should be .avi.
- `cv2.VideoWriter_fourcc('I','4','2','0')`: This option is an uncompressed YUV encoding, 4:2:0 chroma subsampled. This encoding is widely compatible but produces large files. The file extension should be .avi.
- `cv2.VideoWriter_fourcc('P','I','M','1')`: This option is MPEG-1. The file extension should be .avi.
- `cv2.VideoWriter_fourcc('X','V','I','D')`: This option is a relatively old MPEG-4 encoding. It is a good option if you want to limit the size of the resulting video. The file extension should be .avi.
- `cv2.VideoWriter_fourcc('M','P','4','V')`: This option is another relatively old MPEG-4 encoding. It is a good option if you want to limit the size of the resulting video. The file extension should be .mp4.

- `cv2.VideoWriter_fourcc('X','2','6','4')`: This option is a relatively new MPEG-4 encoding. It may be the best option if you want to limit the size of the resulting video. The file extension should be .mp4.
- `cv2.VideoWriter_fourcc('T','H','E','O')`: This option is **Ogg Vorbis**. The file extension should be .ogv.
- `cv2.VideoWriter_fourcc('F','L','V','1')`: This option is a Flash video. The file extension should be .flv.

A frame rate and frame size must be specified too. Since we are copying from another video, these properties can be read from the get method of the VideoCapture class.

Capturing camera frames

A stream of camera frames is represented by a VideoCapture object too. However, for a camera, we construct a VideoCapture object by passing the camera's device index instead of a video's filename. Let's consider the following example, which captures 10 seconds of video from a camera and writes it to an AVI file. The code is similar to the previous section's sample (which was captured from a video file instead of a camera) but changes are marked in **bold**:

```
import cv2

cameraCapture = cv2.VideoCapture(0)
fps = 30   # An assumption
size = (int(cameraCapture.get(cv2.CAP_PROP_FRAME_WIDTH)),
        int(cameraCapture.get(cv2.CAP_PROP_FRAME_HEIGHT)))
videoWriter = cv2.VideoWriter(
    'MyOutputVid.avi', cv2.VideoWriter_fourcc('I','4','2','0'),
    fps, size)

success, frame = cameraCapture.read()
numFramesRemaining = 10 * fps - 1 # 10 seconds of frames
while success and numFramesRemaining > 0:
    videoWriter.write(frame)
    success, frame = cameraCapture.read()
    numFramesRemaining -= 1
```

For some cameras on certain systems, `cameraCapture.get(cv2.CAP_PROP_FRAME_WIDTH)` and `cameraCapture.get(cv2.CAP_PROP_FRAME_HEIGHT)` may return inaccurate results. To be more certain of the actual image dimensions, you can first capture a frame and then get its height and width with code such as `h, w = frame.shape[:2]`. Occasionally, you might even encounter a camera that yields a few bad frames with unstable dimensions before it starts yielding good frames with stable dimensions. If you are concerned about guarding against this kind of quirk, you may want to read and ignore a few frames at the start of a capture session.

Unfortunately, in most cases, the `get` method of `VideoCapture` does not return an accurate value for the camera's frame rate; it typically returns 0. The official documentation at `http://docs.opencv.org/modules/highgui/doc/reading_and_writing_images_and_video.html` warns of the following:

"Value 0 is returned when querying a property that is not supported by the backend used by the VideoCapture instance.

Note
Reading / writing properties involves many layers. Some unexpected result might happens [sic] along this chain.
`VideoCapture -> API Backend -> Operating System -> Device Driver -> Device Hardware`
The returned value might be different from what really is used by the device or it could be encoded using device-dependent rules (for example, steps or percentage). Effective behavior depends from [sic] device driver and the API backend."

To create an appropriate `VideoWriter` class for the camera, we have to either make an assumption about the frame rate (as we did in the preceding code) or measure it using a timer. The latter approach is better and we will cover it later in this chapter.

The number of cameras and their order is, of course, system-dependent. Unfortunately, OpenCV does not provide any means of querying the number of cameras or their properties. If an invalid index is used to construct a `VideoCapture` class, the `VideoCapture` class will not yield any frames; its `read` method will return `(False, None)`. To avoid trying to retrieve frames from a `VideoCapture` object that was not opened correctly, you may want to first call the `VideoCapture.isOpened` method, which returns a Boolean.

The `read` method is inappropriate when we need to synchronize either a set of cameras or a **multihead camera** such as a stereo camera. Then, we use the `grab` and `retrieve` methods instead. For a set of two cameras, we can use code similar to the following:

```
success0 = cameraCapture0.grab()
success1 = cameraCapture1.grab()
if success0 and success1:
    frame0 = cameraCapture0.retrieve()
    frame1 = cameraCapture1.retrieve()
```

Displaying an image in a window

One of the most basic operations in OpenCV is displaying an image in a window. This can be done with the `imshow` function. If you come from any other GUI framework background, you might think it sufficient to call `imshow` to display an image. However, in OpenCV, the window is drawn (or re-drawn) only when you call another function, `waitKey`. The latter function pumps the window's event queue (allowing various events such as drawing to be handled), and it returns the keycode of any key that the user may have typed within a specified timeout. To some extent, this rudimentary design simplifies the task of developing demos that use video or webcam input; at least the developer has manual control over the capture and display of new frames.

Here is a very simple sample script to read an image from a file and display it:

```
import cv2
import numpy as np

img = cv2.imread('my-image.png')
cv2.imshow('my image', img)
cv2.waitKey()
cv2.destroyAllWindows()
```

The `imshow` function takes two parameters: the name of the window in which we want to display the image and the image itself. We will talk about `waitKey` in more detail in the next section, *Displaying camera frames in a window*.

The aptly named `destroyAllWindows` function disposes of all of the windows created by OpenCV.

Displaying camera frames in a window

OpenCV allows named windows to be created, redrawn, and destroyed using the `namedWindow`, `imshow`, and `destroyWindow` functions. Also, any window may capture keyboard input via the `waitKey` function and mouse input via the `setMouseCallback` function. Let's look at an example where we show the frames captured from a live camera:

```
import cv2

clicked = False
def onMouse(event, x, y, flags, param):
    global clicked
    if event == cv2.EVENT_LBUTTONUP:
        clicked = True

cameraCapture = cv2.VideoCapture(0)
cv2.namedWindow('MyWindow')
cv2.setMouseCallback('MyWindow', onMouse)

print('Showing camera feed. Click window or press any key to stop.')
success, frame = cameraCapture.read()
while success and cv2.waitKey(1) == -1 and not clicked:
    cv2.imshow('MyWindow', frame)
    success, frame = cameraCapture.read()

cv2.destroyWindow('MyWindow')
cameraCapture.release()
```

The argument for `waitKey` is a number of milliseconds to wait for keyboard input. By default, it is 0, which is a special value meaning infinity. The return value is either -1 (meaning that no key has been pressed) or an ASCII keycode, such as 27 for *Esc*. For a list of ASCII keycodes, refer to http://www.asciitable.com/. Also, note that Python provides a standard function, `ord`, which can convert a character into its ASCII keycode. For example, `ord('a')` returns 97.

Again, note that OpenCV's window functions and `waitKey` are interdependent. OpenCV windows are only updated when `waitKey` is called. Conversely, `waitKey` only captures input when an OpenCV window has focus.

The mouse callback passed to `setMouseCallback` should take five arguments, as seen in our code sample. The callback's `param` argument is set as an optional third argument to `setMouseCallback`. By default, it is 0. The callback's event argument is one of the following actions:

- `cv2.EVENT_MOUSEMOVE`: This event refers to mouse movement.
- `cv2.EVENT_LBUTTONDOWN`: This event refers to the left button going down when it is pressed.
- `cv2.EVENT_RBUTTONDOWN`: This event refers to the right button going down when it is pressed.
- `cv2.EVENT_MBUTTONDOWN`: This event refers to the middle button going down when it is pressed.
- `cv2.EVENT_LBUTTONUP`: This event refers to the left button coming back up when it is released.
- `cv2.EVENT_RBUTTONUP`: This event refers to the right button coming back up when it is released.
- `cv2.EVENT_MBUTTONUP`: This event refers to the middle button coming back up when it is released.
- `cv2.EVENT_LBUTTONDBLCLK`: This event refers to the left button being double-clicked.
- `cv2.EVENT_RBUTTONDBLCLK`: This event refers to the right button being double-clicked.
- `cv2.EVENT_MBUTTONDBLCLK`: This event refers to the middle button being double-clicked.

The mouse callback's flags argument may be some bitwise combination of the following events:

- `cv2.EVENT_FLAG_LBUTTON`: This event refers to the left button being pressed.
- `cv2.EVENT_FLAG_RBUTTON`: This event refers to the right button being pressed.
- `cv2.EVENT_FLAG_MBUTTON`: This event refers to the middle button being pressed.
- `cv2.EVENT_FLAG_CTRLKEY`: This event refers to the *Ctrl* key being pressed.
- `cv2.EVENT_FLAG_SHIFTKEY`: This event refers to the *Shift* key being pressed.
- `cv2.EVENT_FLAG_ALTKEY`: This event refers to the *Alt* key being pressed.

Unfortunately, OpenCV does not provide any means of manually handling window events. For example, we cannot stop our application when a window's close button is clicked. Due to OpenCV's limited event handling and GUI capabilities, many developers prefer to integrate it with other application frameworks. Later in this chapter, in the *Cameo – an object-oriented design* section, we will design an abstraction layer to help to integrate OpenCV with any application framework.

Project Cameo (face tracking and image manipulation)

OpenCV is often studied through a cookbook approach that covers a lot of algorithms, but nothing about high-level application development. To an extent, this approach is understandable because OpenCV's potential applications are so diverse. OpenCV is used in a wide variety of applications, such as photo/video editors, motion-controlled games, a robot's AI, or psychology experiments where we log participants' eye movements. Across these varied use cases, can we truly study a useful set of abstractions?

The book's authors believe we can, and the sooner we start creating abstractions, the better. We will structure many of our OpenCV examples around a single application, but, at each step, we will design a component of this application to be extensible and reusable.

We will develop an interactive application that performs face tracking and image manipulations on camera input in real time. This type of application covers a broad range of OpenCV's functionality and challenges us to create an efficient, effective implementation.

Specifically, our application will merge faces in real time. Given two streams of camera input (or, optionally, prerecorded video input), the application will superimpose faces from one stream atop faces in the other. Filters and distortions will be applied to give this blended scene a unified look and feel. Users should have the experience of being engaged in a live performance where they enter another environment and persona. This type of user experience is popular in amusement parks such as Disneyland.

In such an application, users would immediately notice flaws, such as a low frame rate or inaccurate tracking. To get the best results, we will try several approaches using conventional imaging and depth imaging.

We will call our application Cameo. A cameo (in jewelry) is a small portrait of a person or (in film) a very brief role played by a celebrity.

Cameo – an object-oriented design

Python applications can be written in a purely procedural style. This is often done with small applications, such as our basic I/O scripts, discussed previously. However, from now on, we will often use an object-oriented style because it promotes modularity and extensibility.

From our overview of OpenCV's I/O functionality, we know that all images are similar, regardless of their source or destination. No matter how we obtain a stream of images or where we send it as output, we can apply the same application-specific logic to each frame in this stream. Separation of I/O code and application code becomes especially convenient in an application, such as Cameo, which uses multiple I/O streams.

We will create classes called `CaptureManager` and `WindowManager` as high-level interfaces to I/O streams. Our application code may use `CaptureManager` to read new frames and, optionally, to dispatch each frame to one or more outputs, including a still image file, a video file, and a window (via a `WindowManager` class). A `WindowManager` class lets our application code handle a window and events in an object-oriented style.

Both `CaptureManager` and `WindowManager` are extensible. We could make implementations that do not rely on OpenCV for I/O.

Abstracting a video stream with managers.CaptureManager

As we have seen, OpenCV can capture, show, and record a stream of images from either a video file or camera, but there are some special considerations in each case. Our `CaptureManager` class abstracts some of the differences and provides a higher-level interface to dispatch images from the capture stream to one or more outputs—a still image file, video file, or window.

A `CaptureManager` object is initialized with a `VideoCapture` object and has `enterFrame` and `exitFrame` methods that should typically be called on every iteration of an application's main loop. Between a call to `enterFrame` and `exitFrame`, the application may (any number of times) set a `channel` property and get a `frame` property. The `channel` property is initially `0` and only multihead cameras use other values. The `frame` property is an image corresponding to the current channel's state when `enterFrame` was called.

A `CaptureManager` class also has the `writeImage`, `startWritingVideo`, and `stopWritingVideo` methods that may be called at any time. Actual file writing is postponed until `exitFrame`. Also, during the `exitFrame` method, `frame` may be shown in a window, depending on whether the application code provides a `WindowManager` class either as an argument to the constructor of `CaptureManager` or by setting the `previewWindowManager` property.

If the application code manipulates `frame`, the manipulations are reflected in recorded files and in the window. A `CaptureManager` class has a constructor argument and property called `shouldMirrorPreview`, which should be `True` if we want `frame` to be mirrored (horizontally flipped) in the window but not in recorded files. Typically, when facing a camera, users prefer a live camera feed to be mirrored.

Recall that a `VideoWriter` object needs a frame rate, but OpenCV does not provide any reliable way to get an accurate frame rate for a camera. The `CaptureManager` class works around this limitation by using a frame counter and Python's standard `time.time` function to estimate the frame rate if necessary. This approach is not foolproof. Depending on frame rate fluctuations and the system-dependent implementation of `time.time`, the accuracy of the estimate might still be poor in some cases. However, if we deploy to unknown hardware, it is better than just assuming that the user's camera has a particular frame rate.

Let's create a file called `managers.py`, which will contain our implementation of `CaptureManager`. This implementation turns out to be quite long, so we will look at it in several pieces:

1. First, let's add imports and a constructor, as follows:

```python
import cv2
import numpy
import time


class CaptureManager(object):
    def __init__(self, capture, previewWindowManager = None,
                 shouldMirrorPreview = False):
        self.previewWindowManager = previewWindowManager
        self.shouldMirrorPreview = shouldMirrorPreview
        self._capture = capture
        self._channel = 0
        self._enteredFrame = False
        self._frame = None
        self._imageFilename = None
        self._videoFilename = None
        self._videoEncoding = None
```

```
self._videoWriter = None
self._startTime = None
self._framesElapsed = 0
self._fpsEstimate = None
```

2. Next, let's add the following getter and setter methods for the properties of `CaptureManager`:

```
@property
def channel(self):
    return self._channel
@channel.setter
def channel(self, value):
    if self._channel != value:
        self._channel = value
        self._frame = None
@property
def frame(self):
    if self._enteredFrame and self._frame is None:
        _, self._frame = self._capture.retrieve(
            self._frame, self.channel)
    return self._frame
@property
def isWritingImage(self):
    return self._imageFilename is not None
@property
def isWritingVideo(self):
    return self._videoFilename is not None
```

Note that most of the `member` variables are nonpublic, as denoted by the underscore prefix in variable names, such as `self._enteredFrame`. These nonpublic variables relate to the state of the current frame and any file-writing operations. As discussed previously, the application code only needs to configure a few things, which are implemented as constructor arguments and settable public properties: the camera channel, the window manager, and the option to mirror the camera preview.

This book assumes a certain level of familiarity with Python; however, if you are getting confused by those @ annotations (for example, @property), refer to the Python documentation about decorators, a built-in feature of the language that allows the wrapping of a function by another function, normally used to apply user-defined behavior in several places of an application. Specifically, you can find relevant documentation at https://docs.python.org/3/reference/compound_stmts.html#grammar-token-decorator.

Python does not enforce the concept of nonpublic member variables, but in cases where the developer intends a variable to be treated as nonpublic, you will often see the single-underscore prefix (_) or double-underscore prefix (__). The single-underscore prefix is just a convention, indicating that the variable should be treated as protected (accessed only within the class and its subclasses). The double-underscore prefix actually causes the Python interpreter to rename the variable, such that MyClass.__myVariable becomes MyClass._MyClass__myVariable. This is called **name mangling** (quite appropriately). By convention, such a variable should be treated as private (accessed only within the class, and **not** its subclasses). The same prefixes, with the same significance, can be applied to methods as well as variables.

3. Continuing with our implementation, let's add the enterFrame method to managers.py:

```
def enterFrame(self):
    """Capture the next frame, if any."""
    # But first, check that any previous frame was exited.
    assert not self._enteredFrame, \
        'previous enterFrame() had no matching exitFrame()'
    if self._capture is not None:
        self._enteredFrame = self._capture.grab()
```

Note that the implementation of enterFrame only grabs (synchronizes) a frame, whereas actual retrieval from a channel is postponed to a subsequent reading of the frame variable.

4. Next, let's add the exitFrame method to managers.py:

```
def exitFrame(self):
    """Draw to the window. Write to files. Release the
    frame."""

    # Check whether any grabbed frame is retrievable.
    # The getter may retrieve and cache the frame.
```

```
        if self.frame is None:
            self._enteredFrame = False
            return

        # Update the FPS estimate and related variables.
        if self._framesElapsed == 0:
            self._startTime = time.time()
        else:
            timeElapsed = time.time() - self._startTime
            self._fpsEstimate = self._framesElapsed / timeElapsed
        self._framesElapsed += 1

        # Draw to the window, if any.
        if self.previewWindowManager is not None:
            if self.shouldMirrorPreview:
                mirroredFrame = numpy.fliplr(self._frame)
                self.previewWindowManager.show(mirroredFrame)
            else:
                self.previewWindowManager.show(self._frame)

        # Write to the image file, if any.
        if self.isWritingImage:
            cv2.imwrite(self._imageFilename, self._frame)
            self._imageFilename = None

        # Write to the video file, if any.
        self._writeVideoFrame()

        # Release the frame.
        self._frame = None
        self._enteredFrame = False
```

The implementation of exitFrame takes the image from the current channel, estimates a frame rate, shows the image via the window manager (if any), and fulfills any pending requests to write the image to files.

5. Several other methods also pertain to file writing. Let's add the following implementations of public methods named writeImage, startWritingVideo, and stopWritingVideo to managers.py:

```
        def writeImage(self, filename):
            """Write the next exited frame to an image file."""
            self._imageFilename = filename
        def startWritingVideo(
                self, filename,
                encoding = cv2.VideoWriter_fourcc('M','J','P','G')):
            """Start writing exited frames to a video file."""
```

```
            self._videoFilename = filename
            self._videoEncoding = encoding
        def stopWritingVideo(self):
            """Stop writing exited frames to a video file."""
            self._videoFilename = None
            self._videoEncoding = None
            self._videoWriter = None
```

The preceding methods simply update the parameters for file-writing operations, whereas the actual writing operations are postponed to the next call of exitFrame.

6. Earlier in this section, we saw that exitFrame calls a helper method named _writeVideoFrame. Let's add the following implementation of _writeVideoFrame to managers.py:

```
        def _writeVideoFrame(self):
            if not self.isWritingVideo:
                return
            if self._videoWriter is None:
                fps = self._capture.get(cv2.CAP_PROP_FPS)
                if fps <= 0.0:
                    # The capture's FPS is unknown so use an estimate.
                    if self._framesElapsed < 20:
                        # Wait until more frames elapse so that the
                        # estimate is more stable.
                        return
                    else:
                        fps = self._fpsEstimate
                size = (int(self._capture.get(
                            cv2.CAP_PROP_FRAME_WIDTH)),
                        int(self._capture.get(
                            cv2.CAP_PROP_FRAME_HEIGHT)))
                self._videoWriter = cv2.VideoWriter(
                    self._videoFilename, self._videoEncoding,
                    fps, size)
            self._videoWriter.write(self._frame)
```

The preceding method creates or appends to a video file in a manner that should be familiar from our earlier scripts (refer to the *Reading/writing a video file* section, earlier in this chapter). However, in situations where the frame rate is unknown, we skip some frames at the start of the capture session so that we have time to build up an estimate of the frame rate.

This concludes our implementation of `CaptureManager`. Although it relies on `VideoCapture`, we could make other implementations that do not use OpenCV for input. For example, we could make a subclass that is instantiated with a socket connection, whose byte stream could be parsed as a stream of images. Also, we could make a subclass that uses a third-party camera library with different hardware support than what OpenCV provides. However, for Cameo, our current implementation is sufficient.

Abstracting a window and keyboard with managers.WindowManager

As we have seen, OpenCV provides functions that cause a window to be created, be destroyed, show an image, and process events. Rather than being methods of a window class, these functions require a window's name to pass as an argument. Since this interface is not object-oriented, it is arguably inconsistent with OpenCV's general style. Also, it is unlikely to be compatible with other window-or event-handling interfaces that we might eventually want to use instead of OpenCV's.

For the sake of object orientation and adaptability, we abstract this functionality into a `WindowManager` class with the `createWindow`, `destroyWindow`, `show`, and `processEvents` methods. As a property, `WindowManager` has a function object called `keypressCallback`, which (if it is not `None`) is called from `processEvents` in response to any keypress. The `keypressCallback` object must be a function that takes a single argument, specifically an ASCII keycode.

Let's add an implementation of `WindowManager` to `managers.py`. The implementation begins with the following class declaration and __init__ method:

```
class WindowManager(object):
    def __init__(self, windowName, keypressCallback = None):
        self.keypressCallback = keypressCallback
        self._windowName = windowName
        self._isWindowCreated = False
```

The implementation continues with the following methods to manage the life cycle of the window and its events:

```python
@property
def isWindowCreated(self):
    return self._isWindowCreated
def createWindow(self):
    cv2.namedWindow(self._windowName)
    self._isWindowCreated = True
def show(self, frame):
    cv2.imshow(self._windowName, frame)
def destroyWindow(self):
    cv2.destroyWindow(self._windowName)
    self._isWindowCreated = False
def processEvents(self):
    keycode = cv2.waitKey(1)
    if self.keypressCallback is not None and keycode != -1:
        self.keypressCallback(keycode)
```

Our current implementation only supports keyboard events, which will be sufficient for Cameo. However, we could modify WindowManager to support mouse events, too. For example, the class interface could be expanded to include a mouseCallback property (and optional constructor argument,) but could otherwise remain the same. With an event framework other than OpenCV's, we could support additional event types in the same way by adding callback properties.

Applying everything with cameo.Cameo

Our application is represented by the Cameo class with two methods: run and onKeypress. On initialization, a Cameo object creates a WindowManager object with onKeypress as a callback, as well as a CaptureManager object using a camera (specifically, a cv2.VideoCapture object) and the same WindowManager object. When run is called, the application executes a main loop in which frames and events are processed.

As a result of event processing, `onKeypress` may be called. The spacebar causes a screenshot to be taken, *Tab* causes a screencast (a video recording) to start/stop, and *Esc* causes the application to quit.

In the same directory as `managers.py`, let's create a file called `cameo.py`, where we will implement the `Cameo` class:

1. The implementation begins with the following `import` statements and __init__ method:

```
import cv2
from managers import WindowManager, CaptureManager

class Cameo(object):
    def __init__(self):
        self._windowManager = WindowManager('Cameo',
                                            self.onKeypress)
        self._captureManager = CaptureManager(
            cv2.VideoCapture(0), self._windowManager, True)
```

2. Next, let's add the following implementation of the `run()` method:

```
def run(self):
    """Run the main loop."""
    self._windowManager.createWindow()
    while self._windowManager.isWindowCreated:
        self._captureManager.enterFrame()
        frame = self._captureManager.frame
        if frame is not None:
            # TODO: Filter the frame (Chapter 3).
            pass
        self._captureManager.exitFrame()
        self._windowManager.processEvents()
```

3. To complete the `Cameo` class implementation, here is the `onKeypress()` method:

```
def onKeypress(self, keycode):
    """Handle a keypress.
    space -> Take a screenshot.
    tab -> Start/stop recording a screencast.
    escape -> Quit.
    """
    if keycode == 32: # space
        self._captureManager.writeImage('screenshot.png')
    elif keycode == 9: # tab
        if not self._captureManager.isWritingVideo:
            self._captureManager.startWritingVideo(
```

```
                        'screencast.avi')
                else:
                    self._captureManager.stopWritingVideo()
        elif keycode == 27: # escape
            self._windowManager.destroyWindow()
```

4. Finally, let's add a __main__ block that instantiates and runs Cameo, as follows:

```
if __name__=="__main__":
    Cameo().run()
```

When running the application, note that the live camera feed is mirrored, while screenshots and screencasts are not. This is the intended behavior, as we pass True for shouldMirrorPreview when initializing the CaptureManager class.

Here is a screenshot of Cameo, showing a window (with the title **Cameo**) and the current frame from a camera:

So far, we do not manipulate the frames in any way except to mirror them for preview. We will start to add more interesting effects in Chapter 3, *Processing Images with OpenCV*.

Summary

By now, we should have an application that displays a camera feed, listens for keyboard input, and (on command) records a screenshot or screencast. We are ready to extend the application by inserting some image-filtering code (Chapter 3, *Processing Images with OpenCV*) between the start and end of each frame. Optionally, we are also ready to integrate other camera drivers or application frameworks besides the ones supported by OpenCV.

We also possess the knowledge to manipulate images as NumPy arrays. This forms the perfect foundation for our next topic, filtering images.

3
Processing Images with OpenCV

Sooner or later, when working with images, you will find you need to alter them: be it by applying artistic filters, extrapolating certain sections, blending two images, or whatever else your mind can conjure. This chapter presents some techniques that you can use to alter images. By the end of it, you should be able to perform tasks such as sharpening an image, marking the contours of subjects, and detecting crosswalks using a line segment detector. Specifically, our discussion and code samples will cover the following topics:

- Converting images between different color models
- Understanding the importance of frequencies and the Fourier transform in image processing
- Applying **high-pass filters (HPFs)**, **low-pass filters (LPFs)**, edge detection filters, and custom convolution filters
- Detecting and analyzing contours, lines, circles, and other geometric shapes
- Writing classes and functions that encapsulate the implementation of a filter

Technical requirements

This chapter uses Python, OpenCV, NumPy, and SciPy. Please refer to Chapter 1, *Setting Up OpenCV*, for installation instructions.

The completed code for this chapter can be found in this book's GitHub repository, https:/ /github.com/PacktPublishing/Learning-OpenCV-4-Computer-Vision-with-Python-Third-Edition, in the chapter03 folder. The sample images are also in this book's GitHub repository, in the images folder.

Converting images between different color models

OpenCV implements literally hundreds of formulas that pertain to the conversion of color models. Some color models are commonly used by input devices such as cameras, while other models are commonly used for output devices such as televisions, computer displays, and printers. In between input and output, when we apply computer vision techniques to images, we will typically work with three kinds of color models: grayscale, **blue-green-red** (BGR), and **hue-saturation-value** (HSV). Let's go over these briefly:

- **Grayscale** is a model that reduces color information by translating it into shades of gray or brightness. This model is extremely useful for the intermediate processing of images in problems where brightness information alone is sufficient, such as face detection. Typically, each pixel in a grayscale image is represented by a single 8-bit value, ranging from 0 for black to 255 for white.
- **BGR** is the blue-green-red color model, in which each pixel has a triplet of values representing the blue, green, and red components or **channels** of the pixel's color. Web developers, and anyone who works with computer graphics, will be familiar with a similar definition of colors, except with the reverse channel order, **red-green-blue** (RGB). Typically, each pixel in a BGR image is represented by a triplet of 8-bit values, such as `[0, 0, 0]` for black, `[255, 0, 0]` for blue, `[0, 255, 0]` for green, `[0, 0, 255]` for red, and `[255, 255, 255]` for white.
- The **HSV** model uses a different triplet of channels. Hue is the color's tone, saturation is its intensity, and value represents its brightness.

By default, OpenCV uses the BGR color model (with 8 bits per channel) to represent any image that it loads from a file or captures from a camera.

Now that we have defined the color models we will use, let's consider how the default model might differ from our intuitive understanding of color.

Light is not paint

For newcomers to the BGR color space, it might seem that things do not add up properly: for example, the (0, 255, 255) triplet (no blue, full green, and full red) produces the color yellow. If you have an artistic background, you won't even need to pick up paints and brushes to know that green and red paint mix together into a muddy shade of brown. However, the color models that are used in computing are called **additive** models and they deal with lights. Lights behave differently from paints (which follow a **subtractive** color model), and since software runs on a computer whose medium is a monitor that emits light, the color model of reference is the additive one.

Exploring the Fourier transform

Much of the processing you apply to images and videos in OpenCV involves the concept of the Fourier transform in some capacity. Joseph Fourier was an 18th-century French mathematician who discovered and popularized many mathematical concepts. He studied the physics of heat, and the mathematics of all things that can be represented by waveform functions. In particular, he observed that all waveforms are just the sum of simple sinusoids of different frequencies.

In other words, the waveforms you observe all around you are the sum of other waveforms. This concept is incredibly useful when manipulating images because it allows us to identify regions in images where a signal (such as the values of image pixels) changes a lot, and also regions where the change is less dramatic. We can then arbitrarily mark these regions as noise or regions of interests, background or foreground, and so on. These are the frequencies that make up the original image, and we have the power to separate them to make sense of the image and extrapolate interesting data.

OpenCV implements a number of algorithms that enable us to process images and make sense of the data contained in them, and these are also reimplemented in NumPy to make our life even easier. NumPy has a **fast Fourier transform** (**FFT**) package, which contains the fft2 method. This method allows us to compute a **discrete Fourier transform** (**DFT**) of the image.

Let's examine the concept of the **magnitude spectrum** of an image using the Fourier transform. The magnitude spectrum of an image is another image that provides a representation of the original image in terms of its changes. Think of it as taking an image and dragging all the brightest pixels to the center. Then, you gradually work your way out to the border where all the darkest pixels have been pushed. Immediately, you will be able to see how many light and dark pixels are contained in your image and the percentage of their distribution.

The Fourier transform is the basis of many algorithms that are used for common image processing operations, such as edge detection or line and shape detection.

Before examining these in detail, let's take a look at two concepts that – in conjunction with the Fourier transform – form the foundation of the aforementioned processing operations: HPFs and LPFs.

HPFs and LPFs

An HPF is a filter that examines a region of an image and boosts the intensity of certain pixels based on the difference in the intensity of the surrounding pixels.

Take, for example, the following kernel:

```
[[ 0,    -0.25,  0   ],
 [-0.25,  1,    -0.25],
 [ 0,    -0.25,  0   ]]
```

 A **kernel** is a set of weights that are applied to a region in a source image to generate a single pixel in the destination image. For example, if we call an OpenCV function with a parameter to specify a kernel size or `ksize` of 7, this implies that 49 (7 x 7) source pixels are considered when generating each destination pixel. We can think of a kernel as a piece of frosted glass moving over the source image and letting a diffused blend of the source's light pass through.

The preceding kernel gives us the average difference in intensity between the central pixel and all its immediate horizontal neighbors. If a pixel stands out from the surrounding pixels, the resulting value will be high. This type of kernel represents a so-called high-boost filter, which is a type of HPF, and it is particularly effective in edge detection.

Note that the values in an edge detection kernel typically sum up to 0. We will cover this in the *Custom kernels – getting convoluted* section of this chapter.

Let's go through an example of applying an HPF to an image:

```
import cv2
import numpy as np
from scipy import ndimage

kernel_3x3 = np.array([[-1, -1, -1],
                       [-1, 8, -1],
                       [-1, -1, -1]])

kernel_5x5 = np.array([[-1, -1, -1, -1, -1],
                       [-1, 1, 2, 1, -1],
                       [-1, 2, 4, 2, -1],
                       [-1, 1, 2, 1, -1],
                       [-1, -1, -1, -1, -1]])

img = cv2.imread("../images/statue_small.jpg", 0)

k3 = ndimage.convolve(img, kernel_3x3)
k5 = ndimage.convolve(img, kernel_5x5)

blurred = cv2.GaussianBlur(img, (17,17), 0)
g_hpf = img - blurred

cv2.imshow("3x3", k3)
cv2.imshow("5x5", k5)
cv2.imshow("blurred", blurred)
cv2.imshow("g_hpf", g_hpf)
cv2.waitKey()
cv2.destroyAllWindows()
```

After the initial imports, we define a `3x3` kernel and a `5x5` kernel, and then we load the image in grayscale. After that, we want to convolve the image with each of the kernels. There are several library functions available for such a purpose. NumPy provides the `convolve` function; however, it only accepts one-dimensional arrays. Although the convolution of multidimensional arrays can be achieved with NumPy, it would be a bit complex. SciPy's `ndimage` module provides another `convolve` function, which supports multidimensional arrays. Finally, OpenCV provides a `filter2D` function (for convolution with 2D arrays) and a `sepFilter2D` function (for the special case of a 2D kernel that can be decomposed into two one-dimensional kernels). The preceding code sample illustrates the `ndimage.convolve` function. We will use the `cv2.filter2D` function in other samples in the *Custom kernels – getting convoluted* section of this chapter.

Our script proceeds by applying two HPFs with the two convolution kernels we defined. Finally, we also implement a different method of obtaining an HPF by applying a LPF and calculating the difference between the original image. Let's see how each filter looks. As input, we start with the following photograph:

Now, here is a screenshot of the output:

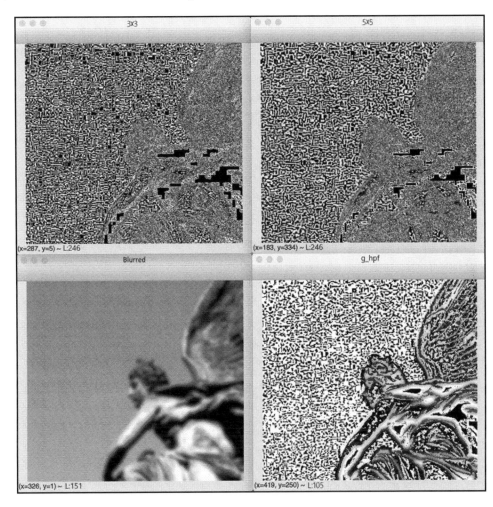

You will notice that the differential HPF, as shown in the bottom-right photograph, yields the best edge-finding result. Since this differential method involves a low-pass filter, let's elaborate on that type of filter. If an HPF boosts the intensity of a pixel, given its difference with neighbors, a LPF will smoothen the pixel if the difference from surrounding pixels is lower than a certain threshold. This is used in denoising and blurring. For example, one of the most popular blurring/smoothening filters, the Gaussian blur, is a low-pass filter that attenuates the intensity of high-frequency signals. The result of the Gaussian blur is shown in the lower-left photograph.

Now that we have tried these filters in a basic example, let's consider how to integrate them into a larger, more interactive application.

Creating modules

Let's revisit the Cameo project that we started in Chapter 2, *Handling Files, Cameras, and GUIs*. We can modify Cameo so that it applies filters to the captured images in real time. As in the case of our `CaptureManager` and `WindowManager` classes, our filters should be reusable outside of Cameo. Thus, we should separate the filters into their own Python module or file.

Let's create a file called `filters.py` in the same directory as `cameo.py`. We need the following `import` statements in `filters.py`:

```
import cv2
import numpy
import utils
```

Let's also create a file called `utils.py` in the same directory. It should contain the following `import` statements:

```
import cv2
import numpy
import scipy.interpolate
```

We will be adding filter functions and classes to `filters.py`, while more general-purpose math functions will go in `utils.py`.

Edge detection

Edges play a major role in both human and computer vision. We, as humans, can easily recognize many object types and their pose just by seeing a backlit silhouette or a rough sketch. Indeed, when art emphasizes edges and poses, it often seems to convey the idea of an archetype, such as Rodin's *The Thinker* or Joe Shuster's *Superman*. Software, too, can reason about edges, poses, and archetypes. We will discuss these kinds of reasoning in later chapters.

OpenCV provides many edge-finding filters, including `Laplacian`, `Sobel`, and `Scharr`. These filters are supposed to turn non-edge regions into black and turn edge regions into white or saturated colors. However, they are prone to misidentifying noise as edges. This flaw can be mitigated by blurring an image before trying to find its edges. OpenCV also provides many blurring filters, including `blur` (a simple average), `medianBlur`, and `GaussianBlur`. The arguments for the edge-finding and blurring filters vary but always include `ksize`, an odd whole number that represents the width and height (in pixels) of a filter's kernel.

For blurring, let's use `medianBlur`, which is effective in removing digital video noise, especially in color images. For edge-finding, let's use `Laplacian`, which produces bold edge lines, especially in grayscale images. After applying `medianBlur`, but before applying `Laplacian`, we should convert the image from BGR into grayscale.

Once we have the result of `Laplacian`, we can invert it to get black edges on a white background. Then, we can normalize it (so that its values range from 0 to 1) and then multiply it with the source image to darken the edges. Let's implement this approach in `filters.py`:

```python
def strokeEdges(src, dst, blurKsize = 7, edgeKsize = 5):
    if blurKsize >= 3:
        blurredSrc = cv2.medianBlur(src, blurKsize)
        graySrc = cv2.cvtColor(blurredSrc, cv2.COLOR_BGR2GRAY)
    else:
        graySrc = cv2.cvtColor(src, cv2.COLOR_BGR2GRAY)
    cv2.Laplacian(graySrc, cv2.CV_8U, graySrc, ksize = edgeKsize)
    normalizedInverseAlpha = (1.0 / 255) * (255 - graySrc)
    channels = cv2.split(src)
    for channel in channels:
        channel[:] = channel * normalizedInverseAlpha
    cv2.merge(channels, dst)
```

 Note that we allow kernel sizes to be specified as arguments for `strokeEdges`.

The `blurKsize` argument is used as `ksize` for `medianBlur`, while `edgeKsize` is used as `ksize` for `Laplacian`. With a typical webcam, a `blurKsize` value of 7 and an `edgeKsize` value of 5 might produce the most pleasing effect. Unfortunately, `medianBlur` is expensive with a large `ksize` argument, such as 7.

If you encounter performance problems when running `strokeEdges`, try decreasing the `blurKsize` value. To turn off the blur effect, set it to a value of less than 3.

We will see the effect of this filter a little later in this chapter, after we have integrated it into Cameo in the *Modifying the* application section.

Custom kernels – getting convoluted

As we have just seen, many of OpenCV's predefined filters use a kernel. Remember that a kernel is a set of weights that determines how each output pixel is calculated from a neighborhood of input pixels. Another term for a kernel is a **convolution matrix**. It mixes up or convolves the pixels in a region. Similarly, a kernel-based filter may be called a convolution filter.

OpenCV provides a very versatile `filter2D()` function, which applies any kernel or convolution matrix that we specify. To understand how to use this function, let's learn about the format of a convolution matrix. It is a 2D array with an odd number of rows and columns. The central element corresponds to a pixel of interest, while the other elements correspond to the neighbors of this pixel. Each element contains an integer or floating-point value, which is a weight that gets applied to an input pixel's value. Consider this example:

```
kernel = numpy.array([[-1, -1, -1],
                      [-1,  9, -1],
                      [-1, -1, -1]])
```

Here, the pixel of interest has a weight of 9 and its immediate neighbors each have a weight of −1. For the pixel of interest, the output color will be nine times its input color, minus the input colors of all eight adjacent pixels. If the pixel of interest is already a bit different from its neighbors, this difference becomes intensified. The effect is that the image looks *sharper* as the contrast between the neighbors is increased.

Continuing with our example, we can apply this convolution matrix to a source and destination image, respectively, as follows:

```
cv2.filter2D(src, -1, kernel, dst)
```

The second argument specifies the per-channel depth of the destination image (such as `cv2.CV_8U` for 8 bits per channel). A negative value (such as to one being used here) means that the destination image has the same depth as the source image.

 For color images, note that `filter2D()` applies the kernel equally to each channel. To use different kernels on different channels, we would also have to use the `split()` and `merge()` functions.

Based on this simple example, let's add two classes to `filters.py`. One class, `VConvolutionFilter`, will represent a convolution filter in general. A subclass, `SharpenFilter`, will represent our sharpening filter specifically. Let's edit `filters.py` so that we can implement these two new classes, as follows:

```
class VConvolutionFilter(object):
    """A filter that applies a convolution to V (or all of BGR)."""
    def __init__(self, kernel):
        self._kernel = kernel
    def apply(self, src, dst):
        """Apply the filter with a BGR or gray source/destination."""
        cv2.filter2D(src, -1, self._kernel, dst)

class SharpenFilter(VConvolutionFilter):
    """A sharpen filter with a 1-pixel radius."""
    def __init__(self):
        kernel = numpy.array([[-1, -1, -1],
                              [-1,  9, -1],
                              [-1, -1, -1]])
        VConvolutionFilter.__init__(self, kernel)
```

Note that the weights sum up to 1. This should be the case whenever we want to leave the image's overall brightness unchanged. If we modify a sharpening kernel slightly so that its weights sum up to 0 instead, we'll have an edge detection kernel that turns edges white and non-edges black. For example, let's add the following edge detection filter to `filters.py`:

```
class FindEdgesFilter(VConvolutionFilter):
    """An edge-finding filter with a 1-pixel radius."""
    def __init__(self):
        kernel = numpy.array([[-1, -1, -1],
                              [-1,  8, -1],
                              [-1, -1, -1]])
        VConvolutionFilter.__init__(self, kernel)
```

Next, let's make a blur filter. Generally, for a blur effect, the weights should sum up to 1 and should be positive throughout the neighborhood. For example, we can take a simple average of the neighborhood as follows:

```
class BlurFilter(VConvolutionFilter):
    """A blur filter with a 2-pixel radius."""
    def __init__(self):
        kernel = numpy.array([[0.04, 0.04, 0.04, 0.04, 0.04],
                              [0.04, 0.04, 0.04, 0.04, 0.04],
                              [0.04, 0.04, 0.04, 0.04, 0.04],
                              [0.04, 0.04, 0.04, 0.04, 0.04],
                              [0.04, 0.04, 0.04, 0.04, 0.04]])
        VConvolutionFilter.__init__(self, kernel)
```

Our sharpening, edge detection, and blur filters use kernels that are highly symmetric. Sometimes, though, kernels with less symmetry produce an interesting effect. Let's consider a kernel that blurs on one side (with positive weights) and sharpens on the other (with negative weights). It will produce a ridged or *embossed* effect. Here is an implementation that we can add to filters.py:

```
class EmbossFilter(VConvolutionFilter):
    """An emboss filter with a 1-pixel radius."""
    def __init__(self):
        kernel = numpy.array([[-2, -1, 0],
                              [-1,  1, 1],
                              [ 0,  1, 2]])
        VConvolutionFilter.__init__(self, kernel)
```

This set of custom convolution filters is very basic. Indeed, it is more basic than OpenCV's ready-made set of filters. However, with a bit of experimentation, you should be able to write your own kernels that produce a unique look.

Modifying the application

Now that we have high-level functions and classes for several filters, it is trivial to apply any of them to the captured frames in Cameo. Let's edit cameo.py and add the lines that appear in bold in the following excerpts. First, we need to add our filters module to our list of imports, as follows:

```
import cv2
import filters
from managers import WindowManager, CaptureManager
```

Now, we need to initialize any filter objects we will use. An example of this can be seen in the following modified __init__ method:

```
class Cameo(object):
    def __init__(self):
        self._windowManager = WindowManager('Cameo',
                                            self.onKeypress)
        self._captureManager = CaptureManager(
            cv2.VideoCapture(0), self._windowManager, True)
        self._curveFilter = filters.BGRPortraCurveFilter()
```

Finally, we need to modify the run method in order to apply our choice of filters. Refer to the following example:

```
    def run(self):
        """Run the main loop."""
        self._windowManager.createWindow()
        while self._windowManager.isWindowCreated:
            self._captureManager.enterFrame()
            frame = self._captureManager.frame
            if frame is not None:
                filters.strokeEdges(frame, frame)
                self._curveFilter.apply(frame, frame)
            self._captureManager.exitFrame()
            self._windowManager.processEvents()

# ... The rest is the same as in Chapter 2
```

Here, we have applied two effects: stroking the edges and emulating the colors of a brand of photo film called Kodak Portra. Feel free to modify the code to apply any filters you like.

 For details about how to implement the Portra film emulation effect, refer to Appendix A, *Bending Color Space with a Curves Filter*.

Here is a screenshot from Cameo with stroked edges and Portra-like colors:

Now that we have sampled some of the visual effects that we can achieve with simple filters, let's consider how we can use other simple functions for analytical purposes – specifically, the detection of edges and shapes.

Edge detection with Canny

OpenCV offers a handy function called Canny (after the algorithm's inventor, John F. Canny), which is very popular not only because of its effectiveness, but also because of the simplicity of its implementation in an OpenCV program since it is a one-liner:

```
import cv2
import numpy as np

img = cv2.imread("../images/statue_small.jpg", 0)
cv2.imwrite("canny.jpg", cv2.Canny(img, 200, 300))  # Canny in one line!
cv2.imshow("canny", cv2.imread("canny.jpg"))
cv2.waitKey()
cv2.destroyAllWindows()
```

The result is a very clear identification of the edges:

The Canny edge detection algorithm is complex but also quite interesting. It is a five-step process:

1. Denoise the image with a Gaussian filter.
2. Calculate the gradients.
3. Apply **non-maximum suppression (NMS)** on the edges. Basically, this means that the algorithm selects the best edges from a set of overlapping edges. We'll discuss the concept of NMS in detail in `Chapter 7`, *Building Custom Object Detectors.*
4. Apply a double threshold to all the detected edges to eliminate any false positives.
5. Analyze all the edges and their connection to each other to keep the real edges and discard the weak ones.

After finding Canny edges, we can do further analysis of the edges in order to determine whether they match a common shape, such as a line or a circle. The Hough transform is one algorithm that uses Canny edges in this way. We will experiment with it later in this chapter, in the *Detecting lines, circles, or other shapes* section.

For now, we will examine other ways of analyzing shapes, not based on edge detection but rather on the concept of finding a blob of similar pixels.

Contour detection

A vital task in computer vision is contour detection. We want to detect contours or outlines of subjects contained in an image or video frame, not only as an end in itself but also as a step toward other operations. These operations are, namely, computing bounding polygons, approximating shapes, and generally calculating **regions of interest** (**ROIs**). ROIs considerably simplify interaction with image data because a rectangular region in NumPy is easily defined with an array slice. We will be using contour detection and ROIs a lot when we explore the concepts of object detection (including face detection) and object tracking.

Let's familiarize ourselves with the API with an example:

```
import cv2
import numpy as np

img = np.zeros((200, 200), dtype=np.uint8)
img[50:150, 50:150] = 255

ret, thresh = cv2.threshold(img, 127, 255, 0)
contours, hierarchy = cv2.findContours(thresh, cv2.RETR_TREE,
                                       cv2.CHAIN_APPROX_SIMPLE)
color = cv2.cvtColor(img, cv2.COLOR_GRAY2BGR)
img = cv2.drawContours(color, contours, -1, (0,255,0), 2)
cv2.imshow("contours", color)
cv2.waitKey()
cv2.destroyAllWindows()
```

First, we create an empty black image that is 200 x 200 pixels in size. Then, we place a white square in the center of it by utilizing array's ability to assign values on a slice.

Then, we threshold the image and call the `findContours` function. This function has three parameters: the input image, the hierarchy type, and the contour approximation method. The second parameter specifies the type of hierarchy tree returned by the function. One of the supported values is `cv2.RETR_TREE`, which tells the function to retrieve the entire hierarchy of external and internal contours. These relationships may matter if we are searching for smaller objects (or smaller regions) inside larger objects (or larger regions). If you only want to retrieve the most external contours, use `cv2.RETR_EXTERNAL`. This may be a good choice in cases where the objects appear on a plain background and we do not care about finding objects within objects.

Referring back to the code sample, note that the `findContours` function returns two elements: the contours and their hierarchy. We use the contours to draw green outlines on the color version of the image. Finally, we display the image.

The result is a white square with its contour drawn in green – a Spartan scene, but effective in demonstrating the concept! Let's move on to more meaningful examples.

Bounding box, minimum area rectangle, and minimum enclosing circle

Finding the contours of a square is a simple task; irregular, skewed, and rotated shapes bring out the full potential of OpenCV's `cv2.findContours` function. Let's take a look at the following image:

In a real-life application, we would be most interested in determining the bounding box of the subject, its minimum enclosing rectangle, and its enclosing circle. The `cv2.findContours` function, in conjunction with a few other OpenCV utilities, makes this very easy to accomplish. First, the following code reads an image from a file, converts it into grayscale, applies a threshold to the grayscale image, and finds the contours in the thresholded image:

```
import cv2
import numpy as np

img = cv2.pyrDown(cv2.imread("hammer.jpg", cv2.IMREAD_UNCHANGED))

ret, thresh = cv2.threshold(cv2.cvtColor(img, cv2.COLOR_BGR2GRAY), 127,
255, cv2.THRESH_BINARY)
contours, hier = cv2.findContours(thresh, cv2.RETR_EXTERNAL,
cv2.CHAIN_APPROX_SIMPLE)
```

Now, for each contour, we can find and draw the bounding box, the minimum enclosing rectangle, and the minimum enclosing circle, as shown in the following code:

```
for c in contours:
    # find bounding box coordinates
    x,y,w,h = cv2.boundingRect(c)
    cv2.rectangle(img, (x,y), (x+w, y+h), (0, 255, 0), 2)

    # find minimum area
    rect = cv2.minAreaRect(c)
    # calculate coordinates of the minimum area rectangle
    box = cv2.boxPoints(rect)
    # normalize coordinates to integers
    box = np.int0(box)
    # draw contours
    cv2.drawContours(img, [box], 0, (0,0, 255), 3)

    # calculate center and radius of minimum enclosing circle
    (x, y), radius = cv2.minEnclosingCircle(c)
    # cast to integers
    center = (int(x), int(y))
    radius = int(radius)
    # draw the circle
    img = cv2.circle(img, center, radius, (0, 255, 0), 2)
```

Finally, we can use the following code to draw the contours and show the image in a window until the user presses a key:

```
cv2.drawContours(img, contours, -1, (255, 0, 0), 1)
cv2.imshow("contours", img)

cv2.waitKey()
cv2.destroyAllWindows()
```

Note that contour detection is performed on a thresholded image, so color information is already lost at this stage, but we draw on the original color image and then show the results in color.

Let's go back and look more closely at the steps we performed in the preceding `for` loop, where we process each detected contour. First, we calculate a simple bounding box:

```
x,y,w,h = cv2.boundingRect(c)
```

This is a pretty straightforward conversion of contour information into the (x, y) coordinates, height, and width of the rectangle. Drawing this rectangle is an easy task and can be done using the following code:

```
cv2.rectangle(img, (x,y), (x+w, y+h), (0, 255, 0), 2)
```

Next, we calculate the minimum-area rectangle enclosing the subject:

```
rect = cv2.minAreaRect(c)
box = cv2.boxPoints(rect)
box = np.int0(box)
```

The mechanism being used here is particularly interesting: OpenCV does not have a function to calculate the coordinates of the minimum rectangle vertices directly from the contour information. Instead, we calculate the minimum rectangle area, and then calculate the vertices of this rectangle. Note that the calculated vertices are floats, but pixels are accessed with integers (you can't access a *portion* of a pixel for the purposes of OpenCV's drawing functions), so we need to perform this conversion. Next, we draw the box, which gives us the perfect opportunity to introduce the `cv2.drawContours` function:

```
cv2.drawContours(img, [box], 0, (0,0, 255), 3)
```

This function – like all of OpenCV's drawing functions – modifies the original image. Note that it takes an array of contours in its second parameter so that you can draw a number of contours in a single operation. Therefore, if you have a single set of points representing a contour polygon, you need to wrap these points in an array, exactly like we did with our box in the preceding example. The third parameter of this function specifies the index of the contours array that we want to draw: a value of −1 will draw all contours; otherwise, a contour at the specified index in the contours array (the second parameter) will be drawn.

Most drawing functions take the color of the drawing (as a BGR tuple) and its thickness (in pixels) as the last two parameters.

The last bounding contour we're going to examine is the minimum enclosing circle:

```
(x, y), radius = cv2.minEnclosingCircle(c)
center = (int(x), int(y))
radius = int(radius)
img = cv2.circle(img, center, radius, (0, 255, 0), 2)
```

The only peculiarity of the cv2.minEnclosingCircle function is that it returns a two-element tuple, of which the first element is a tuple itself, representing the coordinates of the circle's center, and the second element is the radius of this circle. After converting all these values into integers, drawing the circle is quite a trivial operation.

When we apply the preceding code to the original image, the final result looks like this:

This is a good result insofar as the circle and rectangles fit tightly around the object. Obviously, though, the object is not circular or rectangular, so we could achieve a tighter fit with various other shapes. Let's do that next.

Convex contours and the Douglas-Peucker algorithm

When working with contours, we may encounter subjects with diverse shapes, including convex ones. A convex shape is one where there are no two points within this shape whose connecting line goes outside the perimeter of the shape itself.

The first facility that OpenCV offers to calculate the approximate bounding polygon of a shape is `cv2.approxPolyDP`. This function takes three parameters:

- A contour.
- An epsilon value representing the maximum discrepancy between the original contour and the approximated polygon (the lower the value, the closer the approximated value will be to the original contour).
- A Boolean flag. If it is `True`, it signifies that the polygon is closed.

The epsilon value is of vital importance to obtain a useful contour, so let's understand what it represents. Epsilon is the maximum difference between the approximated polygon's perimeter and the original contour's perimeter. The smaller this difference is, the more the approximated polygon will be similar to the original contour.

You may ask yourself why we need an approximate polygon when we have a contour that is already a precise representation. The answer to this is that a polygon is a set of straight lines, and many computer vision tasks become simpler if we can define polygons so that they delimit regions for further manipulation and processing.

Now that we know what an epsilon is, we need to obtain contour perimeter information as a reference value. This can be obtained with the `cv2.arcLength` function of OpenCV:

```
epsilon = 0.01 * cv2.arcLength(cnt, True)
approx = cv2.approxPolyDP(cnt, epsilon, True)
```

Effectively, we're instructing OpenCV to calculate an approximated polygon whose perimeter can only differ from the original contour by an epsilon ratio – specifically, 1% of the original arc length.

OpenCV also offers a `cv2.convexHull` function for obtaining processed contour information for convex shapes. This is a straightforward one-line expression:

```
hull = cv2.convexHull(cnt)
```

Let's combine the original contour, approximated polygon contour, and the convex hull into one image to observe the differences between them. To simplify things, we will draw the contours on top of a black background so that the original subject is not visible but its contours are:

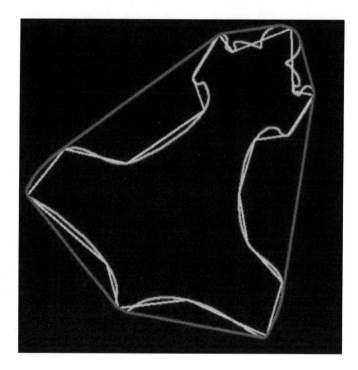

As you can see, the convex hull surrounds the entire subject, the approximated polygon is the innermost polygon shape, and in between the two is the original contour, mainly composed of arcs.

By combining all the preceding steps into one script that loads a file, finds contours, approximates the contours as a polygon, finds a convex hull, and displays a visualization, we have the following code:

```
import cv2
import numpy as np

img = cv2.pyrDown(cv2.imread("hammer.jpg", cv2.IMREAD_UNCHANGED))
```

```
ret, thresh = cv2.threshold(cv2.cvtColor(img, cv2.COLOR_BGR2GRAY),
                            127, 255, cv2.THRESH_BINARY)

contours, hier = cv2.findContours(thresh, cv2.RETR_EXTERNAL,
                                  cv2.CHAIN_APPROX_SIMPLE)

black = np.zeros_like(img)
for cnt in contours:
    epsilon = 0.01 * cv2.arcLength(cnt,True)
    approx = cv2.approxPolyDP(cnt,epsilon,True)
    hull = cv2.convexHull(cnt)
    cv2.drawContours(black, [cnt], -1, (0, 255, 0), 2)
    cv2.drawContours(black, [approx], -1, (255, 255, 0), 2)
    cv2.drawContours(black, [hull], -1, (0, 0, 255), 2)

cv2.imshow("hull", black)
cv2.waitKey()
cv2.destroyAllWindows()
```

Code like this works well on simple images, in which we have only one or a few objects, and only a few colors that are easily separated by thresholds. Unfortunately, color thresholding and contour detection are less effective on complex images that contain several objects or multicolored objects. For these more challenging cases, we will have to look at more complex algorithms.

Detecting lines, circles, and other shapes

Detecting edges and finding contours are not only common and important tasks in their own right; they also form the basis of other complex operations. Line and shape detection walk hand-in-hand with edge and contour detection, so let's examine how OpenCV implements these.

The theory behind line and shape detection has its foundation in a technique called the Hough transform, invented by Richard Duda and Peter Hart, who extended (generalized) the work that was done by Paul Hough in the early 1960s. Let's take a look at OpenCV's API for Hough transforms.

Detecting lines

First of all, let's detect some lines. We can do this with either the `HoughLines` function or the `HoughLinesP` function. The former uses the standard Hough transform, while the latter uses the probabilistic Hough transform (hence the `P` in the name). The probabilistic version is so-called because it only analyzes a subset of the image's points and estimates the probability that these points all belong to the same line. This implementation is an optimized version of the standard Hough transform; it is less computationally intensive and executes faster. `HoughLinesP` is implemented so that it returns the two endpoints of each detected line segment, whereas `HoughLines` is implemented so that it returns a representation of each line as a single point and an angle, without information about endpoints.

Let's take a look at a very simple example:

```
import cv2
import numpy as np

img = cv2.imread('lines.jpg')
gray = cv2.cvtColor(img, cv2.COLOR_BGR2GRAY)
edges = cv2.Canny(gray, 50, 120)
minLineLength = 20
maxLineGap = 5
lines = cv2.HoughLinesP(edges, 1, np.pi/180.0, 20,
                        minLineLength, maxLineGap)
for x1, y1, x2, y2 in lines[0]:
    cv2.line(img, (x1, y1), (x2, y2), (0,255,0),2)

cv2.imshow("edges", edges)
cv2.imshow("lines", img)
cv2.waitKey()
cv2.destroyAllWindows()
```

The crucial part of this simple script – aside from the `HoughLines` function call – is setting the minimum line length (shorter lines will be discarded) and the maximum line gap, which is the maximum size of a gap in a line before the two segments start being considered as separate lines.

Also, note that the `HoughLines` function takes a single channel binary image, which is processed through the Canny edge detection filter. Canny is not a strict requirement, but an image that has been denoised and only represents edges is the ideal source for a Hough transform, so you will find this to be a common practice.

The parameters of `HoughLinesP` are as follows:

- The image.
- The resolution or step size to use when searching for lines. `rho` is the positional step size in pixels, while `theta` is the rotational step size in radians. For example, if we specify `rho=1` and `theta=np.pi/180.0`, we search for lines that are separated by as little as 1 pixel and 1 degree.
- The `threshold`, which represents the threshold below which a line is discarded. The Hough transform works with a system of bins and votes, with each bin representing a line, so if a candidate line has at least the `threshold` number of votes, it is retained; otherwise, it is discarded.
- `minLineLength` and `maxLineGap`, which we mentioned previously.

Detecting circles

OpenCV also has a function for detecting circles, called `HoughCircles`. It works in a very similar fashion to `HoughLines`, but where `minLineLength` and `maxLineGap` were the parameters to be used to discard or retain lines, `HoughCircles` has a minimum distance between a circle's centers, as well as minimum and maximum values for a circle's radius. Here is the obligatory example:

```
import cv2
import numpy as np

planets = cv2.imread('planet_glow.jpg')
gray_img = cv2.cvtColor(planets, cv2.COLOR_BGR2GRAY)
gray_img = cv2.medianBlur(gray_img, 5)

circles = cv2.HoughCircles(gray_img,cv2.HOUGH_GRADIENT,1,120,
                           param1=100,param2=30,minRadius=0,maxRadius=0)

circles = np.uint16(np.around(circles))

for i in circles[0,:]:
    # draw the outer circle
    cv2.circle(planets, (i[0],i[1]),i[2],(0,255,0),2)
    # draw the center of the circle
    cv2.circle(planets, (i[0],i[1]),2,(0,0,255),3)
cv2.imwrite("planets_circles.jpg", planets)
cv2.imshow("HoughCirlces", planets)
cv2.waitKey()
cv2.destroyAllWindows()
```

Here is a visual representation of the result:

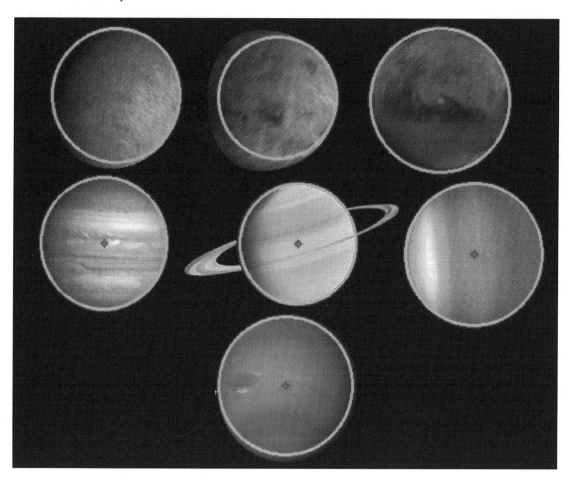

Detecting other shapes

OpenCV's implementations of the Hough transform are limited to detecting lines and circles; however, we already implicitly explored shape detection in general when we talked about `approxPolyDP`. This function allows for the approximation of polygons, so if your image contains polygons, they will be accurately detected through the combined use of `cv2.findContours` and `cv2.approxPolyDP`.

Summary

At this point, you should have gained a good understanding of color models, the Fourier transform, and several kinds of filters that have been made available by OpenCV to process images.

You should also be proficient in detecting edges, lines, circles, and shapes in general. Additionally, you should be able to find contours and exploit the information they provide about the subjects contained in an image. These concepts are complementary to the next chapter's topics – namely, the segmentation of an image according to depth and estimating the distance of a subject in an image.

4
Depth Estimation and Segmentation

This chapter begins by showing you how to use data from a depth camera to identify foreground and background regions, such that we can limit an effect to only the foreground or only the background.

After covering depth cameras, the chapter proceeds with other techniques for depth estimation, namely, **stereo imaging** and **structure from motion (SfM)**. The latter techniques do not require a depth camera; instead, they rely on capturing images of a subject from multiple perspectives with one or more ordinary cameras.

Finally, the chapter covers segmentation techniques that allow us to extract foreground objects from a single image. By the end of the chapter, you will learn several ways to segment an image into multiple depths or multiple objects. Specifically, we will cover the following topics:

- Using a depth camera to capture depth maps, point cloud maps, disparity maps, images based on visible light, and images based on infrared light
- Converting 10-bit images to 8-bit images
- Converting a disparity map into a mask that differentiates between foreground and background regions
- Using either stereo imaging or SfM to create a disparity map
- Using the GrabCut algorithm to segment an image into foreground and background regions
- Using the Watershed algorithm to segment an image into multiple regions that might be different objects

Technical requirements

This chapter uses Python, OpenCV, and NumPy. Some parts of the chapter use a depth camera, such as Asus Xtion PRO, along with OpenCV's optional support for OpenNI 2 in order to capture images from such a camera. Please refer back to Chapter 1, *Setting Up OpenCV*, for installation instructions. The chapter also uses Matplotlib to make charts. To install matplotlib, run $ pip install matplotlib (or $ pip3 install matplotlib, depending on your environment).

The completed code for this chapter can be found in this book's GitHub repository, https://github.com/PacktPublishing/Learning-OpenCV-4-Computer-Vision-with-Python-Third-Edition, in the chapter04 folder. Sample images are in the repository in the images folder.

Creating modules

To help us build an interactive demo of a depth camera, we will reuse much of the Cameo project that we developed in Chapter 2, *Handling Files, Cameras, and GUIs*, and Chapter 3, *Processing Images with OpenCV*. As you will recall, we designed Cameo to support various kinds of input, so we can easily adapt it to support depth cameras in particular. We will add code that analyzes the depth layers in an image in order to find the main region, such as the face of a person sitting in front of the camera. Having found this region, we will paint everything else black. This type of effect is sometimes used in chat applications to hide the background so that users have more privacy.

Some of the code to manipulate depth-camera data will be reusable outside Cameo.py, so we should separate it into a new module. Let's create a depth.py file in the same directory as Cameo.py. We need the following import statement in depth.py:

```
import numpy
```

Our application will use depth-related functionality, so let's add the following import statement to Cameo.py:

```
import depth
```

We will also modify CaptureManager.py, but we do not need to add any new import statements to it.

Now that we have taken a brief look at the modules that we will create or modify, let's go deeper into the subject of depth.

Capturing frames from a depth camera

Back in `Chapter 2`, *Handling Files, Cameras, and GUIs*, we discussed the concept that a computer can have multiple video capture devices and each device can have multiple channels. Suppose a given device is a depth camera. Each channel might correspond to a different lens and sensor. Also, each channel might correspond to different kinds of data, such as a normal color image versus a depth map. OpenCV, via its optional support for OpenNI 2, allows us to request any of the following channels from a depth camera (though a given camera might support only some of these channels):

- `cv2.CAP_OPENNI_DEPTH_MAP`: This is a **depth map**—a grayscale image in which each pixel value is the estimated distance from the camera to a surface. Specifically, each pixel value is a 16-bit unsigned integer representing a depth measurement in millimeters.

- `cv2.CAP_OPENNI_POINT_CLOUD_MAP`: This is a **point cloud map**—a color image in which each color corresponds to an *x*, *y*, or *z* spatial dimension. Specifically, the channel yields a BGR image, where B is *x* (blue is right), G is *y* (green is up), and R is *z* (red is deep), from the camera's perspective. The values are in meters.

- `cv2.CAP_OPENNI_DISPARITY_MAP` or `cv2.CAP_OPENNI_DISPARITY_MAP_32F`: These are **disparity maps**—grayscale images in which each pixel value is the stereo disparity of a surface. To conceptualize stereo disparity, let's suppose we overlay two images of a scene, shot from different viewpoints. The result would be similar to seeing double. For points on any pair of twin objects in the scene, we can measure the distance in pixels. This measurement is the stereo disparity. Nearby objects exhibit greater stereo disparity than far-off objects. Thus, nearby objects appear brighter in a disparity map. `cv2.CAP_OPENNI_DISPARITY_MAP` is a disparity map with 8-bit unsigned integer values and `cv2.CAP_OPENNI_DISPARITY_MAP_32F` is a disparity map with 32-bit floating-point values.

- `cv2.CAP_OPENNI_VALID_DEPTH_MASK`: This is a **valid depth mask** that shows whether the depth information at a given pixel is believed to be valid (shown by a non-zero value) or invalid (shown by a value of zero). For example, if the depth camera depends on an infrared illuminator (an infrared flash), depth information is invalid in regions that are occluded (shadowed) from this light.

- `cv2.CAP_OPENNI_BGR_IMAGE`: This is an ordinary BGR image from a camera that captures visible light. Each pixel's B, G, and R values are unsigned 8-bit integers.

- `cv2.CAP_OPENNI_GRAY_IMAGE`: This is an ordinary monochrome image from a camera that captures visible light. Each pixel value is an unsigned 8-bit integer.
- `cv2.CAP_OPENNI_IR_IMAGE`: This is a monochrome image from a camera that captures **infrared (IR)** light, specifically the **near infrared (NIR)** part of the spectrum. Each pixel value is an unsigned 16-bit integer. Typically, the camera will not actually use this entire 16-bit range but, instead, just a portion of it such as a 10-bit range; still, the data type is a 16-bit integer. Although NIR light is invisible to the human eye, it is physically quite similar to red light. Thus, NIR images from a camera do not necessarily look strange to a human being. However, a typical depth camera not only captures NIR light, but also projects a grid-like pattern of NIR lights for the benefit of the depth-finding algorithm. Thus, we might see a recognizable face in the depth camera's NIR image, but the face might be dotted with bright white lights.

Let's consider samples of some of these image types. The following screenshot shows a point cloud map of a man sitting behind a sculpture of a cat:

Here is a disparity map of the same scene:

Finally, here is a valid depth mask of the now-familiar cat sculpture and man:

Next, let's consider how to use some of the channels from a depth camera in an interactive application such as Cameo.

Converting 10-bit images to 8-bit

As we noted in the previous section, some of the channels of a depth camera use a range larger than 8 bits for their data. A large range tends to be useful for computations, but inconvenient for display, since most computer monitors are only capable of using an 8-bit range, [0, 255], per channel.

OpenCV's `cv2.imshow` function re-scales and truncates the given input data in order to convert the image for display. Specifically, if the input image's data type is unsigned 16-bit or signed 32-bit integers, `cv2.imshow` divides the data by 256 and truncates it to the 8-bit unsigned integer range, [0, 255]. If the input image's data type is 32-bit or 64-bit floating-point numbers, `cv2.imshow` assumes that the data's range is [0.0, 1.0], so it multiplies the data by 255 and truncates it to the 8-bit unsigned integer range, [0, 255]. By re-scaling the data, `cv2.imshow` is relying on its naive assumptions about the original scale. These assumptions will be wrong in some cases. For example, if an image's data type is 16-bit unsigned integers, but the actual data range is 10-bit unsigned integers, [0, 1023], then the image would look very dark if we relied on `cv2.imshow` to convert it.

Consider the following example of an image of an eye, captured with a 10-bit grayscale camera. On the left-hand side, we see the result of a correct conversion from the 10-bit scale to the 8-bit scale. On the right-hand side, we see the result of an incorrect conversion, based on a faulty assumption that the image uses a 16-bit scale:

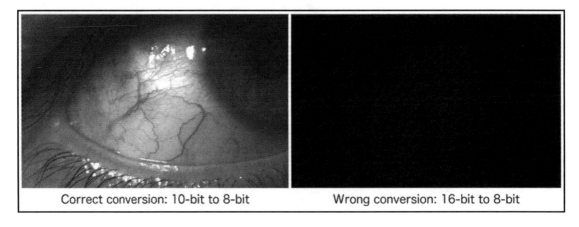

Correct conversion: 10-bit to 8-bit   Wrong conversion: 16-bit to 8-bit

The improperly converted image looks all black because our assumption about the scale was off by a huge amount: 6 bits or a factor of 64. Such a mistake is possible if we rely on `cv2.imshow` to perform conversions to the 8-bit scale automatically for us.

Of course, to avoid such problems, we can do our own image conversions and then pass the resulting 8-bit image to `cv2.imshow`. Let's modify `managers.py` (one of our existing scripts in the Cameo project) in order to provide an option to convert 10-bit images to 8-bit. We will provide a `shouldConvertBitDepth10To8` variable, which the developer can set to `True` or `False`. The following code block (with changes in **bold**) shows how we initialize this variable:

```
class CaptureManager(object):

    def __init__(self, capture, previewWindowManager = None,
                 shouldMirrorPreview = False,
                 shouldConvertBitDepth10To8 = True):

        self.previewWindowManager = previewWindowManager
        self.shouldMirrorPreview = shouldMirrorPreview
        self.shouldConvertBitDepth10To8 = \
                shouldConvertBitDepth10To8

        # ... The rest of the method is unchanged ...
```

Next, we will modify the `frame` property's getter to support the conversion. If `shouldConvertBitDepth10To8` is `True`, and the frame's datatype is 16-bit unsigned integers, then we will assume the frame actually has a 10-bit range, which we will convert to 8-bit. As part of the conversion, we will apply a right bit shift operation, $>> 2$, which truncates the two least significant bits. This is equivalent to integer division by 4. Here is the relevant code:

```
@property
def frame(self):
    if self._enteredFrame and self._frame is None:
        _, self._frame = self._capture.retrieve(
                self._frame, self.channel)
        if self.shouldConvertBitDepth10To8 and \
                self._frame is not None and \
                self._frame.dtype == numpy.uint16:
            self._frame = (self._frame >> 2).astype(
                    numpy.uint8)
    return self._frame
```

With these modifications in place, we will be able to more easily manipulate and display frames from some channels, notably `cv2.CAP_OPENNI_IR_IMAGE`. Next, though, let's look at an example of a function that manipulates frames from the `cv2.CAP_OPENNI_DISPARITY_MAP` and `cv2.CAP_OPENNI_VALID_DEPTH_MASK` channels in order to create a mask that isolates one thing, such as the user's face. Afterwards, we will consider how to use all these channels together in Cameo.

Creating a mask from a disparity map

Let's assume that a user's face, or some other object of interest, occupies most of the depth camera's field of view. However, the image also contains some other content that is not of interest. By analyzing the disparity map, we can tell that some pixels within the rectangle are outliers—too near or too far to really be a part of the face or another object of interest. We can make a mask to exclude these outliers. However, we should only apply this test where the data is valid, as indicated by the valid depth mask.

Let's write a function to generate a mask whose values are 0 for the rejected regions of the image and 255 for the accepted regions. This function should take a disparity map, valid depth mask, and optionally a rectangle as arguments. If a rectangle is specified, we will make a mask that is just the size of the specified region. This will be useful to us later in Chapter 5, *Detecting and Recognizing Faces*, where we will work with a face detector that finds bounding rectangles around faces. Let's call our `createMedianMask` function and implement it in `depth.py` as follows:

```python
def createMedianMask(disparityMap, validDepthMask, rect = None):
    """Return a mask selecting the median layer, plus shadows."""
    if rect is not None:
        x, y, w, h = rect
        disparityMap = disparityMap[y:y+h, x:x+w]
        validDepthMask = validDepthMask[y:y+h, x:x+w]
    median = numpy.median(disparityMap)
    return numpy.where((validDepthMask == 0) | \
                       (abs(disparityMap - median) < 12),
                       255, 0).astype(numpy.uint8)
```

To identify outliers in the disparity map, we first find the median using `numpy.median`, which takes an array as an argument. If the array is of an odd length, `median` returns the value that would lie in the middle of the array if the array were sorted. If the array is of an even length, `median` returns the average of the two values that would be sorted nearest to the middle of the array.

To generate a mask based on per-pixel Boolean operations, we use `numpy.where` with three arguments. In the first argument, `where` takes an array whose elements are evaluated for truth or falsity. An output array of the same dimensions is returned. Wherever an element in the input array is `True`, the `where` function's second argument is assigned to the corresponding element in the output array. Conversely, wherever an element in the input array is `False`, the `where` function's third argument is assigned to the corresponding element in the output array.

Our implementation treats a pixel as an outlier when it has a valid disparity value that deviates from the median disparity value by 12 or more. We have chosen the value of 12 just by experimentation. Feel free to tweak this value later based on the results you encounter when running Cameo with your particular camera setup.

Modifying the application

Let's open the `Cameo.py` file, which contains the `Cameo` class that we last modified in `Chapter 3`, *Processing Images with OpenCV*. This class implements an application that works well with regular cameras. We do not necessarily want to replace this class, but rather we want to create a variant of it that changes the implementations of some methods in order to work with depth cameras instead. For this purpose, we will make a **subclass**, which inherits some of the `Cameo` behaviors and overrides other behaviors. Let's call it a `CameoDepth` subclass. Add the following line to `Cameo.py` (after the `Cameo` class and before the __main__ code block) in order to declare `CameoDepth` as a subclass of `Cameo`:

```
class CameoDepth(Cameo):
```

We will override or reimplement the __init__ method in `CameoDepth`. Whereas Cameo instantiates our `CaptureManager` class with a device index for a regular camera, `CameoDepth` needs to use a device index for a depth camera. The latter can be `cv2.CAP_OPENNI2`, which represents a device index for Microsoft Kinect, or `cv2.CAP_OPENNI2_ASUS`, which represents a device index for Asus Xtion PRO or Occipital Structure. The following code block shows a sample implementation of the __init__ method of `CameoDepth` (with differences from the __init__ method of `Cameo` in **bold**), but you may want to modify it to uncomment the appropriate device index for your setup:

```
def __init__(self):
    self._windowManager = WindowManager('Cameo',
                                        self.onKeypress)
    #device = cv2.CAP_OPENNI2 # uncomment for Kinect
    device = cv2.CAP_OPENNI2_ASUS # uncomment for Xtion or Structure
    self._captureManager = CaptureManager(
```

```
            cv2.VideoCapture(device), self._windowManager, True)
        self._curveFilter = filters.BGRPortraCurveFilter()
```

Similarly, we will override the `run` method in order to use several channels from the depth camera. First, we will try to retrieve a disparity map, then a valid depth mask, and finally a BGR color image. If no BGR image can be retrieved, this probably means that the depth camera does not have any BGR sensor so, in this case, we will proceed to retrieve an infrared grayscale image instead. The following code snippet shows the start of the run method of `CameoDepth`:

```
def run(self):
    """Run the main loop."""
    self._windowManager.createWindow()
    while self._windowManager.isWindowCreated:
        self._captureManager.enterFrame()
        self._captureManager.channel = cv2.CAP_OPENNI_DISPARITY_MAP
        disparityMap = self._captureManager.frame
        self._captureManager.channel = cv2.CAP_OPENNI_VALID_DEPTH_MASK
        validDepthMask = self._captureManager.frame
        self._captureManager.channel = cv2.CAP_OPENNI_BGR_IMAGE
        frame = self._captureManager.frame
        if frame is None:
            # Failed to capture a BGR frame.
            # Try to capture an infrared frame instead.
            self._captureManager.channel = cv2.CAP_OPENNI_IR_IMAGE
            frame = self._captureManager.frame
```

Having captured a disparity map, a valid depth mask, and either a BGR image or an infrared grayscale image, the `run` method continues by calling the `depth.createMedianMask` function that we implemented in the previous section, *Creating a mask from a disparity map*. We pass the disparity map and valid depth mask to the latter function and, in return, we receive a mask that is white in regions whose depth is close to the median depth, and black in other regions. Wherever the mask is black (`mask == 0`), we want to paint the BGR or infrared image black in order to obscure everything except the main object in the image. Finally, for a BGR image, we want to apply the artistic filters that we previously implemented in `Chapter 3`, *Processing Images with OpenCV*. The following code completes the implementation of the `CameoDepth` run method:

```
        if frame is not None:

            # Make everything except the median layer black.
            mask = depth.createMedianMask(disparityMap, validDepthMask)
            frame[mask == 0] = 0

            if self._captureManager.channel == \
                    cv2.CAP_OPENNI_BGR_IMAGE:
```

```
        # A BGR frame was captured.
        # Apply filters to it.
        filters.strokeEdges(frame, frame)
        self._curveFilter.apply(frame, frame)

    self._captureManager.exitFrame()
    self._windowManager.processEvents()
```

CameoDepth does not need any other method implementations of its own; it inherits appropriate implementations from its parent class or Cameo superclass.

Now, we simply need to modify the __main__ section of Cameo.py in order to run an instance of the CameoDepth class instead of the Cameo class. Here is the relevant code:

```
if __name__=="__main__":
    #Cameo().run() # uncomment for ordinary camera
    CameoDepth().run() # uncomment for depth camera
```

Plug in a depth camera and then run the script. Move closer to or farther from the camera until your face is visible, but the background goes black. The following screenshot was taken with CameoDepth and an Asus Xtion PRO camera. We can see an infrared image of one of the authors, Joseph Howse, who is brushing his teeth. The code has successfully blacked out the background so the image does not reveal whether he is brushing his teeth in a house, on a train, or in a tent. The mystery continues:

This is a good opportunity to consider the output of the `createMedianMask` function, which we implemented in the previous section. If we visualize the regions where the mask is 0 as black, and the regions where the mask is 1 as white, then the mask of Joseph Howse brushing his teeth appears as follows:

The result is good, but not perfect. For example, on the right-hand side of the image (from the viewer's perspective), the mask incorrectly includes a shadow region behind the hair, and incorrectly excludes the shoulder. The latter problem could probably be solved by fine-tuning the criteria that we used with `numpy.where` in the implementation of `createMedianMask`.

If you are fortunate enough to have multiple depth cameras, try all of them to see how they differ in terms of their support for color images, and their effectiveness in distinguishing near and far layers. Also, try various objects and lighting conditions to see how they affect (or do not affect) the infrared image. When you are satisfied with the result of your testing, let's move on to other techniques for depth estimation. (We will return to depth cameras again in subsequent chapters.)

Depth estimation with a normal camera

A depth camera is an impressive device, but not every developer or user has one and it has some limitations. Notably, a typical depth camera does not work well outdoors because the infrared component of sunlight is much brighter than the camera's own infrared light source. Blinded by the sun, the camera cannot see the infrared pattern that it normally uses to estimate depth.

As an alternative, we can use one or more normal cameras and we can estimate relative distances to objects based on triangulation from different camera perspectives. If we use two cameras simultaneously, this approach is called **stereo vision**. If we use one camera, but we move it over time to obtain different perspectives, this approach is called structure from motion. Broadly, techniques for stereo vision are also helpful in SfM, but in SfM we face additional problems if we are dealing with a moving subject. For this chapter's purposes, let's assume that we are dealing with a stationary subject.

As many philosophers would agree, geometry is fundamental to our understanding of the world. More to the point, **epipolar geometry** is the foundation of stereo vision. How does epipolar geometry work? Conceptually, it traces imaginary lines from the camera to each object in the image, then does the same on the second image, and calculates the distance to an object based on the intersection of the lines corresponding to the same object. Here is a representation of this concept:

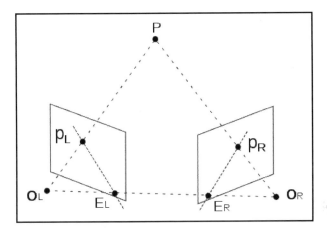

Let's see how OpenCV applies epipolar geometry to calculate a disparity map. This will enable us to segment the image into various layers of foreground and background. As input, we need two images of the same subject taken from different points of view.

Like so many of our scripts, this one begins by importing NumPy and OpenCV:

```
import numpy as np
import cv2
```

We define initial values for several parameters of a stereo algorithm, as seen in the following code:

```
minDisparity = 16
numDisparities = 192 - minDisparity
blockSize = 5
uniquenessRatio = 1
speckleWindowSize = 3
speckleRange = 3
disp12MaxDiff = 200
P1 = 600
P2 = 2400
```

With these parameters, we create an instance of OpenCV's `cv2.StereoSGBM` class. SGBM stands for **semiglobal block matching**, which is an algorithm used for computing disparity maps. Here is the code that initializes the object:

```
stereo = cv2.StereoSGBM_create(
    minDisparity = minDisparity,
    numDisparities = numDisparities,
    blockSize = blockSize,
    uniquenessRatio = uniquenessRatio,
    speckleRange = speckleRange,
    speckleWindowSize = speckleWindowSize,
    disp12MaxDiff = disp12MaxDiff,
    P1 = P1,
    P2 = P2
)
```

We also load two images from file:

```
imgL = cv2.imread('../images/color1_small.jpg')
imgR = cv2.imread('../images/color2_small.jpg')
```

We want to provide several sliders to enable a user to interactively adjust the parameters of the algorithm that calculates the disparity map. Whenever a user adjusts any of the sliders, we will update the parameters of the stereo algorithm by setting properties of the `StereoSGBM` instance, and recalculate the disparity map by calling the `compute` method of the `StereoSGBM` instance. Let's take a look at the implementation of the `update` function, which is the callback function for the sliders:

```
def update(sliderValue = 0):

    stereo.setBlockSize(
        cv2.getTrackbarPos('blockSize', 'Disparity'))
    stereo.setUniquenessRatio(
        cv2.getTrackbarPos('uniquenessRatio', 'Disparity'))
```

```
stereo.setSpeckleWindowSize(
    cv2.getTrackbarPos('speckleWindowSize', 'Disparity'))
stereo.setSpeckleRange(
    cv2.getTrackbarPos('speckleRange', 'Disparity'))
stereo.setDisp12MaxDiff(
    cv2.getTrackbarPos('disp12MaxDiff', 'Disparity'))

disparity = stereo.compute(
    imgL, imgR).astype(np.float32) / 16.0

cv2.imshow('Left', imgL)
cv2.imshow('Right', imgR)
cv2.imshow('Disparity',
           (disparity - minDisparity) / numDisparities)
```

Now, let's look at the code that creates a window and sliders:

```
cv2.namedWindow('Disparity')
cv2.createTrackbar('blockSize', 'Disparity', blockSize, 21,
                   update)
cv2.createTrackbar('uniquenessRatio', 'Disparity',
                   uniquenessRatio, 50, update)
cv2.createTrackbar('speckleWindowSize', 'Disparity',
                   speckleWindowSize, 200, update)
cv2.createTrackbar('speckleRange', 'Disparity',
                   speckleRange, 50, update)
cv2.createTrackbar('disp12MaxDiff', 'Disparity',
                   disp12MaxDiff, 250, update)
```

Note that we provide the update function as an argument to the cv2.createTrackbar function so that update is called whenever a slider is adjusted. Next, we call update manually to initialize the disparity map:

```
# Initialize the disparity map. Show the disparity map and images.
update()
```

When the user presses any key, we will close the window:

```
# Wait for the user to press any key.
# Meanwhile, update() will be called anytime the user moves a slider.
cv2.waitKey()
```

Let's review the functionality of this example. We take two images of the same subject and calculate a disparity map, showing in brighter tones the points in the map that are closer to the camera. The regions marked in black represent the disparities.

Here is the first image that we have used in this example:

This is the second one:

The user sees the original images, as well as a nice and quite easy-to-interpret disparity map:

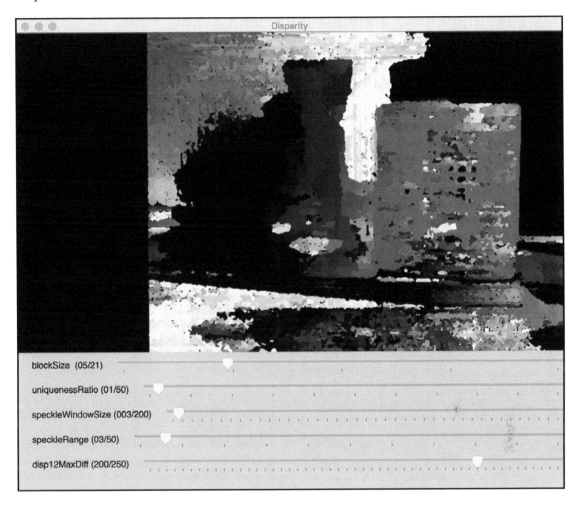

We have used many, but not all, of the parameters supported by `StereoSGBM`. The OpenCV documentation provides the following descriptions of all the parameters:

Parameter	Description from OpenCV Documentation
minDisparity	Minimum possible disparity value. Normally, it is zero, but sometimes rectification algorithms can shift images so this parameter needs to be adjusted accordingly.
numDisparities	Maximum disparity minus minimum disparity. The value is always greater than zero. In the current implementation, this parameter must be divisible by 16.
blockSize	Matched block size. It must be an odd number >=1 . Normally, it should be somewhere in the 3-11 range.
P1	The first parameter controlling the disparity smoothness [see the description of P2].
P2	The second parameter controlling the disparity smoothness. The larger the values, the smoother the disparity. P1 is the penalty on the disparity change by plus or minus 1 between neighbor pixels. P2 is the penalty on the disparity change by more than 1 between neighbor pixels. The algorithm requires P2 > P1. See the `stereo_match.cpp` sample where some reasonably good P1 and P2 values are shown, such as `8*number_of_image_channels*SADWindowSize*SADWindowSize` and `32*number_of_image_channels*SADWindowSize*SADWindowSize,` respectively.
disp12MaxDiff	Maximum allowed difference (in integer pixel units) in the left-right disparity check. Set it to a non-positive value to disable the check.
preFilterCap	Truncation value for the prefiltered image pixels. The algorithm first computes the *x*-derivative at each pixel and clips its value by the `[-preFilterCap, preFilterCap]` interval. The resulting values are passed to the Birchfield-Tomasi pixel cost function.
uniquenessRatio	Margin in percentage by which the best (minimum) computed cost function value should *win* the second best value to consider the found match correct. Normally, a value within the 5-15 range is good enough.
speckleWindowSize	Maximum size of smooth disparity regions to consider their noise speckles and invalidate. Set it to 0 to disable speckle filtering. Otherwise, set it somewhere in the 50-200 range.
speckleRange	Maximum disparity variation within each connected component. If you do speckle filtering, set the parameter to a positive value; it will be implicitly multiplied by 16. Normally, 1 or 2 is good enough.

mode	Set it to `StereoSGBM::MODE_HH` to run the full-scale, two-pass dynamic programming algorithm. It will consume `O(W*H*numDisparities)` bytes, which is large for 640x480 stereo and huge for HD-size pictures. By default, it is set to false.

With the preceding script, you will be able to load images of your choice and play around with, parameters until you are happy with the disparity map generated by `StereoSGBM`.

Foreground detection with the GrabCut algorithm

Calculating a disparity map is a useful way to segment the foreground and background of an image, but `StereoSGBM` is not the only algorithm that can accomplish this and, in fact, `StereoSGBM` is more about gathering three-dimensional information from two-dimensional pictures than anything else. **GrabCut**, however, is a perfect tool for foreground/background segmentation. The GrabCut algorithm consists of the following steps:

1. A rectangle including the subject(s) of the picture is defined.
2. The area lying outside the rectangle is automatically defined as a background.
3. The data contained in the background is used as a reference to distinguish background areas from foreground areas within the user-defined rectangle.
4. A **Gaussian Mixture Model** (**GMM**) models the foreground and background, and labels undefined pixels as probable background and probable foreground.
5. Each pixel in the image is virtually connected to the surrounding pixels through virtual edges, and each edge is assigned a probability of being foreground or background, based on how similar it is in color to the pixels surrounding it.

6. Each pixel (or node as it is conceptualized in the algorithm) is connected to either a foreground or a background node. You can visualize this as follows:

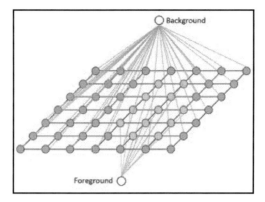

7. After the nodes have been connected to either terminal (the background or foreground, also called the source or sink, respectively), the edges between nodes belonging to different terminals are cut (hence the name, GrabCut). Thus, the image is segmented into two parts. The following figure adequately represents the algorithm:

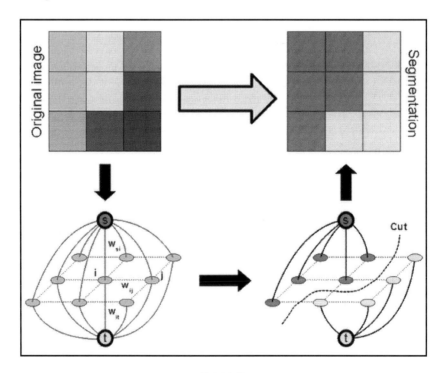

Let's look at an example. We start with the image of a beautiful statue of an angel:

We want to grab our angel and discard the background. To do this, we will create a relatively short script that will segment the image using GrabCut, and then display the resulting foreground image side by side with the original. We will use matplotlib, a popular Python library, which makes displaying charts and images a trivial task.

The code is actually quite straightforward. First, we load the image we want to process and then we create a mask populated with zeros with the same shape as the image we've loaded:

```
import numpy as np
import cv2
from matplotlib import pyplot as plt

original = cv2.imread('../images/statue_small.jpg')
img = original.copy()
mask = np.zeros(img.shape[:2], np.uint8)
```

We then create zero-filled background and foreground models:

```
bgdModel = np.zeros((1, 65), np.float64)
fgdModel = np.zeros((1, 65), np.float64)
```

We could have populated these models with data, but we are going to initialize the GrabCut algorithm with a rectangle identifying the subject we want to isolate. Thus, background and foreground models are going to be determined based on the areas left out of the initial rectangle. This rectangle is defined in the next line:

```
rect = (100, 1, 421, 378)
```

Now to the interesting part! We run the GrabCut algorithm. As arguments, we specify the empty models, the mask, and the rectangle that we want to use to initialize the operation:

```
cv2.grabCut(img, mask, rect, bgdModel, fgdModel, 5, cv2.GC_INIT_WITH_RECT)
```

Notice the 5 integer argument. This is the number of iterations the algorithm is going to run on the image. You can increase it, but at some point pixel classifications will converge so, effectively, you might just be adding iterations without any further improvements to the result.

After this, our mask will have changed to contain values between 0 and 3, inclusive. These values have the following meanings:

- 0 (also defined as `cv2.GC_BGD`) is an obvious background pixel.
- 1 (also defined as `cv2.GC_FGD`) is an obvious foreground pixel.
- 2 (also defined as `cv2.GC_PR_BGD`) is a probable background pixel.
- 3 (also defined as `cv2.GC_PR_FGD`) is a probable foreground pixel.

To visualize the result of the GrabCut, we want to paint the background black and leave the foreground unchanged. We can make another mask to help us do this. The values 0 and 2 (obvious and probable background) will be converted into 0s, and the values 1 and 3 (obvious and probably foreground) into 1s. The result will be stored in `mask2`. We will multiply the original image by `mask2` in order to make the background black (by multiplying by 0) while leaving the foreground unchanged (by multiplying by 1). Here is the relevant code:

```
mask2 = np.where((mask==2) | (mask==0), 0, 1).astype('uint8')
img = img*mask2[:,:,np.newaxis]
```

The final part of our script displays the images side by side:

```
plt.subplot(121)
plt.imshow(cv2.cvtColor(img, cv2.COLOR_BGR2RGB))
plt.title("grabcut")
plt.xticks([])
plt.yticks([])
```

```
plt.subplot(122)
plt.imshow(cv2.cvtColor(original, cv2.COLOR_BGR2RGB))
plt.title("original")
plt.xticks([])
plt.yticks([])

plt.show()
```

Here is the result:

This is quite a satisfactory result. You'll notice that a triangle of background is left under the angel's arm. It is possible to refine the GrabCut result by manually selecting more background regions and applying more iterations. This technique is quite well illustrated in the grabcut.py file in the samples/python folder of your OpenCV installation.

Image segmentation with the Watershed algorithm

Finally, let's take a quick look at the Watershed algorithm. The algorithm is called Watershed because its conceptualization involves water. Imagine areas with low density (little to no change) in an image as valleys, and areas with high density (lots of change) as peaks. Start filling the valleys with water to the point where water from two different valleys is about to merge. To prevent the merging of water from different valleys, you build a barrier to keep them separated. The resulting barrier is the image segmentation.

As an example, let's segment an image of a playing card. We want to separate the pips (the large, countable symbols) from the background:

1. Once more, we begin our script by importing `numpy`, `cv2`, and `matplotlib`. Then, we load our image of a playing card from file:

   ```
   import numpy as np
   import cv2
   from matplotlib import pyplot as plt

   img = cv2.imread('../images/5_of_diamonds.png')
   gray = cv2.cvtColor(img, cv2.COLOR_BGR2GRAY)
   ```

2. After converting the image from color to grayscale, we run a threshold on it. This operation helps by dividing the image into two regions, blacks and whites:

   ```
   ret, thresh = cv2.threshold(gray, 0, 255,
                         cv2.THRESH_BINARY_INV |
   cv2.THRESH_OTSU)
   ```

3. Next, we remove noise from the thresholded image by applying a morphological transformation to it. **Morphology** consists of **dilating** (expanding) or **eroding** (contracting) the white regions of the image in some series of steps. We will apply the morphological **open** operation, which consists of an erosion step followed by a dilation step. The open operation makes big white regions swallow up little black regions (noise), while leaving big black regions (real objects) relatively unchanged. The `cv2.morphologyEx` function, with the `cv2.MORPH_OPEN` argument, allows us to perform this operation:

   ```
   # Remove noise.
   kernel = np.ones((3,3), np.uint8)
   opening = cv2.morphologyEx(thresh, cv2.MORPH_OPEN, kernel,
                         iterations = 2)
   ```

4. By dilating the result of the open transformation, we can obtain regions of the image that are most certainly background:

   ```
   # Find the sure background region.
   sure_bg = cv2.dilate(opening, kernel, iterations=3)
   ```

   Conversely, we can obtain sure foreground regions by applying `distanceTransform`. In practical terms, we can be most confident that a point is really part of the foreground if it is far away from the nearest foreground-background edge.

5. Once we have obtained the `distanceTransform` representation of the image, we apply a threshold to select regions that are most surely part of the foreground:

```
# Find the sure foreground region.
dist_transform = cv2.distanceTransform(opening,cv2.DIST_L2,5)
ret, sure_fg = cv2.threshold(
        dist_transform, 0.7*dist_transform.max(), 255, 0)
sure_fg = sure_fg.astype(np.uint8)
```

At this stage, we have some sure foreground and background regions.

6. Now, what about the regions in between? We can find these unsure or unknown regions by subtracting the sure foreground from background:

```
# Find the unknown region.
unknown = cv2.subtract(sure_bg, sure_fg)
```

7. Now that we have these regions, we can build our famous *barriers* to stop the water from merging. This is done with the `connectedComponents` function. We took a glimpse at graph theory when we analyzed the GrabCut algorithm and conceptualized an image as a set of nodes that are connected by edges. Given the sure foreground areas, some of these nodes will be connected together, but some will not. The disconnected nodes belong to different water valleys, and there should be a barrier between them:

```
# Label the foreground objects.
ret, markers = cv2.connectedComponents(sure_fg)
```

8. Next, we add 1 to the labels for all regions because we only want unknowns to stay at 0:

```
# Add one to all labels so that sure background is not 0, but 1.
markers += 1

# Label the unknown region as 0.
markers[unknown==255] = 0
```

9. Finally, we open the gates! Let the water flow! The `cv2.watershed` function assigns the label −1 to pixels that are edges between components. We color these edges blue in the original image:

```
markers = cv2.watershed(img, markers)
img[markers==-1] = [255,0,0]
```

Let's use `matplotlib` to show the result:

```
plt.imshow(cv2.cvtColor(img, cv2.COLOR_BGR2RGB))
plt.show()
```

The plot should look like the following image:

This type of segmentation could serve as part of a system for recognizing playing cards. Similarly, the Watershed algorithm can help us segment and count any kind of object on a plain background, such as coins on a sheet of paper.

Summary

In this chapter, we learned how to analyze simple spatial relationships within images so that we can differentiate between multiple objects, or between a foreground and a background. Our techniques included extraction of three-dimensional information from a two-dimensional input (a video frame or an image). First, we examined depth cameras, and then epipolar geometry and stereo images, so we are now able to calculate disparity maps. Finally, we looked at image segmentation with two of the most popular methods: GrabCut and Watershed.

As we progress through this book, we will continue to extract increasingly complex information from images. Next, we are ready to explore OpenCV's functionality for detection and recognition of faces and other objects.

5
Detecting and Recognizing Faces

Computer vision makes many futuristic-sounding tasks a reality. Two such tasks are face detection (locating faces in an image) and face recognition (identifying a face as a specific person). OpenCV implements several algorithms for face detection and recognition. These have applications in all sorts of real-world contexts, from security to entertainment.

This chapter introduces some of OpenCV's face detection and recognition functionality, along with the data files that define particular types of trackable objects. Specifically, we look at Haar cascade classifiers, which analyze the contrast between adjacent image regions to determine whether or not a given image or sub image matches a known type. We consider how to combine multiple Haar cascade classifiers in a hierarchy so that one classifier identifies a parent region (for our purposes, a face) and other classifiers identify child regions (such as eyes).

We also take a detour into the humble but important subject of rectangles. By drawing, copying, and resizing rectangular image regions, we can perform simple manipulations on image regions that we are tracking.

All told, we will cover the following topics:

- Understanding Haar cascades.
- Finding the pre-trained Haar cascades that come with OpenCV. These include several face detectors.
- Using Haar cascades to detect faces in still images and videos.
- Gathering images to train and test a face recognizer.
- Using several different face recognition algorithms: Eigenfaces, Fisherfaces, and **Local Binary Pattern Histograms (LBPHs)**.
- Copying rectangular regions from one image to another, with or without a mask.

- Using a depth camera to distinguish between a face and the background based on depth.
- Swapping two people's faces in an interactive application.

By the end of this chapter, we will integrate face tracking and rectangle manipulations into Cameo, the interactive application that we have developed in previous chapters. Finally, we will have some face-to-face interaction!

Technical requirements

This chapter uses Python, OpenCV, and NumPy. As part of OpenCV, it uses the optional `opencv_contrib` modules, which include functionality for face recognition. Some parts of this chapter use OpenCV's optional support for OpenNI 2 to capture images from depth cameras. Please refer back to `Chapter 1`, *Setting Up OpenCV*, for installation instructions.

The complete code for this chapter can be found in this book's GitHub repository, `https://github.com/PacktPublishing/Learning-OpenCV-4-Computer-Vision-with-Python-Third-Edition`, in the `chapter05` folder. Sample images are in the repository in the `images` folder.

Conceptualizing Haar cascades

When we talk about classifying objects and tracking their location, what exactly are we hoping to pinpoint? What constitutes a recognizable part of an object?

Photographic images, even from a webcam, may contain a lot of detail for our (human) viewing pleasure. However, image detail tends to be unstable with respect to variations in lighting, viewing angle, viewing distance, camera shake, and digital noise. Moreover, even real differences in physical detail might not interest us for classification. Joseph Howse, one of this book's authors, was taught in school that no two snowflakes look alike under a microscope. Fortunately, as a Canadian child, he had already learned how to recognize snowflakes without a microscope, as the similarities are more obvious in bulk.

Hence, some means of abstracting image detail is useful in producing stable classification and tracking results. The abstractions are called **features**, which are said to be **extracted** from the image data. There should be far fewer features than pixels, though any pixel might influence multiple features. A set of features is represented as a vector, and the level of similarity between two images can be evaluated based on some measure of the distance between the images' corresponding feature vectors.

Haar-like features are one type of feature that is often applied to real-time face detection. They were first used for this purpose in the paper, *Robust Real-Time Face Detection*, by Paul Viola and Michael Jones (*International Journal of Computer Vision 57(2)*, 137–154, Kluwer Academic Publishers, 2001). An electronic version of this paper is available at `http://www.vision.caltech.edu/html-files/EE148-2005-Spring/pprs/viola04ijcv.pdf`. Each Haar-like feature describes the pattern of contrast among adjacent image regions. For example, edges, vertices, and thin lines each generate a kind of feature. Some features are distinctive in the sense that they typically occur in a certain class of object (such as a face) but not in other objects. These distinctive features can be organized into a hierarchy, called a **cascade**, in which the highest layers contain features of greatest distinctiveness, enabling a classifier to quickly reject subjects that lack these features.

For any given subject, the features may vary depending on the scale of the image and the size of the neighborhood within which contrast is being evaluated. The latter is called the **window size**. To make a Haar cascade classifier **scale-invariant** or, in other words, robust to changes in scale, the window size is kept constant but images are rescaled a number of times; hence, at some level of rescaling, the size of an object (such as a face) may match the window size. Together, the original image and the rescaled images are called an **image pyramid**, and each successive level in this pyramid is a smaller rescaled image. OpenCV provides a scale-invariant classifier that can load a Haar cascade from an XML file in a particular format. Internally, this classifier converts any given image into an image pyramid.

Haar cascades, as implemented in OpenCV, are not robust to changes in rotation or perspective. For example, an upside-down face is not considered similar to an upright face and a face viewed in profile is not considered similar to a face viewed from the front. A more complex and more resource-intensive implementation could improve Haar cascades' robustness to rotation by considering multiple transformations of images as well as multiple window sizes. However, we will confine ourselves to the implementation in OpenCV.

Getting Haar cascade data

The OpenCV 4 source code, or your installation of a prepackaged build of OpenCV 4, should contain a subfolder called `data/haarcascades`. If you are unable to locate this, refer back to `Chapter 1`, *Setting Up OpenCV*, for instructions on obtaining the OpenCV 4 source code.

The `data/haarcascades` folder contains XML files that can be loaded by an OpenCV class called `cv2.CascadeClassifier`. An instance of this class interprets a given XML file as a Haar cascade, which provides a detection model for a type of object such as a face. `cv2.CascadeClassifier` can detect this type of object in any image. As usual, we could obtain a still image from a file, or we could obtain a series of frames from a video file or a video camera.

Once you find `data/haarcascades`, create a directory elsewhere for your project; in this folder, create a subfolder called `cascades`, and copy the following files from `data/haarcascades` into `cascades`:

- `haarcascade_frontalface_default.xml`
- `haarcascade_frontalface_alt.xml`
- `haarcascade_eye.xml`

As their names suggest, these cascades are for tracking faces and eyes. They require a frontal, upright view of the subject. We will use them later when building a face detector.

 If you are curious about how these cascade files are generated, you can find more information in Joseph Howse's book, *OpenCV 4 for Secret Agents* (Packt Publishing, 2019), specifically in *Chapter 3, Training a Smart Alarm to Recognize the Villain and His Cat*. With a lot of patience and a reasonably powerful computer, you can make your own cascades and train them for various types of objects.

Using OpenCV to perform face detection

With `cv2.CascadeClassifier`, it makes little difference whether we perform face detection on a still image or a video feed. The latter is just a sequential version of the former: face detection on a video is simply face detection applied to each frame. Naturally, with more advanced techniques, it would be possible to track a detected face continuously across multiple frames and determine that the face is the same one in each frame. However, it is good to know that a basic sequential approach also works.

Let's go ahead and detect some faces.

Performing face detection on a still image

The first and most basic way to perform face detection is to load an image and detect faces in it. To make the result visually meaningful, we will draw rectangles around faces in the original image. Remembering that the face detector is designed for upright, frontal faces, we will use an image of a row of people, specifically woodcutters, standing shoulder-to-shoulder and facing the viewer.

Having copied the Haar cascade XML files into our cascades folder, let's go ahead and create the following basic script to perform face detection:

```
import cv2


face_cascade = cv2.CascadeClassifier(
    './cascades/haarcascade_frontalface_default.xml')
img = cv2.imread('../images/woodcutters.jpg')
gray = cv2.cvtColor(img, cv2.COLOR_BGR2GRAY)
faces = face_cascade.detectMultiScale(gray, 1.08, 5)
for (x, y, w, h) in faces:
    img = cv2.rectangle(img, (x, y), (x+w, y+h), (255, 0, 0), 2)
cv2.namedWindow('Woodcutters Detected!')
cv2.imshow('Woodcutters Detected!', img)
cv2.imwrite('./woodcutters_detected.jpg', img)
cv2.waitKey(0)
```

Let's walk through the preceding code in small steps. First, we use the obligatory `cv2` import that you will find in every script in this book. Then, we declare a `face_cascade` variable, which is a `CascadeClassifier` object that loads a cascade for face detection:

```
face_cascade = cv2.CascadeClassifier(
    './cascades/haarcascade_frontalface_default.xml')
```

We then load our image file with `cv2.imread` and convert it into grayscale because `CascadeClassifier` expects grayscale images. The next step, `face_cascade.detectMultiScale`, is where we perform the actual face detection:

```
img = cv2.imread('../images/woodcutters.jpg')
gray = cv2.cvtColor(img, cv2.COLOR_BGR2GRAY)
faces = face_cascade.detectMultiScale(gray, 1.08, 5)
```

The parameters of detectMultiScale include scaleFactor and minNeighbors. The scaleFactor argument, which should be greater than 1.0, determines the downscaling ratio of the image at each iteration of the face detection process. As we discussed earlier in the *Conceptualizing Haar cascades* section, this downscaling is intended to achieve scale invariance by matching various faces to the window size. The minNeighbors argument is the minimum number of overlapping detections that are required in order to retain a detection result. Normally, we expect that a face may be detected in multiple overlapping windows, and a greater number of overlapping detections makes us more confident that the detected face is truly a face.

The value returned from the detection operation is a list of tuples that represent the face rectangles. OpenCV's cv2.rectangle function allows us to draw rectangles at the specified coordinates. x and y represent the left and top coordinates, while w and h represent the width and height of the face rectangle. We draw blue rectangles around all of the faces we find by looping through the faces variable, making sure we use the original image for drawing, not the gray version:

```
for (x, y, w, h) in faces:
    img = cv2.rectangle(img, (x, y), (x+w, y+h), (255, 0, 0), 2)
```

Lastly, we call cv2.imshow to display the resulting processed image. As usual, to prevent the image window from closing automatically, we insert a call to waitKey, which returns when the user presses any key:

```
cv2.imshow('Woodcutters Detected!', img)
cv2.imwrite('./woodcutters_detected.jpg', img)
cv2.waitKey(0)
```

And there we go, a whole band of woodcutters have been detected in our image, as shown in the following screenshot:

 The photograph in this example is the work of Sergey Prokudin-Gorsky (1863-1944), a pioneer of color photography. Tsar Nicholas II sponsored Prokudin-Gorsky to photograph people and places throughout the Russian Empire as a vast documentary project. Prokudin-Gorsky photographed these woodcutters near the Svir River, in northwestern Russia, in 1909.

Performing face detection on a video

We now understand how to perform face detection on a still image. As mentioned previously, we can repeat the process of face detection on each frame of a video (be it a camera feed or a pre-recorded video file).

The next script will open a camera feed, read a frame, examine that frame for faces, and scan for eyes within the detected faces. Finally, it will draw blue rectangles around the faces and green rectangles around the eyes. Here is the script in its entirety:

```
import cv2


face_cascade = cv2.CascadeClassifier(
    './cascades/haarcascade_frontalface_default.xml')
eye_cascade = cv2.CascadeClassifier(
    './cascades/haarcascade_eye.xml')

camera = cv2.VideoCapture(0)
while (cv2.waitKey(1) == -1):
    success, frame = camera.read()
    if success:
        gray = cv2.cvtColor(frame, cv2.COLOR_BGR2GRAY)
        faces = face_cascade.detectMultiScale(
            gray, 1.3, 5, minSize=(120, 120))
        for (x, y, w, h) in faces:
            cv2.rectangle(frame, (x, y), (x+w, y+h), (255, 0, 0), 2)
            roi_gray = gray[y:y+h, x:x+w]
            eyes = eye_cascade.detectMultiScale(
                roi_gray, 1.03, 5, minSize=(40, 40))
            for (ex, ey, ew, eh) in eyes:
                cv2.rectangle(frame, (x+ex, y+ey),
                              (x+ex+ew, y+ey+eh), (0, 255, 0), 2)
        cv2.imshow('Face Detection', frame)
```

Let's break up the preceding sample into smaller, digestible chunks:

1. As usual, we import the `cv2` module. After that, we initialize two `CascadeClassifier` objects, one for faces and another for eyes:

   ```
   face_cascade = cv2.CascadeClassifier(
       './cascades/haarcascade_frontalface_default.xml')
   eye_cascade = cv2.CascadeClassifier(
       './cascades/haarcascade_eye.xml')
   ```

2. As in most of our interactive scripts, we open a camera feed and start iterating over frames. We continue until the user presses any key. Whenever we successfully capture a frame, we convert it into grayscale as our first step in processing it:

   ```
   camera = cv2.VideoCapture(0)
   while (cv2.waitKey(1) == -1):
       success, frame = camera.read()
   ```

```
if success:
    gray = cv2.cvtColor(frame, cv2.COLOR_BGR2GRAY)
```

3. We detect faces with the `detectMultiScale` method of our face detector. As we have previously done, we use the `scaleFactor` and `minNeighbors` arguments. We also use the `minSize` argument to specify a minimum size of a face, specifically 120x120. No attempt will be made to detect faces smaller than this. (Assuming that our user is sitting close to the camera, it is safe to say that the user's face will be larger than 120x120 pixels.) Here is the call to `detectMultiScale`:

```
faces = face_cascade.detectMultiScale(
    gray, 1.3, 5, minSize=(120, 120))
```

4. We iterate over the rectangles of the detected faces. We draw a blue border around each rectangle in the original color image. Then, within the same rectangular region of the grayscale image, we perform eye detection:

```
for (x, y, w, h) in faces:
    cv2.rectangle(frame, (x, y), (x+w, y+h), (255, 0, 0), 2)
    roi_gray = gray[y:y+h, x:x+w]
    eyes = eye_cascade.detectMultiScale(
        roi_gray, 1.1, 5, minSize=(40, 40))
```

The eye detector is a bit less accurate than the face detector. You might see shadows, parts of the frames of glasses, or other regions of the face falsely detected as eyes. To improve the results, you could try defining `roi_gray` as a smaller region of the face, since we can make a good guess about the eyes' location in an upright face. You could also try using a `maxSize` argument to avoid false positives that are too large to be eyes. Also, you could adjust `minSize` and `maxSize` so that the dimensions are proportional to `w` and `h`, the size of the detected face. As an exercise, feel free to experiment with changes to these and other parameters.

5. We loop through the resulting eye rectangles and draw green outlines around them:

```
for (ex, ey, ew, eh) in eyes:
    cv2.rectangle(frame, (x+ex, y+ey),
                  (x+ex+ew, y+ey+eh), (0, 255, 0), 2)
```

6. Finally, we show the resulting frame in the window:

```
cv2.imshow('Face Detection', frame)
```

Run the script. If our detectors produce accurate results, and if any face is within the field of view of the camera, you should see a blue rectangle around the face and a green rectangle around each eye, as shown in this screenshot:

Experiment with this script to see how the face and eye detectors perform under various conditions. Try a brighter or darker room. If you wear glasses, try removing them. Try various people's faces and various expressions. Adjust the detection parameters in the script to see how they affect the results. When you are satisfied, let's consider what else we can do with faces in OpenCV.

Performing face recognition

Detecting faces is a fantastic feature of OpenCV and one that constitutes the basis for a more advanced operation: face recognition. What is face recognition? It is the ability of a program, given an image or a video feed containing a person's face, to identify that person. One of the ways to achieve this (and the approach adopted by OpenCV) is to *train* the program by feeding it a set of classified pictures (a facial database) and to perform recognition based on features of those pictures.

Another important feature of OpenCV's face recognition module is that each recognition has a confidence score, which allows us to set thresholds in real-life applications to limit the incidence of false identifications.

Let's start from the very beginning; to perform face recognition, we need faces to recognize. We can do this in two ways: supply the images ourselves or obtain freely available face databases. A large directory of face databases is available online at `http://www.face-rec.org/databases/`. Here are a few notable examples from the directory:

- Yale Face Database (Yalefaces):
  `http://vision.ucsd.edu/content/yale-face-database`
- Extended Yale Face Database B: `http://vision.ucsd.edu/content/extended-yale-face-database-b-b`
- Database of Faces (from AT&T Laboratories Cambridge):
  `http://www.cl.cam.ac.uk/research/dtg/attarchive/facedatabase.html`

To perform face recognition on these samples, we would then have to run face recognition on an image that contains the face of one of the sampled people. This process might be educational, but perhaps not as satisfying as providing images of our own. You probably had the same thought that many computer vision learners have had: I wonder if I can write a program that recognizes my face with a certain degree of confidence.

Generating the data for face recognition

Let's go ahead and write a script that will generate those images for us. A few images containing different expressions are all that we need, but it is preferable that the training images are square and are all the same size. Our sample script uses a size of 200x200, but most freely available datasets have smaller images than this.

Here is the script itself:

```
import cv2
import os


output_folder = '../data/at/jm'
if not os.path.exists(output_folder):
    os.makedirs(output_folder)

face_cascade = cv2.CascadeClassifier(
    './cascades/haarcascade_frontalface_default.xml')
eye_cascade = cv2.CascadeClassifier(
    './cascades/haarcascade_eye.xml')

camera = cv2.VideoCapture(0)
count = 0
while (cv2.waitKey(1) == -1):
    success, frame = camera.read()
    if success:
        gray = cv2.cvtColor(frame, cv2.COLOR_BGR2GRAY)
        faces = face_cascade.detectMultiScale(
            gray, 1.3, 5, minSize=(120, 120))
        for (x, y, w, h) in faces:
            cv2.rectangle(frame, (x, y), (x+w, y+h), (255, 0, 0), 2)
            face_img = cv2.resize(gray[y:y+h, x:x+w], (200, 200))
            face_filename = '%s/%d.pgm' % (output_folder, count)
            cv2.imwrite(face_filename, face_img)
            count += 1
        cv2.imshow('Capturing Faces...', frame)
```

Here, we are generating sample images by building on our newfound knowledge of how to detect a face in a video feed. We are detecting a face, cropping that region of the grayscale-converted frame, resizing it to be 200x200 pixels, and saving it as a PGM file with a name in a particular folder (in this case, jm, one of the author's initials; you can use your own initials). Like many of our windowed applications, this one runs until the user presses any key.

The count variable is present because we needed progressive names for the images. Run the script for a few seconds, change your facial expression a few times, and check the destination folder you specified in the script. You will find a number of images of your face, grayed, resized, and named with the format <count>.pgm.

Modify the `output_folder` variable to make it match your name. For example, you might choose `'../data/at/my_name'`. Run the script, wait for it to detect your face in a number of frames (say, 20 or more), and then press any key to quit. Now, modify the `output_folder` variable again to make it match the name of a friend whom you also want to recognize. For example, you might choose `'../data/at/name_of_my_friend'`. Do not change the base part of the folder (in this case, `'../data/at'`) because later, in the *Loading the training data for face recognition* section, we will write code that loads the training images from all of the subfolders of this base folder. Ask your friend to sit in front of the camera, run the script again, let it detect your friend's face in a number of frames, and then quit. Repeat this process for any additional people you might want to recognize.

Let's now move on to try and recognize the user's face in a video feed. This should be fun!

Recognizing faces

OpenCV 4 implements three different algorithms for recognizing faces: Eigenfaces, Fisherfaces, and **Local Binary Pattern Histograms** (LBPHs). Eigenfaces and Fisherfaces are derived from a more general-purpose algorithm called **Principal Component Analysis** (**PCA**). For a detailed description of the algorithms, refer to the following links:

- **PCA**: An intuitive introduction by Jonathon Shlens is available at `http://arxiv.org/pdf/1404.1100v1.pdf`. This algorithm was invented in 1901 by Karl Pearson, and the original paper, *On Lines and Planes of Closest Fit to Systems of Points in Space*, is available at `http://pca.narod.ru/pearson1901.pdf`.
- **Eigenfaces**: The paper, *Eigenfaces for Recognition* (1991), by Matthew Turk and Alex Pentland, is available at `http://www.cs.ucsb.edu/~mturk/Papers/jcn.pdf`.
- **Fisherfaces**: The seminal paper, *The Use of Multiple Measurements in Taxonomic Problems* (1936), by R. A. Fisher, is available at `http://onlinelibrary.wiley.com/doi/10.1111/j.1469-1809.1936.tb02137.x/pdf`.
- **Local Binary Pattern**: The first paper describing this algorithm is *Performance evaluation of texture measures with classification based on Kullback discrimination of distributions* (1994), by T. Ojala, M. Pietikainen, and D. Harwood. It is available at `https://ieeexplore.ieee.org/document/576366`.

For this book's purposes, let's just take a high-level overview of the algorithms. First and foremost, they all follow a similar process; they take a set of classified observations (our face database, containing numerous samples per individual), train a model based on it, perform an analysis of face images (which may be face regions that we detected in an image or video), and determine two things: the subject's identity, and a measure of confidence that this identification is correct. The latter is commonly known as the **confidence score**.

Eigenfaces performs PCA, which identifies principal components of a certain set of observations (again, your face database), calculates the divergence of the current observation (the face being detected in an image or frame) compared to the dataset, and produces a value. The smaller the value, the smaller the difference between the face database and detected face; hence, a value of 0 is an exact match.

Fisherfaces also derives from PCA and evolves the concept, applying more complex logic. While computationally more intensive, it tends to yield more accurate results than Eigenfaces.

LBPH instead divides a detected face into small cells and, for each cell, builds a histogram that describes whether the brightness of the image is increasing when comparing neighboring pixels in a given direction. This cell's histogram can be compared to the corresponding cell's in the model, producing a measure of similarity. Of the face recognizers in OpenCV, the implementation of LBPH is the only one that allows the model sample faces and the detected faces to be of different shape and size. Hence, it is a convenient option, and the authors of this book find that its accuracy compares favorably to the other two options.

Loading the training data for face recognition

Regardless of our choice of face recognition algorithm, we can load the training images in the same way. Earlier, in the *Generating the data for face recognition* section, we generated training images and saved them in folders that were organized according to people's names or initials. For example, the following folder structure could contain sample face images of this book's authors, Joseph Howse (J. H.) and Joe Minichino (J. M.):

```
../
  data/
    at/
      jh/
      jm/
```

Let's write a script that loads these images and labels them in a way that OpenCV's face recognizers will understand. To work with the filesystem and the data, we will use the Python standard library's `os` module, as well as the `cv2` and `numpy` modules. Let's create a script that starts with the following `import` statements:

```
import os

import cv2
import numpy
```

Let's add the following `read_images` function, which walks through a directory's subdirectories, loads the images, resizes them to a specified size, and puts the resized images in a list. At the same time, it builds two other lists: first, a list of people's names or initials (based on the subfolder names), and second, a list of labels or numeric IDs associated with the loaded images. For example, `jh` could be a name and `0` could be the label for all images that were loaded from the `jh` subfolder. Finally, the function converts the lists of images and labels into NumPy arrays, and it returns three variables: the list of names, the NumPy array of images, and the NumPy array of labels. Here is the function's implementation:

```
def read_images(path, image_size):
    names = []
    training_images, training_labels = [], []
    label = 0
    for dirname, subdirnames, filenames in os.walk(path):
        for subdirname in subdirnames:
            names.append(subdirname)
            subject_path = os.path.join(dirname, subdirname)
            for filename in os.listdir(subject_path):
                img = cv2.imread(os.path.join(subject_path, filename),
                                 cv2.IMREAD_GRAYSCALE)
                if img is None:
                    # The file cannot be loaded as an image.
                    # Skip it.
                    continue
                img = cv2.resize(img, image_size)
                training_images.append(img)
                training_labels.append(label)
            label += 1
    training_images = numpy.asarray(training_images, numpy.uint8)
    training_labels = numpy.asarray(training_labels, numpy.int32)
    return names, training_images, training_labels
```

Let's call our `read_images` function by adding code such as the following:

```
path_to_training_images = '../data/at'
training_image_size = (200, 200)
names, training_images, training_labels = read_images(
    path_to_training_images, training_image_size)
```

 Edit the `path_to_training_images` variable in the preceding code block to ensure that it matches the base folder of the `output_folder` variables you defined earlier in the code for the section, *Generating the data for face recognition*.

So far, we have training data in a useful format but we have not yet created a face recognizer or performed any training. We will do so in the next section, where we continue the implementation of the same script.

Performing face recognition with Eigenfaces

Now that we have an array of training images and an array of their labels, we can create and train a face recognizer with just two more lines of code:

```
model = cv2.face.EigenFaceRecognizer_create()
model.train(training_images, training_labels)
```

What have we done here? We created the Eigenfaces face recognizer with OpenCV's `cv2.EigenFaceRecognizer_create` function, and we trained the recognizer by passing the arrays of images and labels (numeric IDs). Optionally, we could have passed two arguments to `cv2.EigenFaceRecognizer_create`:

- `num_components`: This is the number of components to keep for the PCA.
- `threshold`: This is a floating-point value specifying a confidence threshold. Faces with a confidence score below the threshold will be discarded. By default, the threshold is the maximum floating-point value so that no faces are discarded.

To test this recognizer, let's use a face detector and a video feed from a camera. As we have done in previous scripts, we can use the following line of code to initialize the face detector:

```
face_cascade = cv2.CascadeClassifier(
    './cascades/haarcascade_frontalface_default.xml')
```

The following code initializes the camera feed, iterates over frames (until the user presses any key), and performs face detection and recognition on each frame:

```python
camera = cv2.VideoCapture(0)
while (cv2.waitKey(1) == -1):
    success, frame = camera.read()
    if success:
        faces = face_cascade.detectMultiScale(frame, 1.3, 5)
        for (x, y, w, h) in faces:
            cv2.rectangle(frame, (x, y), (x+w, y+h), (255, 0, 0), 2)
            gray = cv2.cvtColor(frame, cv2.COLOR_BGR2GRAY)
            roi_gray = gray[x:x+w, y:y+h]
            if roi_gray.size == 0:
                # The ROI is empty. Maybe the face is at the image edge.
                # Skip it.
                continue
            roi_gray = cv2.resize(roi_gray, training_image_size)
            label, confidence = model.predict(roi_gray)
            text = '%s, confidence=%.2f' % (names[label], confidence)
            cv2.putText(frame, text, (x, y - 20),
                        cv2.FONT_HERSHEY_SIMPLEX, 1, (255, 0, 0), 2)
        cv2.imshow('Face Recognition', frame)
```

Let's walk through the most important functionality of the preceding block of code. For each detected face, we convert and resize it so that we have a grayscale version that matches the expected size (in this case, 200x200 pixels as defined by the training_image_size variable in the previous section, *Loading the training data for face recognition*). Then, we pass the resized, grayscale face to the face recognizer's predict function. This returns a label and confidence score. We look up the person's name corresponding to the numeric label of that face. (Remember that we created the names array in the previous section, *Loading the training data for face recognition.*) We draw the name and confidence score in blue text above the recognized face. After iterating over all detected faces, we display the annotated image.

 We have taken a simple approach to face detection and recognition, and it serves the purpose of enabling you to have a basic application running and understand the process of face recognition in OpenCV 4. To improve upon this approach and make it more robust, you could take further steps such as correctly aligning and rotating detected faces so that the accuracy of the recognition is maximized.

When you run the script, you should see something similar to the following screenshot:

Next, let's consider how we would adapt these script to replace Eigenfaces with another face recognition algorithm.

Performing face recognition with Fisherfaces

What about Fisherfaces? The process does not change much; we simply need to instantiate a different algorithm. With default arguments, the declaration of our `model` variable would look like this:

```
model = cv2.face.FisherFaceRecognizer_create()
```

`cv2.face.FisherFaceRecognizer_create` takes the same two optional arguments as `cv2.createEigenFaceRecognizer_create`: the number of principal components to keep and the confidence threshold.

Performing face recognition with LBPH

Finally, let's take a quick look at the LBPH algorithm. Again, the process is similar. However, the algorithm factory takes the following optional parameters (in order):

- `radius`: The pixel distance between the neighbors that are used to calculate a cell's histogram (by default, 1)
- `neighbors`: The number of neighbors used to calculate a cell's histogram (by default, 8)
- `grid_x`: The number of cells into which the face is divided horizontally (by default, 8)
- `grid_y`: The number of cells into which the face is divided vertically (by default, 8)
- `confidence`: The confidence threshold (by default, the highest possible floating-point value so that no results are discarded)

With default arguments, the model declaration would look like this:

```
model = cv2.face.LBPHFaceRecognizer_create()
```

Note that, with LBPH, we do not need to resize images as the division into grids allows a comparison of patterns identified in each cell.

Discarding results based on the confidence score

The `predict` method returns a tuple, in which the first element is the label of the recognized individual and the second is the confidence score. All algorithms come with the option of setting a confidence score threshold, which measures the distance of the recognized face from the original model, therefore, a score of 0 signifies an exact match.

There may be cases in which you would rather retain all recognitions and then apply further processing, so you can come up with your own algorithms to estimate the confidence score of a recognition. For example, if you are trying to identify people in a video, you may want to analyze the confidence score in subsequent frames to establish whether the recognition was successful or not. In this case, you can inspect the confidence score obtained by the algorithm and draw your own conclusions.

The typical range of the confidence score depends on the algorithm. Eigenfaces and Fisherfaces produce values (roughly) in the range 0 to 20,000, with any score below 4,000-5,000 being a quite confident recognition. For LBPH, the reference value for a good recognition is below 50, and any value above 80 is considered a poor confidence score.

A normal custom approach would be to hold off drawing a rectangle around a recognized face until we have a number of frames with a satisfying arbitrary confidence score, but you have total freedom to use OpenCV's face recognition module to tailor your application to your needs.

Swapping faces in the infrared

Face detection and recognition are not limited to the visible spectrum of light. With a **Near-Infrared** (**NIR**) camera and NIR light source, face detection and recognition are possible even when a scene appears totally dark to the human eye. This capability is quite useful in security and surveillance applications.

We studied basic usage of NIR depth cameras, such as the Asus Xtion PRO, in `Chapter 4`, *Depth Estimation and Segmentation*. We extended the object-oriented code of our interactive application, Cameo. We captured frames from a depth camera. Based on depth, we segmented each frame into a main layer (such as the user's face) and other layers. We painted the other layers black. This achieved the effect of hiding the background so that only the main layer (the user's face) appeared on-screen in the interactive video feed.

Now, let's modify Cameo to do something that exercises our previous skills in depth segmentation and our new skills in face detection. Let's detect faces and, when we detect at least two faces in a frame, let's swap the faces so that one person's head appears atop another person's body. Rather than copying all pixels in a detected face rectangle, we will only copy the pixels that are part of the main depth layer for that rectangle. This should achieve the effect of swapping faces but not the background pixels surrounding the faces.

Once the changes are complete, Cameo will be able to produce output such as the following screenshot:

Here, we see the face of Joseph Howse swapped with the face of Janet Howse, his mother. Although Cameo is copying pixels from rectangular regions (and this is clearly visible at the bottom of the swapped regions, in the foreground), some of the background pixels are not swapped, so we do not see rectangular edges everywhere.

You can find all of the relevant changes to the Cameo source code in this book's repository at `https://github.com/PacktPublishing/Learning-OpenCV-4-Computer-Vision-with-Python-Third-Edition`, specifically in the `chapter05/cameo` folder. For brevity, we will not discuss all of the changes here in this book, but we will cover some of the highlights in the next two subsections, *Modifying the application's loop* and *Masking a copy operation*.

Modifying the application's loop

To support face swapping, the Cameo project has two new modules called `rects` and `trackers`. The `rects` module contains functions for copying and swapping rectangles, with an optional mask to limit the copy or swap operation to particular pixels. The `trackers` module contains a class called `FaceTracker`, which adapts OpenCV's face detection functionality to an object-oriented style of programming.

As we have covered OpenCV's face detection functionality earlier in this chapter, and we have demonstrated an object-oriented programming style in previous chapters, we will not go into the `FaceTracker` implementation here. Instead, you may look at it in this book's repository.

Let's open `cameo.py` so that we can walk through the overall changes to the application:

1. Near the top of the file, we need to import our new modules, as shown in **bold** in the following code block:

```
import cv2
import depth
import filters
from managers import WindowManager, CaptureManager
import rects
from trackers import FaceTracker
```

2. Now, let's turn our attention to changes in the __init__ method of our `CameoDepth` class. Our updated application uses an instance of `FaceTracker`. As part of its functionality, `FaceTracker` can draw rectangles around detected faces. Let's give Cameo's user the option to enable or disable the drawing of face rectangles. We will keep track of the currently selected option via a Boolean variable. The following code block shows (in **bold**) the necessary changes to initialize the `FaceTracker` object and the Boolean variable:

```
class CameoDepth(Cameo):

    def __init__(self):
        self._windowManager = WindowManager('Cameo',
                                              self.onKeypress)
        #device = cv2.CAP_OPENNI2 # uncomment for Kinect
        device = cv2.CAP_OPENNI2_ASUS # uncomment for Xtion
        self._captureManager = CaptureManager(
            cv2.VideoCapture(device), self._windowManager, True)
        self._faceTracker = FaceTracker()
        self._shouldDrawDebugRects = False
        self._curveFilter = filters.BGRPortraCurveFilter()
```

We make use of the `FaceTracker` object in the `run` method of `CameoDepth`, which contains the application's main loop that captures and processes frames. Every time we successfully capture a frame, we call methods of `FaceTracker` to update the face detection result and get the latest detected faces. Then, for each face, we create a mask based on the depth camera's disparity map. (Previously, in *Chapter 4*, *Depth Estimation and Segmentation*, we created such a mask for the entire image instead of a mask for each face rectangle.) Then, we call a function, `rects.swapRects`, to perform a masked swap of the face rectangles. (We will look at the implementation of swapRects a little later, in the *Masking a copy operation* section.)

3. Depending on the currently selected option, we might tell `FaceTracker` to draw rectangles around the faces. All of the relevant changes are shown in **bold** in the following code block:

```
def run(self):
    """Run the main loop."""
    self._windowManager.createWindow()
    while self._windowManager.isWindowCreated:
        # ... The logic for capturing a frame is unchanged ...

        if frame is not None:
            self._faceTracker.update(frame)
            faces = self._faceTracker.faces
            masks = [
                depth.createMedianMask(
                    disparityMap, validDepthMask,
                    face.faceRect) \
                for face in faces
            ]
            rects.swapRects(frame, frame,
                            [face.faceRect for face in faces],
                            masks)

            if self._captureManager.channel ==
    cv2.CAP_OPENNI_BGR_IMAGE:
                # A BGR frame was captured.
                # Apply filters to it.
                filters.strokeEdges(frame, frame)
                self._curveFilter.apply(frame, frame)

            if self._shouldDrawDebugRects:
                self._faceTracker.drawDebugRects(frame)

        self._captureManager.exitFrame()
        self._windowManager.processEvents()
```

4. Finally, let's modify the `onKeypress` method so that the user can hit the *X* key to start or stop displaying rectangles around detected faces. Again, the relevant changes are shown in **bold** in the following code block:

```
def onKeypress(self, keycode):
    """Handle a keypress.

    space -> Take a screenshot.
    tab -> Start/stop recording a screencast.
    x -> Start/stop drawing debug rectangles around faces.
    escape -> Quit.

    """
    if keycode == 32: # space
        self._captureManager.writeImage('screenshot.png')
    elif keycode == 9: # tab
        if not self._captureManager.isWritingVideo:
            self._captureManager.startWritingVideo(
                'screencast.avi')
        else:
            self._captureManager.stopWritingVideo()
    elif keycode == 120: # x
        self._shouldDrawDebugRects = \
            not self._shouldDrawDebugRects
    elif keycode == 27: # escape
        self._windowManager.destroyWindow()
```

Next, let's look at the implementation of the `rects` module that we imported earlier in this section.

Masking a copy operation

The `rects` module is implemented in `rects.py`. We already saw a call to the `rects.swapRects` function in the previous section. However, before we consider the implementation of `swapRects`, we first need to a more basic `copyRect` function.

As far back as Chapter 2, *Handling Files, Cameras, and GUIs*, we learned how to copy data from one rectangular **region of interest** (**ROI**) to another using NumPy's slicing syntax. Outside the ROIs, the source and destination images were unaffected. Now, we want to apply further limits to this copy operation. We want to use a given mask that has the same dimensions as the source rectangle.

We shall copy only those pixels in the source rectangle where the mask's value is not zero. Other pixels shall retain their old values from the destination image. This logic, with an array of conditions and two arrays of possible output values, can be expressed concisely with the `numpy.where` function.

With this approach in mind, let's consider our `copyRect` function. As arguments, it takes a source and destination image, a source and destination rectangle, and a mask. The latter may be `None`, in which case, we simply resize the content of the source rectangle to match the destination rectangle and then assign the resulting resized content to the destination rectangle. Otherwise, we next ensure that the mask and the images have the same number of channels. We assume that the mask has one channel but the images may have three channels (BGR). We can add duplicate channels to mask using the `repeat` and `reshape` methods of `numpy.array`. Finally, we perform the copy operation using `numpy.where`. The complete implementation is as follows:

```python
def copyRect(src, dst, srcRect, dstRect, mask = None,
             interpolation = cv2.INTER_LINEAR):
    """Copy part of the source to part of the destination."""

    x0, y0, w0, h0 = srcRect
    x1, y1, w1, h1 = dstRect

    # Resize the contents of the source sub-rectangle.
    # Put the result in the destination sub-rectangle.
    if mask is None:
        dst[y1:y1+h1, x1:x1+w1] = \
            cv2.resize(src[y0:y0+h0, x0:x0+w0], (w1, h1),
                       interpolation = interpolation)
    else:
        if not utils.isGray(src):
            # Convert the mask to 3 channels, like the image.
            mask = mask.repeat(3).reshape(h0, w0, 3)
        # Perform the copy, with the mask applied.
        dst[y1:y1+h1, x1:x1+w1] = \
            numpy.where(cv2.resize(mask, (w1, h1),
                                   interpolation = \
                                   cv2.INTER_NEAREST),
                        cv2.resize(src[y0:y0+h0, x0:x0+w0], (w1, h1),
                                   interpolation = interpolation),
                        dst[y1:y1+h1, x1:x1+w1])
```

We also need to define a `swapRects` function, which uses `copyRect` to perform a circular swap of a list of rectangular regions. `swapRects` has a `masks` argument, which is a list of masks whose elements are passed to the respective `copyRect` calls. If the value of the `masks` argument is None, we pass None to every `copyRect` call. The following code shows the full implementation of `swapRects`:

```
def swapRects(src, dst, rects, masks = None,
              interpolation = cv2.INTER_LINEAR):
    """Copy the source with two or more sub-rectangles swapped."""

    if dst is not src:
        dst[:] = src

    numRects = len(rects)
    if numRects < 2:
        return

    if masks is None:
        masks = [None] * numRects

    # Copy the contents of the last rectangle into temporary storage.
    x, y, w, h = rects[numRects - 1]
    temp = src[y:y+h, x:x+w].copy()

    # Copy the contents of each rectangle into the next.
    i = numRects - 2
    while i >= 0:
        copyRect(src, dst, rects[i], rects[i+1], masks[i],
                 interpolation)
        i -= 1

    # Copy the temporarily stored content into the first rectangle.
    copyRect(temp, dst, (0, 0, w, h), rects[0], masks[numRects - 1],
             interpolation)
```

Note that the `mask` argument in `copyRect` and the `masks` argument in `swapRects` both have a default value of None. If no mask is specified, these functions copy or swap the entire contents of the rectangle or rectangles.

Summary

By now, you should have a good understanding of how face detection and face recognition work and how to implement them in Python and OpenCV 4.

Face detection and face recognition are constantly evolving branches of computer vision, with algorithms being developed continuously, and they will evolve even faster in the near future with a growing interest in robotics and the **Internet of Things (IoT)**.

For now, the accuracy of detection and recognition algorithms heavily depends on the quality of the training data, so make sure you provide your applications with a large number of training images covering a variety of expressions, poses, and lighting conditions.

As human beings, we might be predisposed to think that human faces are particularly recognizable. We might even be overconfident in our own face recognition abilities. However, in computer vision, there is nothing very special about human faces, and we can just as readily use algorithms to find and identify other things. We will begin to do so next in Chapter 6, *Retrieving Images and Searching Using Image Descriptors*.

6
Retrieving Images and Searching Using Image Descriptors

Similar to the human eyes and brain, OpenCV can detect the main features of an image and extract them into so-called image descriptors. These features can then be used as a database, enabling image-based searches. Moreover, we can use key points to stitch images together and compose a bigger image. (Think of putting together many pictures to form a 360° panorama.)

This chapter will show you how to detect the features of an image with OpenCV and make use of them to match and search images. Over the course of this chapter, we will take sample images and detect their main features, and then try to find a region of another image that matches the sample image. We will also find the homography or spatial relationship between a sample image and a matching region of another image.

More specifically, we will cover the following tasks:

- Detecting keypoints and extracting local descriptors around the keypoints using any of the following algorithms: Harris corners, SIFT, SURF, or ORB
- Matching keypoints using brute-force algorithms or the FLANN algorithm
- Filtering out bad matches using KNN and the ratio test
- Finding the homography between two sets of matching keypoints
- Searching a set of images to determine which one contains the best match for a reference image

We will finish this chapter by building a proof-of-concept forensic application. Given a reference image of a tattoo, we will search for a set of images of people in order to find a person with a matching tattoo.

Technical requirements

This chapter uses Python, OpenCV, and NumPy. In regards to OpenCV, we use the optional `opencv_contrib` modules, which include additional algorithms for keypoint detection and matching. To enable the SIFT and SURF algorithms (which are patented and *not* free for commercial use), we must configure the `opencv_contrib` modules with the `OPENCV_ENABLE_NONFREE` flag in CMake. Please refer to Chapter 1, *Setting Up OpenCV*, for installation instructions. Additionally, if you have not already installed Matplotlib, install it by running `$ pip install matplotlib` (or `$ pip3 install matplotlib`, depending on your environment).

The complete code for this chapter can be found in this book's GitHub repository, `https://github.com/PacktPublishing/Learning-OpenCV-4-Computer-Vision-with-Python-Third-Edition`, in the `chapter06` folder. The sample images can be found in the `images` folder.

Understanding types of feature detection and matching

A number of algorithms can be used to detect and describe features, and we will explore several of them in this section. The most commonly used feature detection and descriptor extraction algorithms in OpenCV are as follows:

- **Harris**: This algorithm is useful for detecting corners.
- **SIFT**: This algorithm is useful for detecting blobs.
- **SURF**: This algorithm is useful for detecting blobs.
- **FAST**: This algorithm is useful for detecting corners.
- **BRIEF**: This algorithm is useful for detecting blobs.
- **ORB**: This algorithm stands for **Oriented FAST and Rotated BRIEF**. It is useful for detecting a combination of corners and blobs.

Matching features can be performed with the following methods:

- Brute-force matching
- FLANN-based matching

Spatial verification can then be performed with homography.

We have just introduced a lot of new terminology and algorithms. Now, we will go over their basic definitions.

Defining features

What is a feature, exactly? Why is a particular area of an image classifiable as a feature, while others are not? Broadly speaking, a feature is an area of interest in the image that is unique or easily recognizable. **Corners** and regions with a high density of textural detail are good features, while patterns that repeat themselves a lot and low-density regions (such as a blue sky) are not. Edges are good features as they tend to divide two regions of an image. A **blob** (a region of an image that greatly differs from its surrounding areas) is also an interesting feature.

Most feature detection algorithms revolve around the identification of corners, edges, and blobs, with some also focusing on the concept of a **ridge**, which you can conceptualize as the axis of symmetry of an elongated object. (Think, for example, about identifying a road in an image.)

Some algorithms are better at identifying and extracting features of a certain type, so it is important to know what your input image is so that you can utilize the best tool in your OpenCV belt.

Detecting Harris corners

Let's start by finding corners using the Harris corner detection algorithm. We will do this by implementing an example. If you continue to study OpenCV beyond this book, you will find that chessboards are a common subject of analysis in computer vision, partly because a checkered pattern is suited to many types of feature detection, and partly because chess is a popular pastime, especially in Russia, where many of OpenCV's developers live.

Here is our sample image of a chessboard and chess pieces:

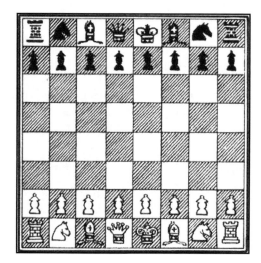

OpenCV has a handy function called `cv2.cornerHarris`, which detects corners in an image. We can see this function at work in the following basic example:

```
import cv2

img = cv2.imread('../images/chess_board.png')
gray = cv2.cvtColor(img, cv2.COLOR_BGR2GRAY)
dst = cv2.cornerHarris(gray, 2, 23, 0.04)
img[dst > 0.01 * dst.max()] = [0, 0, 255]
cv2.imshow('corners', img)
cv2.waitKey()
```

Let's analyze the code. After the usual imports, we load the chessboard image and convert it into grayscale. Then, we call the `cornerHarris` function:

```
dst = cv2.cornerHarris(gray, 2, 23, 0.04)
```

The most important parameter here is the third one, which defines the aperture or kernel size of the Sobel operator. The Sobel operator detects edges by measuring horizontal and vertical differences between pixel values in a neighborhood, and it does this using a kernel. The `cv2.cornerHarris` function uses a Sobel operator whose aperture is defined by this parameter. In plain English, the parameters define how sensitive corner detection is. It must be between 3 and 31 and be an odd value. With a low (highly sensitive) value of 3, all those diagonal lines in the black squares of the chessboard will register as corners when they touch the border of the square. For a higher (less sensitive) value of 23, only the corners of each square will be detected as corners.

`cv2.cornerHarris` returns an image in floating-point format. Each value in this image represents a score for the corresponding pixel in the source image. A moderate or high score indicates that the pixel is likely to be a corner. Conversely, we can treat pixels with the lowest scores as non-corners. Consider the following line:

```
img[dst > 0.01 * dst.max()] = [0, 0, 255]
```

Here, we select pixels with scores that are at least 1% of the highest score, and we color these pixels red in the original image. Here is the result:

Great! Nearly all the detected corners are marked in red. The marked points include nearly all the corners of the chessboard's squares.

If we tweak the second parameter in `cv2.cornerHarris`, we will see that smaller regions (for a smaller parameter value) or larger regions (for a larger parameter value) will be detected as corners. This parameter is called the block size.

Detecting DoG features and extracting SIFT descriptors

The preceding technique, which uses `cv2.cornerHarris`, is great for detecting corners and has a distinct advantage because corners are corners; they are detected even if the image is rotated. However, if we scale an image to a smaller or larger size, some parts of the image may lose or even gain a corner quality.

For example, take a look at the following corner detections in an image of the F1 Italian Grand Prix track:

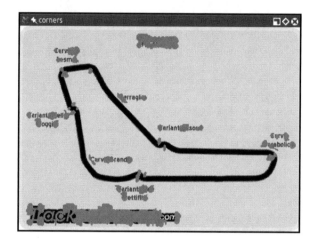

Here is the corner detection result with a smaller version of the same image:

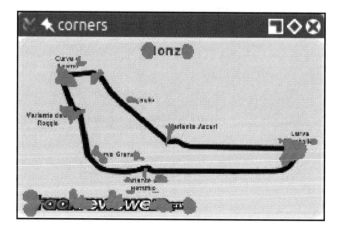

You will notice how the corners are a lot more condensed; however, even though we gained some corners, we lost others! In particular, let's examine the **Variante Ascari** chicane, which looks like a squiggle at the end of the part of the track that runs straight from northwest to southeast. In the larger version of the image, both the entrance and the apex of the double bend were detected as corners. In the smaller image, the apex is not detected as such. If we further reduce the image, at some scale, we will lose the entrance to that chicane too.

This loss of features raises an issue; we need an algorithm that works regardless of the scale of the image. Enter **Scale-Invariant Feature Transform (SIFT)**. While the name may sound a bit mysterious, now that we know what problem we are trying to solve, it actually makes sense. We need a function (a transform) that will detect features (a feature transform) and will not output different results depending on the scale of the image (a scale-invariant feature transform). Note that SIFT does not detect keypoints (which is done with the **Difference of Gaussians (DoG)**; instead, it describes the region surrounding them by means of a feature vector.

A quick introduction to the DoG is in order. Previously, in `Chapter 3`, *Processing Images with OpenCV*, we talked about low pass filters and blurring operations, and specifically the `cv2.GaussianBlur()` function. DoG is the result of applying different Gaussian filters to the same image. Previously, we applied this type of technique for edge detection, and the idea is the same here. The final result of a DoG operation contains areas of interest (keypoints), which are then going to be described through SIFT.

Let's see how DoG and SIFT behave in the following image, which is full of corners and features:

Here, the beautiful panorama of Varese (in Lombardy, Italy) gains a new type of fame as a subject of computer vision. Here is the code that produces this processed image:

```
import cv2

img = cv2.imread('../images/varese.jpg')
gray = cv2.cvtColor(img, cv2.COLOR_BGR2GRAY)

sift = cv2.xfeatures2d.SIFT_create()
keypoints, descriptors = sift.detectAndCompute(gray, None)

cv2.drawKeypoints(img, keypoints, img, (51, 163, 236),
                  cv2.DRAW_MATCHES_FLAGS_DRAW_RICH_KEYPOINTS)

cv2.imshow('sift_keypoints', img)
cv2.waitKey()
```

After the usual imports, we load the image we want to process. Then, we convert the image into grayscale. By now, you may have gathered that many methods in OpenCV expect a grayscale image as input. The next step is to create a SIFT detection object and compute the features and descriptors of the grayscale image:

```
sift = cv2.xfeatures2d.SIFT_create()
keypoints, descriptors = sift.detectAndCompute(gray, None)
```

Behind the scenes, these simple lines of code carry out an elaborate process; we create a `cv2.SIFT` object, which uses DoG to detect keypoints and then computes a feature vector for the surrounding region of each keypoint. As the name of the `detectAndCompute` method clearly suggests, two main operations are performed: feature detection and the computation of descriptors. The return value of the operation is a tuple containing a list of keypoints and another list of the keypoints' descriptors.

Finally, we process this image by drawing the keypoints on it with the `cv2.drawKeypoints` function and then displaying it with the usual `cv2.imshow` function. As one of its arguments, the `cv2.drawKeypoints` function accepts a flag that specifies the type of visualization we want. Here, we specify `cv2.DRAW_MATCHES_FLAGS_DRAW_RICH_KEYPOINT` in order to draw a visualization of the scale and orientation of each keypoint.

Anatomy of a keypoint

Each keypoint is an instance of the `cv2.KeyPoint` class, which has the following properties:

- The `pt` (point) property contains the *x* and *y* coordinates of the keypoint in the image.
- The `size` property indicates the diameter of the feature.
- The `angle` property indicates the orientation of the feature, as shown by the radial lines in the preceding processed image.
- The `response` property indicates the strength of the keypoint. Some features are classified by SIFT as stronger than others, and `response` is the property you would check to evaluate the strength of a feature.
- The `octave` property indicates the layer in the image pyramid where the feature was found. Let's briefly review the concept of an image pyramid, which we discussed previously in Chapter 5, *Detecting and Recognizing Faces*, in the *Conceptualizing Haar cascades* section. The SIFT algorithm operates in a similar fashion to face detection algorithms in that it processes the same image iteratively but alters the input at each iteration. In particular, the scale of the image is a parameter that changes at each iteration (`octave`) of the algorithm. Thus, the `octave` property is related to the image scale at which the keypoint was detected.
- Finally, the `class_id` property can be used to assign a custom identifier to a keypoint or a group of keypoints.

Detecting Fast Hessian features and extracting SURF descriptors

Computer vision is a relatively young branch of computer science, so many famous algorithms and techniques have only been invented recently. SIFT is, in fact, only 21 years old, having been published by David Lowe in 1999.

SURF is a feature detection algorithm that was published in 2006 by Herbert Bay. SURF is several times faster than SIFT, and it is partially inspired by it.

Note that both SIFT and SURF are patented algorithms and, for this reason, are made available only in builds of `opencv_contrib` where the `OPENCV_ENABLE_NONFREE` CMake flag is used.

It is not particularly relevant to this book to understand how SURF works under the hood, inasmuch as we can use it in our applications and make the best of it. What is important to understand is that `cv2.SURF` is an OpenCV class that performs keypoint detection with the Fast Hessian algorithm and descriptor extraction with SURF, much like the `cv2.SIFT` class performs keypoint detection with DoG and descriptor extraction with SIFT.

Also, the good news is that OpenCV provides a standardized API for all its supported feature detection and descriptor extraction algorithms. Thus, with only trivial changes, we can adapt our previous code sample to use SURF instead of SIFT. Here is the modified code, with the changes in bold:

```
import cv2

img = cv2.imread('../images/varese.jpg')
gray = cv2.cvtColor(img, cv2.COLOR_BGR2GRAY)

surf = cv2.xfeatures2d.SURF_create(8000)
keypoints, descriptor = surf.detectAndCompute(gray, None)

cv2.drawKeypoints(img, keypoints, img, (51, 163, 236),
                cv2.DRAW_MATCHES_FLAGS_DRAW_RICH_KEYPOINTS)

cv2.imshow('surf_keypoints', img)
cv2.waitKey()
```

The parameter to `cv2.xfeatures2d.SURF_create` is a threshold for the Fast Hessian algorithm. By increasing the threshold, we can reduce the number of features that will be retained. With a threshold of `8000`, we get the following result:

Try adjusting the threshold to see how it affects the result. As an exercise, you may want to build a GUI application with a slider that controls the value of the threshold. This way, a user can adjust the threshold and see the number of features increase and decrease in an inversely proportional fashion. We built a GUI application with sliders in Chapter 4, *Depth Estimation and Segmentation*, in the *Depth estimation with a normal camera* section, so you may want to refer back to that section as a guide.

Next, we'll examine the FAST corner detector, the BRIEF keypoint descriptor, and ORB (which uses FAST and BRIEF together).

Using ORB with FAST features and BRIEF descriptors

If SIFT is young, and SURF younger, ORB is in its infancy. ORB was first published in 2011 as a fast alternative to SIFT and SURF.

The algorithm was published in the paper *ORB: an efficient alternative to SIFT or SURF*, available in PDF format at http://www.willowgarage.com/sites/default/files/orb_final.pdf.

ORB mixes the techniques used in the FAST keypoint detector and the BRIEF keypoint descriptor, so it is worth taking a quick look at FAST and BRIEF first. Then, we will talk about brute-force matching – an algorithm used for feature matching – and look at an example of feature matching.

FAST

The **Features from Accelerated Segment Test (FAST)** algorithm works by analyzing circular neighborhoods of 16 pixels. It marks each pixel in a neighborhood as brighter or darker than a particular threshold, which is defined relative to the center of the circle. A neighborhood is deemed to be a corner if it contains a number of contiguous pixels marked as brighter or darker.

FAST also uses a high-speed test, which can sometimes determine that a neighborhood is not a corner by checking just 2 or 4 pixels instead of 16. To understand how this test works, let's take a look at the following diagram, taken from the OpenCV documentation:

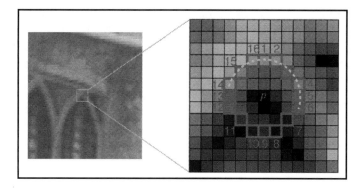

Here, we can see a 16-pixel neighborhood at two different magnifications. The pixels at positions 1, 5, 9, and 13 correspond to the four cardinal points at the edge of the circular neighborhood. If the neighborhood is a corner, we expect that out of these four pixels, exactly three *or* exactly one will be brighter than the threshold. (Another way of saying this is that exactly one *or* exactly three of them will be darker than the threshold.) If exactly two of them are brighter than the threshold, then we have an edge, not a corner. If exactly four or exactly zero of them are brighter than the threshold, then we have a relatively uniform neighborhood that is neither a corner nor an edge.

FAST is a clever algorithm, but it's not devoid of weaknesses, and to compensate for these weaknesses, developers analyzing images can implement a machine learning approach in order to feed a set of images (relevant to a given application) to the algorithm so that parameters such as the threshold are optimized. Whether the developer specifies parameters directly or provides a training set for a machine learning approach, FAST is an algorithm that is sensitive to the developer's input, perhaps more so than SIFT.

BRIEF

Binary Robust Independent Elementary Features (**BRIEF**), on the other hand, is not a feature detection algorithm, but a descriptor. Let's delve deeper into the concept of what a descriptor is, and then look at BRIEF.

When we previously analyzed images with SIFT and SURF, the heart of the entire process was the call to the `detectAndCompute` function. This function performs two different steps – detection and computation – and they return two different results, coupled in a tuple.

The result of detection is a set of keypoints; the result of the computation is a set of descriptors for those keypoints. This means that OpenCV's `cv2.SIFT` and `cv2.SURF` classes implement algorithms for both detection and description. Remember, though, that the original SIFT and SURF are *not* feature detection algorithms. OpenCV's `cv2.SIFT` implements DoG feature detection plus SIFT description, while OpenCV's `cv2.SURF` implements Fast Hessian feature detection plus SURF description.

Keypoint descriptors are a representation of the image that serves as the gateway to feature matching because you can compare the keypoint descriptors of two images and find commonalities.

BRIEF is one of the fastest descriptors currently available. The theory behind BRIEF is quite complicated, but suffice it to say that BRIEF adopts a series of optimizations that make it a very good choice for feature matching.

Brute-force matching

A brute-force matcher is a descriptor matcher that compares two sets of keypoint descriptors and generates a result that is a list of matches. It is called brute-force because little optimization is involved in the algorithm. For each keypoint descriptor in the first set, the matcher makes comparisons to every keypoint descriptor in the second set. Each comparison produces a distance value and the best match can be chosen on the basis of least distance.

More generally, in computing, the term **brute-force** is associated with an approach that prioritizes the exhaustion of all possible combinations (for example, all the possible combinations of characters to crack a password of a known length). Conversely, an algorithm that prioritizes speed might skip some possibilities and try to take a shortcut to the solution that seems the most plausible.

OpenCV provides a `cv2.BFMatcher` class that supports several approaches to brute-force feature matching.

Matching a logo in two images

Now that we have a general idea of what FAST and BRIEF are, we can understand why the team behind ORB (composed of Ethan Rublee, Vincent Rabaud, Kurt Konolige, and Gary R. Bradski) chose these two algorithms as a foundation for ORB.

In their paper, the authors aim to achieve the following results:

- The addition of a fast and accurate orientation component to FAST
- The efficient computation of oriented BRIEF features
- Analysis of variance and correlation of oriented BRIEF features
- A learning method to decorrelate BRIEF features under rotational invariance, leading to better performance in nearest-neighbor applications

The main points are quite clear: ORB aims to optimize and speed up operations, including the very important step of utilizing BRIEF in a rotation-aware fashion so that matching is improved, even in situations where a training image has a very different rotation to the query image.

At this stage, though, perhaps you have had enough of the theory and want to sink your teeth in to some feature matching, so let's look at some code. The following script attempts to match features in a logo to the features in a photograph that contain the logo:

```python
import cv2
from matplotlib import pyplot as plt

# Load the images.
img0 = cv2.imread('../images/nasa_logo.png',
                  cv2.IMREAD_GRAYSCALE)
img1 = cv2.imread('../images/kennedy_space_center.jpg',
                  cv2.IMREAD_GRAYSCALE)

# Perform ORB feature detection and description.
orb = cv2.ORB_create()
```

```
kp0, des0 = orb.detectAndCompute(img0, None)
kp1, des1 = orb.detectAndCompute(img1, None)

# Perform brute-force matching.
bf = cv2.BFMatcher(cv2.NORM_HAMMING, crossCheck=True)
matches = bf.match(des0, des1)

# Sort the matches by distance.
matches = sorted(matches, key=lambda x:x.distance)

# Draw the best 25 matches.
img_matches = cv2.drawMatches(
    img0, kp0, img1, kp1, matches[:25], img1,
    flags=cv2.DRAW_MATCHES_FLAGS_NOT_DRAW_SINGLE_POINTS)

# Show the matches.
plt.imshow(img_matches)
plt.show()
```

Let's examine this code step by step. After the usual imports, we load two images (the query image and the scene) in grayscale format. Here is the query image, which is the NASA logo:

Here is the photo of the scene, which is the Kennedy Space Center:

Now, we proceed to create the ORB feature detector and descriptor:

```
# Perform ORB feature detection and description.
orb = cv2.ORB_create()
kp0, des0 = orb.detectAndCompute(img0, None)
kp1, des1 = orb.detectAndCompute(img1, None)
```

In a similar fashion to what we did with SIFT and SURF, we detect and compute the keypoints and descriptors for both images.

From here, the concept is pretty simple: iterate through the descriptors and determine whether they are a match or not, and then calculate the quality of this match (distance) and sort the matches so that we can display the top *n* matches with a degree of confidence that they are, in fact, matching features on both images. cv2.BFMatcher does this for us:

```
# Perform brute-force matching.
bf = cv2.BFMatcher(cv2.NORM_HAMMING, crossCheck=True)
matches = bf.match(des0, des1)

# Sort the matches by distance.
matches = sorted(matches, key=lambda x:x.distance)
```

At this stage, we already have all the information we need, but as computer vision enthusiasts, we place quite a bit of importance on visually representing data, so let's draw these matches in a matplotlib chart:

```
# Draw the best 25 matches.
img_matches = cv2.drawMatches(
    img0, kp0, img1, kp1, matches[:25], img1,
    flags=cv2.DRAW_MATCHES_FLAGS_NOT_DRAW_SINGLE_POINTS)

# Show the matches.
plt.imshow(img_matches)
plt.show()
```

 Python's slicing syntax is quite robust. If the matches list contains fewer than 25 entries, the matches[:25] slicing command will run without problems and give us a list with just as many elements as the original.

The result is as follows:

You might think that this is a disappointing result. Indeed, we can see that most of the matches are false matches. Unfortunately, this is quite typical. To improve our results, we need to apply additional techniques to filter out bad matches. We'll turn our attention to this task next.

Filtering matches using K-Nearest Neighbors and the ratio test

Imagine that a large group of renowned philosophers asks you to judge their debate on a question of great importance to life, the universe, and everything. You listen carefully as each philosopher speaks in turn. Finally, when all the philosophers have exhausted all their lines of argument, you review your notes and perceive two things, as follows:

- Every philosopher disagrees with every other
- No one philosopher is much more convincing than the others

From your first observation, you infer that *at most* one of the philosophers is right; however, it is possible that all the philosophers could be wrong. Then, from your second observation, you begin to fear that you are at risk of picking a philosopher who is wrong, *even if* one of the philosophers is correct. Any way you look at it, these people have made you late for dinner. You call it a tie and say that the debate's all-important question remains unresolved.

We can compare our imaginary problem of judging the philosophers' debate to our practical problem of filtering out bad keypoint matches.

First, let's assume that each keypoint in our query image has, at most, one correct match in the scene. By implication, if our query image is the NASA logo, we assume that the other image – the scene – contains, at most, one NASA logo. Given that a query keypoint has, at most, one correct or good match, when we consider all *possible* matches, we are primarily observing bad matches. Thus, a brute-force matcher, which computes a distance score for every possible match, can give us plenty of observations of the distance scores for bad matches. We expect that a good match will have a significantly better (lower) distance score than the numerous bad matches, so the scores for the bad matches can help us pick a threshold for a good match. Such a threshold does not necessarily generalize well across different query keypoints or different scenes, but at least it helps us on a case-by-case basis.

Now, let's consider the implementation of a modified brute-force matching algorithm that adaptively chooses a distance threshold in the manner we have described. In the previous section's code sample, we used the `match` method of the `cv2.BFMatcher` class in order to get a list containing the single best (least-distance) match for each query keypoint. By doing so, we discarded information about the distance scores of all the worse possible matches – the kind of information we need for our adaptive approach. Fortunately, `cv2.BFMatcher` also provides a `knnMatch` method, which accepts an argument, `k`, that specifies the maximum number of best (least-distance) matches that we want to retain for each query keypoint. (In some cases, we may get fewer matches than the maximum.) **KNN** stands for **k-nearest neighbors**.

We will use the `knnMatch` method to request a list of the two best matches for each query keypoint. Based on our assumption that each query keypoint has, at most, one correct match, we are confident that the second-best match is wrong. We multiply the second-best match's distance score by a value less than 1 in order to obtain the threshold.

Then, we accept the best match as a good match only if its distant score is less than the threshold. This approach is known as the **ratio test**, and it was first proposed by David Lowe, the author of the SIFT algorithm. He describes the ratio test in his paper, *Distinctive Image Features from Scale-Invariant Keypoints*, which is available at https://www.cs.ubc.ca/~lowe/papers/ijcv04.pdf. Specifically, in the *Application to object recognition* section, he states the following:

> *"The probability that a match is correct can be determined by taking the ratio of the distance from the closest neighbor to the distance of the second closest."*

We can load the images, detect keypoints, and compute ORB descriptors in the same way as we did in the previous section's code sample. Then, we can perform brute-force KNN matching using the following two lines of code:

```
# Perform brute-force KNN matching.
bf = cv2.BFMatcher(cv2.NORM_HAMMING, crossCheck=False)
pairs_of_matches = bf.knnMatch(des0, des1, k=2)
```

knnMatch returns a list of lists; each inner list contains at least one match and no more than k matches, sorted from best (least distance) to worst. The following line of code sorts the outer list based on the distance score of the best matches:

```
# Sort the pairs of matches by distance.
pairs_of_matches = sorted(pairs_of_matches, key=lambda x:x[0].distance)
```

Let's draw the top 25 best matches, along with any second-best matches that knnMatch may have paired with them. We can't use the cv2.drawMatches function because it only accepts a one-dimensional list of matches; instead, we must use cv2.drawMatchesKnn. The following code is used to select, draw, and show the matches:

```
# Draw the 25 best pairs of matches.
img_pairs_of_matches = cv2.drawMatchesKnn(
    img0, kp0, img1, kp1, pairs_of_matches[:25], img1,
    flags=cv2.DRAW_MATCHES_FLAGS_NOT_DRAW_SINGLE_POINTS)

# Show the pairs of matches.
plt.imshow(img_pairs_of_matches)
plt.show()
```

So far, we have not filtered out any bad matches – and, indeed, we have deliberately included the second-best matches, which we believe to be bad – so the result looks a mess. Here it is:

Now, let's apply the ratio test. We will set the threshold at 0.8 times the distance score of the second-best match. If `knnMatch` has failed to provide a second-best match, we reject the best match anyway because we are unable to apply the test. The following code applies these conditions and provides us with a list of best matches that passed the test:

```
# Apply the ratio test.
matches = [x[0] for x in pairs_of_matches
           if len(x) > 1 and x[0].distance < 0.8 * x[1].distance]
```

Having applied the ratio test, now we are only dealing with best matches (not pairs of best and second-best matches), so we can draw them with `cv2.drawMatches` instead of `cv2.drawMatchesKnn`. Again, we will select the top 25 matches from the list. The following code is used to select, draw, and show the matches:

```
# Draw the best 25 matches.
img_matches = cv2.drawMatches(
    img0, kp0, img1, kp1, matches[:25], img1,
    flags=cv2.DRAW_MATCHES_FLAGS_NOT_DRAW_SINGLE_POINTS)

# Show the matches.
plt.imshow(img_matches)
plt.show()
```

Here, we can see the matches that passed the ratio test:

Comparing this output image to the one in the previous section, we can see that KNN and the ratio test have allowed us to filter out many bad matches. The remaining matches are not perfect but nearly all of them point to the correct region – the NASA logo on the side of the Kennedy Space Center.

We have made a promising start. Next, we will replace the brute-force matcher with a faster matcher called **FLANN**. After that, we will learn how to describe a set of matches in terms of homography – that is, a 2D transformation matrix that expresses the position, rotation, scale, and other geometric characteristics of the matched object.

Matching with FLANN

FLANN stands for **Fast Library for Approximate Nearest Neighbors**. It is an open source library under the permissive 2-clause BSD license. The official internet home of FLANN is http://www.cs.ubc.ca/research/flann/. The following is a quote from the website:

"FLANN is a library for performing fast approximate nearest neighbor searches in high-dimensional spaces. It contains a collection of algorithms we found to work best for the nearest neighbor search and a system for automatically choosing the best algorithm and optimum parameters depending on the dataset.
FLANN is written in C++ and contains bindings for the following languages: C, MATLAB, and Python."

In other words, FLANN has a big toolbox, it knows how to choose the right tools for the job, and it speaks several languages. These features make the library fast and convenient. Indeed, FLANN's authors claim that it is 10 times faster than other nearest-neighbor search software for many datasets.

As a standalone library, FLANN is available on GitHub at
`https://github.com/mariusmuja/flann/`. However, we will use FLANN as part of OpenCV because OpenCV provides a handy wrapper for it.

To begin our practical example of FLANN matching, let's import NumPy, OpenCV, and Matplotlib, and load two images from files. Here is the relevant code:

```
import numpy as np
import cv2
from matplotlib import pyplot as plt

img0 = cv2.imread('../images/gauguin_entre_les_lys.jpg',
                  cv2.IMREAD_GRAYSCALE)
img1 = cv2.imread('../images/gauguin_paintings.png',
                  cv2.IMREAD_GRAYSCALE)
```

Here is the first image – the query image – that our script is loading:

This work of art is *Entre les lys* (*Among the lilies*), painted by Paul Gauguin in 1889. We will search for matching keypoints in a larger image that contains multiple works by Gauguin, alongside some haphazard shapes drawn by one of the authors of this book. Here is the larger image:

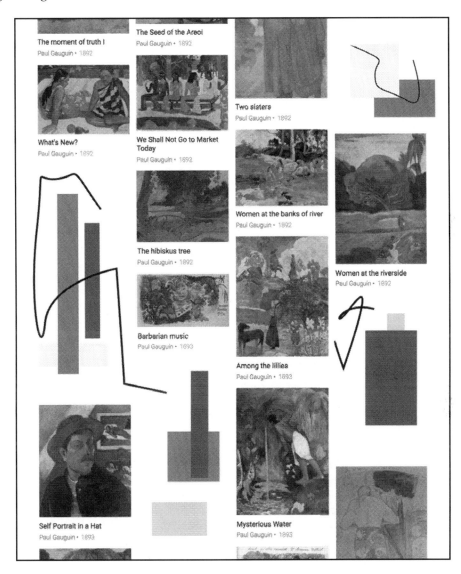

Within the larger image, *Entre les lys* appears in the third column, third row. The query image and the corresponding region of the larger image are not identical; they depict *Entre les lys* in slightly different colors and at a different scale. Nonetheless, this should be an easy case for our matcher.

Let's detect the necessary keypoints and extract our features using the `cv2.SIFT` class:

```
# Perform SIFT feature detection and description.
sift = cv2.xfeatures2d.SIFT_create()
kp0, des0 = sift.detectAndCompute(img0, None)
kp1, des1 = sift.detectAndCompute(img1, None)
```

So far, the code should seem familiar, since we have already dedicated several sections of this chapter to SIFT and other descriptors. In our previous examples, we fed the descriptors to `cv2.BFMatcher` for brute-force matching. This time, we will use `cv2.FlannBasedMatcher` instead. The following code performs FLANN-based matching with custom parameters:

```
# Define FLANN-based matching parameters.
FLANN_INDEX_KDTREE = 1
index_params = dict(algorithm=FLANN_INDEX_KDTREE, trees=5)
search_params = dict(checks=50)

# Perform FLANN-based matching.
flann = cv2.FlannBasedMatcher(index_params, search_params)
matches = flann.knnMatch(des0, des1, k=2)
```

Here, we can see that the FLANN matcher takes two parameters: an `indexParams` object and a `searchParams` object. These parameters, passed in the form of dictionaries in Python (and structs in C++), determine the behavior of the index and search objects that are used internally by FLANN to compute the matches. We have chosen parameters that offer a reasonable balance between accuracy and processing speed. Specifically, we are using a **kernel density tree (kd-tree)** indexing algorithm with five trees, which FLANN can process in parallel. (The FLANN documentation recommends between one tree, which would offer no parallelism, and 16 trees, which would offer a high degree of parallelism if the system could exploit it.)

We are performing 50 checks or traversals of each tree. A greater number of checks can provide greater accuracy but at a greater computational cost.

After performing FLANN-based matching, we apply Lowe's ratio test with a multiplier of 0.7. To demonstrate a different coding style, we will use the result of the ratio test in a slightly different way compared to how we did in the previous section's code sample. Previously, we assembled a new list with just the good matches in it. This time, we will assemble a list called `mask_matches`, in which each element is a sublist of length `k` (the same `k` that we passed to `knnMatch`). If a match is good, we set the corresponding element of the sublist to `1`; otherwise, we set it to `0`.

For example, if we have `mask_matches = [[0, 0], [1, 0]]`, this means that we have two matched keypoints; for the first keypoint, the best and second-best matches are both bad, while for the second keypoint, the best match is good but the second-best match is bad. Remember, we assume that all the second-best matches are bad. We use the following code to apply the ratio test and build the mask:

```
# Prepare an empty mask to draw good matches.
mask_matches = [[0, 0] for i in range(len(matches))]

# Populate the mask based on David G. Lowe's ratio test.
for i, (m, n) in enumerate(matches):
    if m.distance < 0.7 * n.distance:
        mask_matches[i]=[1, 0]
```

Now, it is time to draw and show the good matches. We can pass our `mask_matches` list to `cv2.drawMatchesKnn` as an optional argument, as shown in bold in the following code segment:

```
# Draw the matches that passed the ratio test.
img_matches = cv2.drawMatchesKnn(
    img0, kp0, img1, kp1, matches, None,
    matchColor=(0, 255, 0), singlePointColor=(255, 0, 0),
    matchesMask=mask_matches, flags=0)

# Show the matches.
plt.imshow(img_matches)
plt.show()
```

`cv2.drawMatchesKnn` only draws the matches that we marked as good (with a value of 1) in our mask. Let's unveil the result. Our script produces the following visualization of the FLANN-based matches:

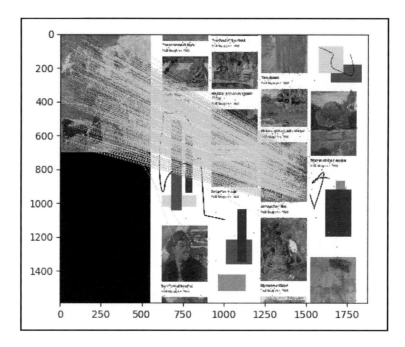

This is an encouraging picture: it appears that nearly all the matches fall in the right places. Next, let's try to reduce this type of result to a more succinct geometric representation – a homography – which would describe the pose of a whole matched object rather than a bunch of disconnected matched points.

Performing homography with FLANN-based matches

First of all, what is homography? Let's read a definition from the internet:

> *"A relation between two figures, such that to any point of the one corresponds one and but one point in the other, and vice versa. Thus, a tangent line rolling on a circle cuts two fixed tangents of the circle in two sets of points that are homographic."*

If you – like the authors of this book – are none the wiser from the preceding definition, you will probably find the following explanation a bit clearer: homography is a condition in which two figures find each other when one is a perspective distortion of the other.

First, let's take a look at what we want to achieve so that we can fully understand what homography is. Then, we will go through the code.

Imagine that we want to search for the following tattoo:

We, as human beings, can easily locate the tattoo in the following image, despite there being a difference in rotation:

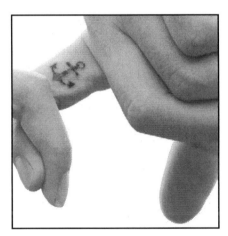

As an exercise in computer vision, we want to write a script that produces the following visualization of keypoint matches and the homography:

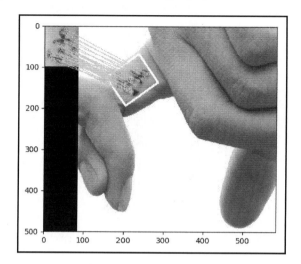

As shown in the preceding screenshot, we took the subject in the first image, correctly identified it in the second image, drew matching lines between the keypoints, and even drew a white border showing the perspective deformation of the subject in the second image relative to the first image.

You might have guessed – correctly – that the script's implementation starts by importing libraries, reading images in grayscale format, detecting features, and computing SIFT descriptors. We did all of this in our previous examples, so we will omit that here. Let's take a look at what we do next:

1. We proceed by assembling a list of matches that pass Lowe's ratio test, as shown in the following code:

```
# Find all the good matches as per Lowe's ratio test.
good_matches = []
for m, n in matches:
    if m.distance < 0.7 * n.distance:
        good_matches.append(m)
```

2. Technically, we can calculate the homography with as few as four matches. However, if any of these four matches is flawed, it will throw off the accuracy of the result. A more practical minimum is `10`. Given the extra matches, the homography-finding algorithm can discard some outliers in order to produce a result that closely fits a substantial subset of the matches. Thus, we proceed to check whether we have at least `10` good matches:

```
MIN_NUM_GOOD_MATCHES = 10

if len(good_matches) >= MIN_NUM_GOOD_MATCHES:
```

3. If this condition has been satisfied, we look up the 2D coordinates of the matched keypoints and place these coordinates in two lists of floating-point coordinate pairs. One list contains the keypoint coordinates in the query image, while the other list contains the matching keypoint coordinates in the scene:

```
src_pts = np.float32(
    [kp0[m.queryIdx].pt for m in good_matches]).reshape(-1, 1, 2)
dst_pts = np.float32(
    [kp1[m.trainIdx].pt for m in good_matches]).reshape(-1, 1, 2)
```

4. Now, we find the homography:

```
M, mask = cv2.findHomography(src_pts, dst_pts, cv2.RANSAC, 5.0)
mask_matches = mask.ravel().tolist()
```

Note that we create a `mask_matches` list, which will be used in the final drawing of the matches so that only points lying within the homography will have matching lines drawn.

5. At this stage, we have to perform a perspective transformation, which takes the rectangular corners of the query image and projects them into the scene so that we can draw the border:

```
h, w = img0.shape
src_corners = np.float32(
    [[0, 0], [0, h-1], [w-1, h-1], [w-1, 0]]).reshape(-1, 1, 2)
dst_corners = cv2.perspectiveTransform(src_corners, M)
dst_corners = dst_corners.astype(np.int32)

# Draw the bounds of the matched region based on the homography.
num_corners = len(dst_corners)
for i in range(num_corners):
    x0, y0 = dst_corners[i][0]
    if i == num_corners - 1:
        next_i = 0
```

```
else:
    next_i = i + 1
x1, y1 = dst_corners[next_i][0]
cv2.line(img1, (x0, y0), (x1, y1), 255, 3, cv2.LINE_AA)
```

Then, we proceed to draw the keypoints and show the visualization, as per our previous examples.

A sample application – tattoo forensics

Let's conclude this chapter with a real-life (or perhaps fantasy-life) example. Imagine you are working for the Gotham forensics department and you need to identify a tattoo. You have the original picture of a criminal's tattoo (perhaps captured in CCTV footage), but you don't know the identity of the person. However, you possess a database of tattoos, indexed with the name of the person that the tattoo belongs to.

Let's divide this task into two parts:

- Build a database by saving image descriptors to files
- Load the database and scan for matches between a query image's descriptors and the descriptors in the database

We will cover these tasks in the next two subsections.

Saving image descriptors to file

The first thing we will do is save the image descriptors to an external file. This way, we don't have to recreate the descriptors every time we want to scan two images for matches.

For the purposes of our example, let's scan a folder for images and create the corresponding descriptor files so that we have them readily available for future searches. To create descriptors, we will use a process we have already used a number of times in this chapter: namely, load an image, create a feature detector, detect features, and compute descriptors. To save the descriptors to a file, we will use a handy method of NumPy arrays called `save`, which dumps array data into a file in an optimized way.

 The `pickle` module, in the Python standard library, provides more general-purpose serialization functionality that supports any Python object and not just NumPy arrays. However, NumPy's array serialization is a good choice for numeric data.

Let's break our script up into functions. The main function will be
named `create_descriptors` (plural, descriptors), and it will iterate over the files in a
given folder. For each file, `create_descriptors` will call a helper function
named `create_descriptor` (singular, descriptor), which will compute and save our
descriptors for the given image file. Let's get started:

1. First, here is the implementation of `create_descriptors`:

    ```
    import os

    import numpy as np
    import cv2

    def create_descriptors(folder):
        feature_detector = cv2.xfeatures2d.SIFT_create()
        files = []
        for (dirpath, dirnames, filenames) in os.walk(folder):
            files.extend(filenames)
        for f in files:
            create_descriptor(folder, f, feature_detector)
    ```

    Note that `create_descriptors` creates the feature detector because we only
    need to do this once, not every time we load a file. The helper
    function, `create_descriptor`, receives the feature detector as an argument.

2. Now, let's look at the latter function's implementation:

    ```
    def create_descriptor(folder, image_path, feature_detector):
        if not image_path.endswith('png'):
            print('skipping %s' % image_path)
            return
        print('reading %s' % image_path)
        img = cv2.imread(os.path.join(folder, image_path),
                         cv2.IMREAD_GRAYSCALE)
        keypoints, descriptors = feature_detector.detectAndCompute(
            img, None)
        descriptor_file = image_path.replace('png', 'npy')
        np.save(os.path.join(folder, descriptor_file), descriptors)
    ```

    Note that we save the descriptor files in the same folder as the images. Moreover,
    we assume that the image files have the `png` extension. To make the script more
    robust, you could modify it so that it supports additional image file extensions
    such as `jpg`. If a file has an unexpected extension, we skip it because it might be a
    descriptor file (from a previous run of the script) or some other non-image file.

3. We have finished implementing the functions. To complete the script, we will call `create_descriptors` with a folder name as an argument:

```
folder = 'tattoos'
create_descriptors(folder)
```

When we run this script, it produces the necessary descriptor files in NumPy's array file format, with the file extension `npy`. These files constitute our database of tattoo descriptors, indexed by name. (Each filename is a person's name.) Next, we'll write a separate script so that we can run a query against this database.

Scanning for matches

Now that we have descriptors saved to files, we just need to perform matching against each set of descriptors to determine which set best matches our query image.

This is the process we will put in place:

1. Load a query image (`query.png`).
2. Scan the folder containing descriptor files. Print the names of the descriptor files.
3. Create SIFT descriptors for the query image.
4. For each descriptor file, load the SIFT descriptors and find FLANN-based matches. Filter the matches based on the ratio test. Print the person's name and the number of matches. If the number of matches exceeds an arbitrary threshold, print that the person is a suspect. (Remember, we are investigating a crime.)
5. Print the name of the prime suspect (the one with the most matches).

Let's consider the implementation:

1. First, the following code block loads the query image:

```
import os

import numpy as np
import cv2

# Read the query image.
folder = 'tattoos'
query = cv2.imread(os.path.join(folder, 'query.png'),
                   cv2.IMREAD_GRAYSCALE)
```

2. We proceed to assemble and print a list of the descriptor files:

```
# create files, images, descriptors globals
files = []
images = []
descriptors = []
for (dirpath, dirnames, filenames) in os.walk(folder):
    files.extend(filenames)
    for f in files:
        if f.endswith('npy') and f != 'query.npy':
            descriptors.append(f)
print(descriptors)
```

3. We set up our typical `cv2.SIFT` and `cv2.FlannBasedMatcher` objects, and we generate descriptors of the query image:

```
# Create the SIFT detector.
sift = cv2.xfeatures2d.SIFT_create()

# Perform SIFT feature detection and description on the
# query image.
query_kp, query_ds = sift.detectAndCompute(query, None)

# Define FLANN-based matching parameters.
FLANN_INDEX_KDTREE = 1
index_params = dict(algorithm=FLANN_INDEX_KDTREE, trees=5)
search_params = dict(checks=50)

# Create the FLANN matcher.
flann = cv2.FlannBasedMatcher(index_params, search_params)
```

4. Now, we search for suspects, whom we define as people with at least 10 good matches for the query tattoo. Our search entails iterating over the descriptor files, loading the descriptors, performing FLANN-based matching, and filtering the matches based on the ratio test. We print a result for each person (each descriptor file):

```
# Define the minimum number of good matches for a suspect.
MIN_NUM_GOOD_MATCHES = 10

greatest_num_good_matches = 0
prime_suspect = None

print('>> Initiating picture scan...')
for d in descriptors:
    print('---------- analyzing %s for matches ------------' % d)
    matches = flann.knnMatch(
```

```
        query_ds, np.load(os.path.join(folder, d)), k=2)
    good_matches = []
    for m, n in matches:
        if m.distance < 0.7 * n.distance:
            good_matches.append(m)
    num_good_matches = len(good_matches)
    name = d.replace('.npy', '').upper()
    if num_good_matches >= MIN_NUM_GOOD_MATCHES:
        print('%s is a suspect! (%d matches)' % \
            (name, num_good_matches))
        if num_good_matches > greatest_num_good_matches:
            greatest_num_good_matches = num_good_matches
            prime_suspect = name
    else:
        print('%s is NOT a suspect. (%d matches)' % \
            (name, num_good_matches))
```

Note the use of the `np.load` method, which loads a specified NPY file into a NumPy array.

5. In the end, we print the name of the prime suspect (if we found a suspect, that is):

```
if prime_suspect is not None:
    print('Prime suspect is %s.' % prime_suspect)
else:
    print('There is no suspect.')
```

Running the preceding script produces the following output:

```
>> Initiating picture scan...
--------- analyzing anchor-woman.npy for matches ------------
ANCHOR-WOMAN is NOT a suspect. (2 matches)
--------- analyzing anchor-man.npy for matches ------------
ANCHOR-MAN is a suspect! (44 matches)
--------- analyzing lady-featherly.npy for matches ------------
LADY-FEATHERLY is NOT a suspect. (2 matches)
--------- analyzing steel-arm.npy for matches ------------
STEEL-ARM is NOT a suspect. (0 matches)
--------- analyzing circus-woman.npy for matches ------------
CIRCUS-WOMAN is NOT a suspect. (1 matches)
Prime suspect is ANCHOR-MAN.
```

If we wanted, we could represent the matches and the homography graphically, as we did in the previous section.

Summary

In this chapter, we learned about detecting keypoints, computing keypoint descriptors, matching these descriptors, filtering out bad matches, and finding the homography between two sets of matching keypoints. We explored a number of algorithms that are available in OpenCV that can be used to accomplish these tasks, and we applied these algorithms to a variety of images and use cases.

If we combine our new knowledge of keypoints with additional knowledge about cameras and perspective, we can track objects in 3D space. This will be the topic of Chapter 9, *Camera Models and Augmented Reality*. You can skip ahead to that chapter if you are particularly keen to reach the third dimension.

If, instead, you think the next logical step is to round off your knowledge of two-dimensional solutions for object detection, recognition, and tracking, you can continue sequentially with Chapter 7, *Building Custom Object Detectors*, and then Chapter 8, *Tracking Objects*. It is good to know of a combination 2D and 3D techniques so that you can choose an approach that offers the right kind of output and the right computational speed for a given application.

7
Building Custom Object Detectors

This chapter delves deeper into the concept of object detection, which is one of the most common challenges in computer vision. Having come this far in the book, you are perhaps wondering when you will be able to put computer vision into practice on the streets. Do you dream of building a system to detect cars and people? Well, you are not too far from your goal, actually.

We have already looked at some specific cases of object detection and recognition in previous chapters. We focused on upright, frontal human faces in Chapter 5, *Detecting and Recognizing Faces*, and on objects with corner-like or blob-like features in Chapter 6, *Retrieving Images and Searching Using Image Descriptors*. Now, in the current chapter, we will explore algorithms that have a good ability to generalize or extrapolate, in the sense that they can cope with the real-world diversity that exists within a given class of object. For example, different cars have different designs, and people can appear to be different shapes depending on the clothes they wear.

Specifically, we will pursue the following objectives:

- Learning about another kind of feature descriptor: the **histogram of oriented gradients** (**HOG**) descriptor.
- Understanding **non-maximum suppression**, also called **non-maxima suppression** (**NMS**), which helps us choose the best of an overlapping set of detection windows.

- Gaining a high-level understanding of **support vector machines (SVMs)**. These general-purpose classifiers are based on supervised machine learning, in a way that is similar to linear regression.
- Detecting people with a pre-trained classifier based on HOG descriptors.
- Training a **bag-of-words (BoW)** classifier to detect a car. For this sample, we will work with a custom implementation of an image pyramid, a sliding window, and NMS so that we can better understand the inner workings of these techniques.

Most of the techniques in this chapter are not mutually exclusive; rather, they work together as components of a detector. By the end of the chapter, you will know how to train and use classifiers that have practical applications on the streets!

Technical requirements

This chapter uses Python, OpenCV, and NumPy. Please refer back to `Chapter 1`, *Setting Up OpenCV*, for installation instructions.

The completed code for this chapter can be found in this book's GitHub repository, at `https://github.com/PacktPublishing/Learning-OpenCV-4-Computer-Vision-with-Python-Third-Edition`, in the `chapter07` folder. Sample images can be found in the repository in the `images` folder.

Understanding HOG descriptors

HOG is a feature descriptor, so it belongs to the same family of algorithms as **scale-invariant feature transform (SIFT)**, **speeded-up robust features (SURF)**, and **Oriented FAST and rotated BRIEF (ORB)**, which we covered in `Chapter 6`, *Retrieving Images and Searching Using Image Descriptors*. Like other feature descriptors, HOG is capable of delivering the type of information that is vital for feature matching, as well as for object detection and recognition. Most commonly, HOG is used for object detection. The algorithm – and, in particular, its use as a people detector – was popularized by Navneet Dalal and Bill Triggs in their paper *Histograms of Oriented Gradients for Human Detection* (INRIA, 2005), which is available online at `https://lear.inrialpes.fr/people/triggs/pubs/Dalal-cvpr05.pdf`.

HOG's internal mechanism is really clever; an image is divided into cells and a set of gradients is calculated for each cell. Each gradient describes the change in pixel intensities in a given direction. Together, these gradients form a histogram representation of the cell. We encountered a similar approach when we studied face recognition with the **local binary pattern histogram** (**LBPH**) in Chapter 5, *Detecting and Recognizing Faces*.

Before diving into the technical details of how HOG works, let's first take a look at how HOG sees the world.

Visualizing HOG

Carl Vondrick, Aditya Khosla, Hamed Pirsiavash, Tomasz Malisiewicz, and Antonio Torralba have developed a HOG visualization technique called HOGgles (HOG goggles). For a summary of HOGgles, as well as links to code and publications, refer to Carl Vondrick's MIT web page at http://www.cs.columbia.edu/~vondrick/ihog/index.html. As one of their test images, Vondrick et al. use the following photograph of a truck:

Vondrick et al. produce the following visualization of the HOG descriptors, based on an approach from Dalal and Triggs' earlier paper:

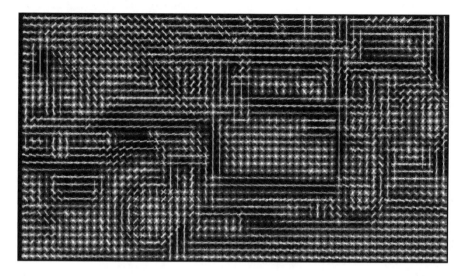

Then, applying HOGgles, Vondrick et al. invert the feature description algorithm to reconstruct the image of the truck as HOG sees it, as shown here:

In both of these two visualizations, you can see that HOG has divided the image into cells, and you can easily recognize the wheels and the main structure of the vehicle. In the first visualization, the calculated gradients for each cell are visualized as a set of crisscrossing lines that sometimes look like an elongated star; the star's longer axes represent stronger gradients. In the second visualization, the gradients are visualized as a smooth transition in brightness, along various axes in a cell.

Now, let's give further consideration to the way HOG works, and the way it can contribute to an object detection solution.

Using HOG to describe regions of an image

For each HOG cell, the histogram contains a number of bins equal to the number of gradients or, in other words, the number of axis directions that HOG considers. After calculating all the cells' histograms, HOG processes groups of histograms to produce higher-level descriptors. Specifically, the cells are grouped into larger regions, called blocks. These blocks can be made of any number of cells, but Dalal and Triggs found that 2x2 cell blocks yielded the best results when performing people detection. A block-wide vector is created so that it can be normalized, compensating for local variations in illumination and shadowing. (A single cell is too small a region to detect such variations.) This normalization improves a HOG-based detector's robustness, with respect to variations in lighting conditions.

Like other detectors, a HOG-based detector needs to cope with variations in objects' location and scale. The need to search in various locations is addressed by moving a fixed-size sliding window across an image. The need to search at various scales is addressed by scaling the image to various sizes, forming a so-called image pyramid. We studied these techniques previously in Chapter 5, *Detecting and Recognizing Faces*, specifically in the *Conceptualizing Haar cascades* section. However, let's elaborate on one difficulty: how to handle multiple detections in overlapping windows.

Suppose we are using a sliding window to perform people detection on an image. We slide our window in small steps, just a few pixels at a time, so we expect that it will frame any given person multiple times. Assuming that overlapping detections are indeed one person, we do not want to report multiple locations but, rather, only one location that we believe to be correct. In other words, even if a detection at a given location has a *good* confidence score, we might reject it if an overlapping detection has a *better* confidence score; thus, from a set of overlapping detections, we would choose the one with the *best* confidence score.

This is where NMS comes into play. Given a set of overlapping regions, we can suppress (or reject) all the regions for which our classifier did not produce a maximal score.

Understanding NMS

The concept of NMS might sound simple. From a set of overlapping solutions, just pick the best one! However, the implementation is more complex than you might initially think. Remember the image pyramid? Overlapping detections can occur at different scales. We must gather up all our positive detections, and convert their bounds back to a common scale before we check for overlap. A typical implementation of NMS takes the following approach:

1. Construct an image pyramid.
2. Scan each level of the pyramid with the sliding window approach, for object detection. For each window that yields a positive detection (beyond a certain arbitrary confidence threshold), convert the window back to the original image's scale. Add the window and its confidence score to a list of positive detections.
3. Sort the list of positive detections by order of descending confidence score so that the best detections come first in the list.
4. For each window, W, in the list of positive detections, remove all subsequent windows that significantly overlap with W. We are left with a list of positive detections that satisfy the criterion of NMS.

Besides NMS, another way to filter the positive detections is to eliminate any subwindows. When we speak of a **subwindow** (or subregion), we mean a window (or region in an image) that is entirely contained inside another window (or region). To check for subwindows, we simply need to compare the corner coordinates of various window rectangles. We will take this simple approach in our first practical example, in the *Detecting people with HOG descriptors* section. Optionally, NMS and suppression of subwindows can be combined.

Several of these steps are iterative, so we have an interesting optimization problem on our hands. A fast sample implementation in MATLAB is provided by Tomasz Malisiewicz at http://www.computervisionblog.com/2011/08/blazing-fast-nmsm-from-exemplar-svm.h tml. A port of this sample implementation to Python is provided by Adrian Rosebrock at https://www.pyimagesearch.com/2015/02/16/faster-non-maximum-suppression-python/ . We will build atop the latter sample later in this chapter, in the *Detecting a car in a scene* section.

Now, how do we determine the confidence score for a window? We need a classification system that determines whether a certain feature is present or not, and a confidence score for this classification. This is where SVMs come into play.

Understanding SVMs

Without going into details of how an SVM works, let's just try to grasp what it can help us accomplish in the context of machine learning and computer vision. Given labeled training data, an SVM learns to classify the same kind of data by finding an optimal hyperplane, which, in plain English, is the plane that divides differently labeled data by the largest possible margin. To aid our understanding, let's consider the following diagram, which is provided by Zach Weinberg under the Creative Commons Attribution-Share Alike 3.0 Unported License:

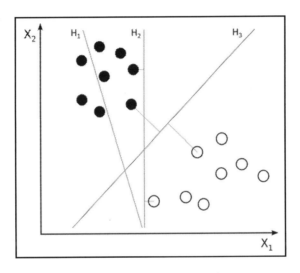

Hyperplane H_1 (shown as a green line) does not divide the two classes (the black dots versus the white dots). Hyperplanes H_2 (shown as a blue line) and H_3 (shown as a red line) both divide the classes; however, only hyperplane H_3 divides the classes by a maximal margin.

Let's suppose we are training an SVM as a people detector. We have two classes, *person* and *non-person*. As training samples, we provide vectors of HOG descriptors of various windows that do or do not contain a person. These windows may come from various images. The SVM learns by finding the optimal hyperplane that maximally divides the multidimensional HOG descriptor space into people (on one side of the hyperplane) and non-people (on the other side). Thereafter, when we give the trained SVM a vector of HOG descriptors for any other window in any image, the SVM can judge whether the window contains a person or not. The SVM can even give us a confidence value that relates to the vector's distance from the optimal hyperplane.

The SVM model has been around since the early 1960s. However, it has undergone improvements since then, and the basis of modern SVM implementations can be found in the paper *Support-vector networks* (*Machine Learning*, 1995) by Corinna Cortes and Vladimir Vapnik. It is available at http://link.springer.com/article/10.1007/BF00994018.

Now that we have a conceptual understanding of the key components we can combine to make an object detector, we can start looking at a few examples. We will start with one of OpenCV's ready-made object detectors, and then we will progress to designing and training our own custom object detectors.

Detecting people with HOG descriptors

OpenCV comes with a class called cv2.HOGDescriptor, which is capable of performing people detection. The interface has some similarities to the cv2.CascadeClassifier class that we used in Chapter 5, *Detecting and Recognizing Faces*. However, unlike cv2.CascadeClassifier, cv2.HOGDescriptor sometimes returns nested detection rectangles. In other words, cv2.HOGDescriptor might tell us that it detected one person whose bounding rectangle is located completely inside another person's bounding rectangle. This situation really is possible; for example, a child could be standing in front of an adult, and the child's bounding rectangle could be completely inside the adult's bounding rectangle. However, in a typical situation, nested detections are probably errors, so cv2.HOGDescriptor is often used along with code to filter out any nested detections.

Let's begin our sample script by implementing a test to determine whether one rectangle is nested inside another. For this purpose, we will wire a function, is_inside(i, o), where i is the possible inner rectangle and o is the possible outer rectangle. The function will return True if i is inside o; otherwise, it will return False. Here is the start of the script:

```
import cv2

def is_inside(i, o):
    ix, iy, iw, ih = i
    ox, oy, ow, oh = o
    return ix > ox and ix + iw < ox + ow and \
        iy > oy and iy + ih < oy + oh
```

Now, we create an instance of cv2.HOGDescriptor, and we specify that it will use a default people detector that is built into OpenCV by running the following code:

```
hog = cv2.HOGDescriptor()
hog.setSVMDetector(cv2.HOGDescriptor_getDefaultPeopleDetector())
```

Note that we specified the people detector with the `setSVMDetector` method. Hopefully, this makes sense based on the previous section of this chapter; an SVM is a classifier, so the choice of SVM determines the type of object our `cv2.HOGDescriptor` will detect.

Now, we proceed to load an image – in this case, an old photograph of women working in a hayfield – and we attempt to detect people in the image by running the following code:

```
img = cv2.imread('../images/haying.jpg')

found_rects, found_weights = hog.detectMultiScale(
    img, winStride=(4, 4), scale=1.02, finalThreshold=1.9)
```

Note that `cv2.HOGDescriptor` has a `detectMultiScale` method, which returns two lists:

1. A list of bounding rectangles for detected objects (in this case, detected people).
2. A list of weights or confidence scores for detected objects. A higher value indicates greater confidence that the detection result is correct.

`detectMultiScale` accepts several optional arguments, including the following:

- `winStride`: This tuple defines the x and y distance that the sliding window moves between successive detection attempts. HOG works well with overlapping windows, so the stride may be small relative to the window size. A smaller value produces more detections, at a higher computational cost. The default stride has no overlap; it is the same as the window size, which is (64, 128) for the default people detector.
- `scale`: This scale factor is applied between successive levels of the image pyramid. A smaller value produces more detections, at a higher computational cost. The value must be greater than 1.0. The default is 1.5.
- `finalThreshold`: This value determines how stringent our detection criteria are. A smaller value is less stringent, resulting in more detections. The default is 2.0.

Now, we can filter the detection results to remove nested rectangles. To determine whether a rectangle is a nested rectangle, we potentially need to compare it to every other rectangle. Note the use of our `is_inside` function in the following nested loop:

```
found_rects_filtered = []
found_weights_filtered = []
for ri, r in enumerate(found_rects):
    for qi, q in enumerate(found_rects):
        if ri != qi and is_inside(r, q):
            break
    else:
```

```
        found_rects_filtered.append(r)
        found_weights_filtered.append(found_weights[ri])
```

Finally, let's draw the remaining rectangles and weights in order to highlight the detected people, and let's show and save this visualization, as follows:

```
for ri, r in enumerate(found_rects_filtered):
    x, y, w, h = r
    cv2.rectangle(img, (x, y), (x + w, y + h), (0, 255, 255), 2)
    text = '%.2f' % found_weights_filtered[ri]
    cv2.putText(img, text, (x, y - 20),
                cv2.FONT_HERSHEY_SIMPLEX, 1, (0, 255, 255), 2)

cv2.imshow('Women in Hayfield Detected', img)
cv2.imwrite('./women_in_hayfield_detected.jpg', img)
cv2.waitKey(0)
```

If you run the script yourself, you will see rectangles around people in the image. Here is the result:

 The photograph is another example of the work of Sergey Prokudin-Gorsky (1863-1944), a pioneer of color photography. Here, the scene is a field at the Leushinskii Monastery, in northwestern Russia, in 1909.

Of the six women who are nearest to the camera, five have been successfully detected. At the same time, a tower in the background has been falsely detected as a person. In many real-world applications, people-detection results can be improved by analyzing a series of frames in a video. For example, imagine that we are looking at a surveillance video of the Leushinskii Monastery's hayfield, instead of a single photograph. We should be able to add code to determine that the tower cannot be a person because it does not move. Also, we should be able to detect additional people in other frames and track each person's movement from frame to frame. We will look at a people-tracking problem in Chapter 8, *Tracking Objects*.

Meanwhile, let's proceed to look at another kind of detector that we can train to detect a given class of objects.

Creating and training an object detector

Using a pre-trained detector makes it easy to build a quick prototype, and we are all very grateful to the OpenCV developers for making such useful capabilities as face detection and people detection readily available. However, whether you are a hobbyist or a computer vision professional, it is unlikely that you will only deal with people and faces.

Moreover, if you are like the authors of this book, you will wonder how the people detector was created in the first place and whether you can improve it. Furthermore, you may also wonder whether you can apply the same concepts to detect diverse objects, ranging from cars to goblins.

Indeed, in industry, you may have to deal with problems of detecting very specific objects, such as registration plates, book covers, or whatever thing may be most important to your employer or client.

Thus, the question is, how do we come up with our own classifiers?

There are many popular approaches. Throughout the remainder of this chapter, we will see that one answer lies in SVMs and the BoW technique.

We have already talked about SVMs and HOG. Let's now take a closer look at BoW.

Understanding BoW

BoW is a concept that was not initially intended for computer vision; rather, we use an evolved version of this concept in the context of computer vision. Let's first talk about its basic version, which – as you may have guessed – originally belongs to the field of language analysis and information retrieval.

 Sometimes, in the context of computer vision, BoW is called **bag of visual words (BoVW)**. However, we will simply use the term BoW, since this is the term used by OpenCV.

BoW is the technique by which we assign a weight or count to each word in a series of documents; we then represent these documents with vectors of these counts. Let's look at an example, as follows:

- Document 1: I like OpenCV and I like Python.
- Document 2: I like C++ and Python.
- Document 3: I don't like artichokes.

These three documents allow us to build a dictionary – also called a **codebook** or vocabulary – with these values, as follows:

```
{
    I: 4,
    like: 4,
    OpenCV: 1,
    and: 2,
    Python: 2,
    C++: 1,
    don't: 1,
    artichokes: 1
}
```

We have eight entries. Let's now represent the original documents using eight-entry vectors. Each vector contains values representing the counts of all words in the dictionary, in order, for a given document. The vector representation of the preceding three sentences is as follows:

```
[2, 2, 1, 1, 1, 0, 0, 0]
[1, 1, 0, 1, 1, 1, 0, 0]
[1, 1, 0, 0, 0, 0, 1, 1]
```

These vectors can be conceptualized as a histogram representation of documents or as a descriptor vector that can be used to train classifiers. For example, a document can be classified as *spam* or *not spam* based on such a representation. Indeed, spam filtering is one of the many real-world applications of BoW.

Now that we have a grasp of the basic concept of BoW, let's see how this applies to the world of computer vision.

Applying BoW to computer vision

We are by now familiar with the concepts of features and descriptors. We have used algorithms such as SIFT and SURF to extract descriptors from an image's features so that we can match these features in another image.

We have also recently familiarized ourselves with another kind of descriptor, based on a codebook or dictionary. We know about an SVM, a model that can accept labeled descriptor vectors as training data, can find an optimal division of the descriptor space into the given classes, and can predict the classes of new data.

Armed with this knowledge, we can take the following approach to build a classifier:

1. Take a sample dataset of images.
2. For each image in the dataset, extract descriptors (with SIFT, SURF, ORB, or a similar algorithm).
3. Add each descriptor vector to the BoW trainer.
4. Cluster the descriptors into *k* clusters whose centers (centroids) are our visual words. This last point probably sounds a bit obscure, but we will explore it further in the next section.

At the end of this process, we have a dictionary of visual words ready to be used. As you can imagine, a large dataset will help make our dictionary richer in visual words. Up to a point, the more words, the better!

Having trained a classifier, we should proceed to test it. The good news is that the test process is conceptually very similar to the training process outlined previously. Given a test image, we can extract descriptors and **quantize** them (or reduce their dimensionality) by calculating a histogram of their distances to the centroids. Based on this, we can attempt to recognize visual words, and locate them in the image.

This is the point in the chapter where you have built up an appetite for a deeper practical example, and are raring to code. However, before proceeding, let's take a quick but necessary digression into the theory of *k*-means clustering so that you can fully understand how visual words are created. Thereby, you will gain a better understanding of the process of object detection using BoW and SVMs.

k-means clustering

k-means clustering is a method of quantization whereby we analyze a large number of vectors in order to find a small number of clusters. Given a dataset, *k* represents the number of clusters into which the dataset is going to be divided. The term *means* refers to the mathematical concept of the mean or the average; when visually represented, the mean of a cluster is its centroid or the geometric center of points in the cluster.

 Clustering refers to the process of grouping points in a dataset into clusters.

OpenCV provides a class called `cv2.BOWKMeansTrainer`, which we will use to help train our classifier. As you might expect, the OpenCV documentation gives the following summary of this class:

> A "kmeans-based class to train a visual vocabulary using the bag of words approach."

After this long theoretical introduction, we can look at an example, and start training our custom classifier.

Detecting cars

To train any kind of classifier, we must begin by creating or acquiring a training dataset. We are going to train a car detector, so our dataset must contain positive samples that represent cars, as well as negative samples that represent other (non-car) things that the detector is likely to encounter while looking for cars. For example, if the detector is intended to search for cars on a street, then a picture of a curb, a crosswalk, a pedestrian, or a bicycle might be a more representative negative sample than a picture of the rings of Saturn. Besides representing the expected subject matter, ideally, the training samples should represent the way our particular camera and algorithm will see the subject matter.

Ultimately, in this chapter, we intend to use a sliding window of fixed size, so it is important that our training samples conform to a fixed size, and that the positive samples are tightly cropped in order to frame a car without much background.

Up to a point, we expect that the classifier's accuracy will improve as we keep adding good training images. On the other hand, a large dataset can make the training slow, and it is possible to overtrain a classifier such that it fails to extrapolate beyond the training set. Later in this section, we will write our code in a way that allows us to easily modify the number of training images so that we find a good size experimentally.

Assembling a dataset of car images would be a time-consuming task if we were to do it all by ourselves (though it is entirely doable). To avoid reinventing the wheel – or the whole car – we can avail ourselves of ready-made datasets, such as the following:

- UIUC Image Database for Car Detection: `https://cogcomp.seas.upenn.edu/Data/Car/`
- Stanford Cars Dataset: `http://ai.stanford.edu/~jkrause/cars/car_dataset.html`

Let's use the UIUC dataset in our example. Several steps are involved in obtaining this dataset and using it in a script, so let's walk through them one by one, as follows:

1. Download the UIUC dataset from `http://l2r.cs.uiuc.edu/~cogcomp/Data/Car/CarData.tar.gz`. Unzip it to some folder, which we will refer to as `<project_path>`. Now, the unzipped data should be located at `<project_path>/CarData`. Specifically, we will use some of the images in `<project_path>/CarData/TrainImages` and `<project_path>/CarData/TestImages`.

2. Also in `<project_path>`, let's create a Python script called `detect_car_bow_svm.py`. To begin the script's implementation, write the following code to check whether the `CarData` subfolder exists:

```
import cv2
import numpy as np
import os

if not os.path.isdir('CarData'):
    print(
        'CarData folder not found. Please download and unzip '
        'http://l2r.cs.uiuc.edu/~cogcomp/Data/Car/CarData.tar.gz '
        'into the same folder as this script.')
    exit(1)
```

If you can run this script and it does not print anything, this means everything is in its correct place.

3. Next, let's define the following constants in the script:

```
BOW_NUM_TRAINING_SAMPLES_PER_CLASS = 10
SVM_NUM_TRAINING_SAMPLES_PER_CLASS = 100
```

Note that our classifier will make use of two training stages: one stage for the BoW vocabulary, which will use a number of images as samples, and another stage for the SVM, which will use a number of BoW descriptor vectors as samples. Arbitrarily, we have defined a different number of training samples for each stage. At each stage, we could have also defined a different number of training samples for the two classes (*car* and *not car*), but instead, we will use the same number.

4. We will use `cv2.SIFT` to extract descriptors and `cv2.FlannBasedMatcher` to match these descriptors. Let's initialize these algorithms with the following code:

```
sift = cv2.xfeatures2d.SIFT_create()

FLANN_INDEX_KDTREE = 1
index_params = dict(algorithm=FLANN_INDEX_KDTREE, trees=5)
search_params = {}
flann = cv2.FlannBasedMatcher(index_params, search_params)
```

Note that we have initialized SIFT and the **Fast Library for Appropriate Nearest Neighbors (FLANN)** in the same way as we did in Chapter 6, *Retrieving Images and Searching Using image Descriptors*. However, this time, descriptor matching is not our end goal; instead, it will be part of the functionality of our BoW.

5. OpenCV provides a class called `cv2.BOWKMeansTrainer` to train a BoW vocabulary, and a class called `cv2.BOWImgDescriptorExtractor` to convert some kind of lower-level descriptors – in our example, SIFT descriptors – into BoW descriptors. Let's initialize these objects with the following code:

```
bow_kmeans_trainer = cv2.BOWKMeansTrainer(40)
bow_extractor = cv2.BOWImgDescriptorExtractor(sift, flann)
```

When initializing `cv2.BOWKMeansTrainer`, we must specify the number of clusters – in our example, 40. When initializing `cv2.BOWImgDescriptorExtractor`, we must specify a descriptor extractor and a descriptor matcher – in our example, the `cv2.SIFT` and `cv2.FlannBasedMatcher` objects that we created earlier.

6. To train the BoW vocabulary, we will provide samples of SIFT descriptors for various *car* and *not car* images. We will load the images from the `CarData/TrainImages` subfolder, which contains positive (*car*) images with names such as `pos-x.pgm`, and negative (*not car*) images with names such as `neg-x.pgm`, where x is a number starting at 1. Let's write the following utility function to return a pair of paths to the i th positive and negative training images, where i is a number starting at 0:

```
def get_pos_and_neg_paths(i):
    pos_path = 'CarData/TrainImages/pos-%d.pgm' % (i+1)
    neg_path = 'CarData/TrainImages/neg-%d.pgm' % (i+1)
    return pos_path, neg_path
```

Later in this section, we will call the preceding function in a loop, with a varying value of i, when we need to acquire a number of training samples.

7. For each path to a training sample, we will need to load the image, extract SIFT descriptors, and add the descriptors to the BoW vocabulary trainer. Let's write another utility function to do precisely this, as follows:

```
def add_sample(path):
    img = cv2.imread(path, cv2.IMREAD_GRAYSCALE)
    keypoints, descriptors = sift.detectAndCompute(img, None)
    if descriptors is not None:
        bow_kmeans_trainer.add(descriptors)
```

 If no features are found in the image, then the `keypoints` and `descriptors` variables will be `None`.

8. At this stage, we have everything we need to start training the BoW vocabulary. Let's read a number of images for each class (*car* as the positive class and *not car* as the negative class) and add them to the training set, as follows:

```
for i in range(BOW_NUM_TRAINING_SAMPLES_PER_CLASS):
    pos_path, neg_path = get_pos_and_neg_paths(i)
    add_sample(pos_path)
    add_sample(neg_path)
```

9. Now that we have assembled the training set, we will call the vocabulary trainer's `cluster` method, which performs the *k*-means classification and returns the vocabulary. We will assign this vocabulary to the BoW descriptor extractor, as follows:

```
voc = bow_kmeans_trainer.cluster()
bow_extractor.setVocabulary(voc)
```

Remember that earlier, we initialized the BoW descriptor extractor with a SIFT descriptor extractor and FLANN matcher. Now, we have also given the BoW descriptor extractor a vocabulary that we trained with samples of SIFT descriptors. At this stage, our BoW descriptor extractor has everything it needs in order to extract BoW descriptors from **Difference of Gaussian (DoG)** features.

Remember that `cv2.SIFT` detects DoG features and extracts SIFT descriptors, as we discussed in `Chapter 6`, *Retrieving Images and Searching Using Image Descriptors*, specifically in the *Detecting DoG features and extracting SIFT descriptors* section.

10. Next, we will declare another utility function that takes an image and returns the descriptor vector, as computed by the BoW descriptor extractor. This involves extracting the image's DoG features, and computing the BoW descriptor vector based on the DoG features, as follows:

```
def extract_bow_descriptors(img):
    features = sift.detect(img)
    return bow_extractor.compute(img, features)
```

11. We are ready to assemble another kind of training set, containing samples of BoW descriptors. Let's create two arrays to accommodate the training data and labels, and populate them with the descriptors generated by our BoW descriptor extractor. We will label each descriptor vector with 1 for a positive sample and -1 for a negative sample, as shown in the following code block:

```
training_data = []
training_labels = []
for i in range(SVM_NUM_TRAINING_SAMPLES_PER_CLASS):
    pos_path, neg_path = get_pos_and_neg_paths(i)
    pos_img = cv2.imread(pos_path, cv2.IMREAD_GRAYSCALE)
    pos_descriptors = extract_bow_descriptors(pos_img)
    if pos_descriptors is not None:
        training_data.extend(pos_descriptors)
        training_labels.append(1)
    neg_img = cv2.imread(neg_path, cv2.IMREAD_GRAYSCALE)
    neg_descriptors = extract_bow_descriptors(neg_img)
    if neg_descriptors is not None:
        training_data.extend(neg_descriptors)
        training_labels.append(-1)
```

Should you wish to train a classifier to distinguish between multiple positive classes, you can simply add other descriptors with other labels. For example, we could train a classifier that uses the label 1 for *car*, 2 for *person*, and -1 for *background*. There is no requirement to have a negative or background class but, if you do not, your classifier will assume that everything belongs to one of the positive classes.

12. OpenCV provides a class called `cv2.ml_SVM`, representing an SVM. Let's create an SVM, and train it with the data and labels that we previously assembled, as follows:

```
svm = cv2.ml.SVM_create()
svm.train(np.array(training_data), cv2.ml.ROW_SAMPLE,
          np.array(training_labels))
```

Note that we must convert the training data and labels from lists to NumPy arrays before we pass them to the `train` method of `cv2.ml_SVM`.

13. Finally, we are ready to test the SVM by classifying some images that were not part of the training set. We will iterate over a list of paths to test images. For each path, we will load the image, extract BoW descriptors, and get the SVM's **prediction** or classification result, which will be either 1.0 (*car*) or -1.0 (*not car*), based on the training labels we used earlier. We will draw text on the image to show the classification result, and we will show the image in a window. After showing all the images, we will wait for the user to hit any key, and then the script will end. All of this is achieved in the following block of code:

```
for test_img_path in ['CarData/TestImages/test-0.pgm',
                      'CarData/TestImages/test-1.pgm',
                      '../images/car.jpg',
                      '../images/haying.jpg',
                      '../images/statue.jpg',
                      '../images/woodcutters.jpg']:
    img = cv2.imread(test_img_path)
    gray_img = cv2.cvtColor(img, cv2.COLOR_BGR2GRAY)
    descriptors = extract_bow_descriptors(gray_img)
    prediction = svm.predict(descriptors)
    if prediction[1][0][0] == 1.0:
        text = 'car'
        color = (0, 255, 0)
    else:
        text = 'not car'
        color = (0, 0, 255)
    cv2.putText(img, text, (10, 30), cv2.FONT_HERSHEY_SIMPLEX, 1,
                color, 2, cv2.LINE_AA)
    cv2.imshow(test_img_path, img)
cv2.waitKey(0)
```

Save and run the script. You should see six windows with various classification results. Here is a screenshot of one of the true positive results:

The next screenshot shows one of the true negative results:

Of the six images in our simple test, only the following one is incorrectly classified:

Try adjusting the number of training samples, and try testing the classifier on more images, to see what results you can get.

Let's take stock of what we have done so far. We have used a mixture of SIFT, BoW, and SVMs to train a classifier to distinguish between two classes: *car* and *not car*. We have applied this classifier to whole images. The next logical step is to apply a sliding window technique so that we can narrow down our classification results to specific regions of an image.

Combining an SVM with a sliding window

By combining our SVM classifier with a sliding window technique and an image pyramid, we can achieve the following improvements:

- Detect multiple objects of the same kind in an image.
- Determine the position and size of each detected object in an image.

We will adopt the following approach:

1. Take a region of the image, classify it, and then move this window to the right by a predefined step size. When we reach the rightmost end of the image, reset the x coordinate to 0, move down a step, and repeat the entire process.
2. At each step, perform a classification with the SVM that was trained with BoW.
3. Keep track of all the windows that are positive detections, according to the SVM.
4. After classifying every window in the entire image, scale the image down, and repeat the entire process of using a sliding window. Thus, we are using an image pyramid. Continue rescaling and classifying until we get to a minimum size.

When we reach the end of this process, we have collected important information about the content of the image. However, there is a problem: in all likelihood, we have found a number of overlapping blocks that each yield a positive detection with high confidence. That is to say, the image may contain one object that gets detected multiple times. If we reported these multiple detections, our report would be quite misleading, so we will filter our results using NMS.

For a refresher, you may wish to refer back to the *Understanding NMS* section, earlier in this chapter.

Next, let's look at how to modify and extend our previous script, in order to implement the approach we have just described.

Detecting a car in a scene

We are now ready to apply all the concepts we learned so far by creating a car detection script that scans an image and draws rectangles around cars. Let's create a new Python script, `detect_car_bow_svm_sliding_window.py`, by copying our previous script, `detect_car_bow_svm.py`. (We covered the implementation of `detect_car_bow_svm.py` earlier, in the *Detecting cars* section.) Much of the new script's implementation will remain unchanged because we still want to train a BoW descriptor extractor and an SVM in almost the same way as we did previously. However, after the training is complete, we will process the test images in a new way. Rather than classifying each image in its entirety, we will decompose each image into pyramid layers and windows, we will classify each window, and we will apply NMS to a list of windows that yielded positive detections.

For NMS, we will rely on Malisiewicz and Rosebrock's implementation, as described earlier in this chapter, in the *Understanding NMS* section. You can find a slightly modified copy of their implementation in this book's GitHub repository, specifically in the Python script at `chapter7/non_max_suppression.py`. This script provides a function with the following signature:

```
def non_max_suppression_fast(boxes, overlapThresh):
```

As its first argument, the function takes a NumPy array containing rectangle coordinates and scores. If we have N rectangles, the shape of this array is Nx5. For a given rectangle at index i, the values in the array have the following meanings:

- `boxes[i][0]` is the leftmost x coordinate.
- `boxes[i][1]` is the topmost y coordinate.
- `boxes[i][2]` is the rightmost x coordinate.
- `boxes[i][3]` is the bottommost y coordinate.
- `boxes[i][4]` is the score, where a higher score represents greater confidence that the rectangle is a correct detection result.

As its second argument, the function takes a threshold that represents the maximum proportion of overlap between rectangles. If two rectangles have a greater proportion of overlap than this, the one with the lower score will be filtered out. Ultimately, the function will return an array of the remaining rectangles.

Now, let's turn our attention to the modifications to the
`detect_car_bow_svm_sliding_window.py` script, as follows:

1. First, we want to add a new import statement for the NMS function, as shown in **bold** in the following code:

```
import cv2
import numpy as np
import os

from non_max_suppression import non_max_suppression_fast as nms
```

2. Let's define some additional parameters near the start of the script, as shown in **bold** here:

```
BOW_NUM_TRAINING_SAMPLES_PER_CLASS = 10
SVM_NUM_TRAINING_SAMPLES_PER_CLASS = 100

SVM_SCORE_THRESHOLD = 1.8
NMS_OVERLAP_THRESHOLD = 0.15
```

We will use `SVM_SCORE_THRESHOLD` as a threshold to distinguish between a positive window and a negative window. We will see how the score is obtained a little later in this section. We will use `NMS_OVERLAP_THRESHOLD` as the maximum acceptable proportion of overlap in the NMS step. Here, we have arbitrarily chosen 15%, so we will cull windows that overlap by more than this proportion. As you experiment with your SVMs, you may tweak these parameters to your liking until you find values that yield the best results in your application.

3. We will reduce the number of *k*-means clusters from `40` to `12` (a number chosen arbitrarily based on experimentation), as follows:

```
bow_kmeans_trainer = cv2.BOWKMeansTrainer(12)
```

4. We will also adjust the parameters of the SVM, as follows:

```
svm = cv2.ml.SVM_create()
svm.setType(cv2.ml.SVM_C_SVC)
svm.setC(50)
svm.train(np.array(training_data), cv2.ml.ROW_SAMPLE,
          np.array(training_labels))
```

With the preceding changes to the SVM, we are specifying the classifier's level of strictness or severity. As the value of the C parameter increases, the risk of false positives decreases but the risk of false negatives increases. In our application, a false positive would be a window detected as a car when it is really *not* a car, and a false negative would be a car detected as a window when it really *is* a car.

After the code that trains the SVM, we want to add two more helper functions. One of them will generate levels of the image pyramid, and the other will generate regions of interest, based on the sliding window technique. Besides adding these helper functions, we also need to handle the test images differently in order to make use of the sliding window and NMS. The following steps cover the changes:

1. First, let's look at the helper function that deals with the image pyramid. This function is shown in the following code block:

```python
def pyramid(img, scale_factor=1.25, min_size=(200, 80),
            max_size=(600, 600)):
    h, w = img.shape
    min_w, min_h = min_size
    max_w, max_h = max_size
    while w >= min_w and h >= min_h:
        if w <= max_w and h <= max_h:
            yield img
        w /= scale_factor
        h /= scale_factor
        img = cv2.resize(img, (int(w), int(h)),
                         interpolation=cv2.INTER_AREA)
```

The preceding function takes an image and generates a series of resized versions of it. The series is bounded by a maximum and minimum image size.

 You will have noticed that the resized image is not returned with the return keyword but with the yield keyword. This is because this function is a so-called generator. It produces a series of images that we can easily use in a loop. If you are not familiar with generators, take a look at the official Python Wiki at https://wiki.python.org/moin/Generators.

2. Next up is the function to generate regions of interest, based on the sliding window technique. This function is shown in the following code block:

```
def sliding_window(img, step=20, window_size=(100, 40)):
    img_h, img_w = img.shape
    window_w, window_h = window_size
    for y in range(0, img_w, step):
        for x in range(0, img_h, step):
            roi = img[y:y+window_h, x:x+window_w]
            roi_h, roi_w = roi.shape
            if roi_w == window_w and roi_h == window_h:
                yield (x, y, roi)
```

Again, this is a generator. Although it is a bit deep-nested, the mechanism is very simple: given an image, return the upper-left coordinates and the sub-image representing the next window. Successive windows are shifted by an arbitrarily sized step from left to right until we reach the end of a row, and from the top to bottom until we reach the end of the image.

3. Now, let's consider the treatment of test images. As in the previous version of the script, we loop through a list of paths to test images, in order to load and process each one. The beginning of the loop is unchanged. For context, here it is:

```
for test_img_path in ['CarData/TestImages/test-0.pgm',
                      'CarData/TestImages/test-1.pgm',
                      '../images/car.jpg',
                      '../images/haying.jpg',
                      '../images/statue.jpg',
                      '../images/woodcutters.jpg']:
    img = cv2.imread(test_img_path)
    gray_img = cv2.cvtColor(img, cv2.COLOR_BGR2GRAY)
```

4. For each test image, we iterate over the pyramid levels, and for each pyramid level, we iterate over the sliding window positions. For each window or **region of interest (ROI)**, we extract BoW descriptors and classify them using the SVM. If the classification produces a positive result that passes a certain confidence threshold, we add the rectangle's corner coordinates and confidence score to a list of positive detections. Continuing from the previous code block, we proceed to handle a given test image with the following code:

```
pos_rects = []
for resized in pyramid(gray_img):
    for x, y, roi in sliding_window(resized):
        descriptors = extract_bow_descriptors(roi)
        if descriptors is None:
            continue
```

```
prediction = svm.predict(descriptors)
if prediction[1][0][0] == 1.0:
    raw_prediction = svm.predict(
        descriptors,
        flags=cv2.ml.STAT_MODEL_RAW_OUTPUT)
    score = -raw_prediction[1][0][0]
    if score > SVM_SCORE_THRESHOLD:
        h, w = roi.shape
        scale = gray_img.shape[0] / \
            float(resized.shape[0])
        pos_rects.append([int(x * scale),
                          int(y * scale),
                          int((x+w) * scale),
                          int((y+h) * scale),
                          score])
```

Let's take note of a couple of complexities in the preceding code, as follows:

- To obtain a confidence score for the SVM's prediction, we must run the `predict` method with an optional flag, `cv2.ml.STAT_MODEL_RAW_OUTPUT`. Then, instead of returning a label, the method returns a score as part of its output. This score may be negative, and a low value represents a high level of confidence. To make the score more intuitive – and to match the NMS function's assumption that a higher score is better – we negate the score so that a high value represents a high level of confidence.

- Since we are working with multiple pyramid levels, the window coordinates do not have a common scale. We have converted them back to a common scale – the original image's scale – before adding them to our list of positive detections.

So far, we have performed car detection at various scales and positions; as a result, we have a list of detected car rectangles, including coordinates and scores. We expect a lot of overlap within this list of rectangles.

5. Now, let's call the NMS function, in order to cherry-pick the highest-scoring rectangles in the case of overlap, as follows:

```
pos_rects = nms(np.array(pos_rects), NMS_OVERLAP_THRESHOLD)
```

Note that we have converted our list of rectangle coordinates and scores to a NumPy array, which is the format expected by this function.

At this stage, we have an array of detected car rectangles and their scores, and we have ensured that these are the best non-overlapping detections we can select (within the parameters of our model).

6. Now, let's draw the rectangles and their scores by adding the following inner loop to the code:

```
for x0, y0, x1, y1, score in pos_rects:
    cv2.rectangle(img, (int(x0), int(y0)), (int(x1), int(y1)),
                  (0, 255, 255), 2)
    text = '%.2f' % score
    cv2.putText(img, text, (int(x0), int(y0) - 20),
                cv2.FONT_HERSHEY_SIMPLEX, 1, (0, 255, 255), 2)
```

As in the previous version of this script, the body of the outer loop ends by showing the current test image, including the annotations we have drawn on it. After the loop runs through all the test images, we wait for the user to press any key; then, the program ends, as shown here:

```
    cv2.imshow(test_img_path, img)
cv2.waitKey(0)
```

Let's run the modified script, and see how well it can answer the eternal question: *Dude, where's my car?*

The following screenshot shows a successful detection:

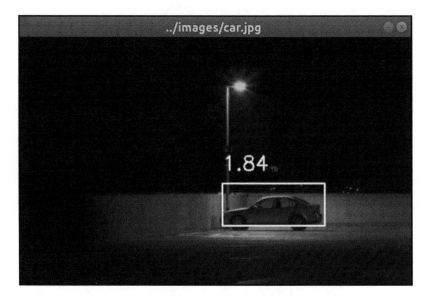

Another of our test images has two cars in it. As it happens, one car is successfully detected while the other is not, as shown in the following screenshot:

Sometimes, a background region with many features in it is falsely detected as a car. Here is an example:

Remember that in this sample script, our training sets are small. Larger training sets, with more diverse backgrounds, could improve the results. Also, remember that the image pyramid and sliding window are producing a large number of ROIs. When we consider this, we should realize that our detector's false positive rate is actually quite low. If we were performing detection on frames of a video, we could further lower the false positive rate by filtering out detections that occur only in a single frame or a few frames, rather than a series of some arbitrary minimum length.

Feel free to experiment with the parameters and training sets of the preceding script. When you are ready, let's wrap up this chapter with a few closing notes.

Saving and loading a trained SVM

A final piece of advice on SVMs: you do not need to train a detector every time you want to use it – and, indeed, you should avoid doing so because training is slow. You can use code such as the following to save a trained SVM model to an XML file:

```
svm = cv2.ml.SVM_create()
svm.train(np.array(training_data), cv2.ml.ROW_SAMPLE,
          np.array(training_labels))
svm.save('my_svm.xml')
```

Subsequently, you can reload the trained SVM, using code such as the following:

```
svm = cv2.ml.SVM_create()
svm.load('my_svm.xml')
```

Typically, you might have one script that trains and saves your SVM model, and other scripts that load and use it for various detection problems.

Summary

In this chapter, we covered a wide range of concepts and techniques, including HOG, BoW, SVMs, image pyramids, sliding windows, and NMS. We learned that these techniques have applications in object detection, as well as other fields. We wrote a script that combined most of these techniques – BoW, SVMs, an image pyramid, a sliding window, and NMS – and we gained practical experience in machine learning through the exercise of training and testing a custom detector. Finally, we demonstrated that we can detect cars!

Our new knowledge forms the foundation of the next chapter, in which we will utilize object detection and classification techniques on sequences of frames in videos. We will learn how to track objects and retain information about them – an important objective in many real-world applications.

8
Tracking Objects

In this chapter, we will explore a selection of techniques from the vast topic of object tracking, which is the process of locating a moving object in a movie or a video feed from a camera. Real-time object tracking is a critical task in many computer vision applications such as surveillance, perceptual user interfaces, augmented reality, object-based video compression, and driver assistance.

Tracking objects can be accomplished in several ways, with the most optimal technique being largely dependent on the task at hand. We will take the following route in our study of this topic:

- Detect moving objects based on differences between the current frame and a frame that represents the background. First, we will try a simple implementation of this approach. Then, we will use OpenCV's implementations of more advanced algorithms, namely, the **Mixture of Gaussians** (**MOG**) and **k-nearest neighbors** (**KNN**) background subtractors. We will also consider how to modify our scripts to use any other background subtractor that OpenCV supports, such as the **Godbehere-Matsukawa-Goldberg** (**GMG**) background subtractor.

- Track a moving object based on a color histogram of the object. This approach involves histogram back-projection, which is the process of computing the similarity between various image regions and a histogram. In other words, the histogram serves as a template of how we expect the object to look. We will use tracking algorithms called MeanShift and CamShift, which operate on the result of the histogram back-projection.

- Use a Kalman filter to find a trend in an object's motion and to predict where the object is going next.

- Review the manner in which OpenCV favors **object-oriented programming** (**OOP**) paradigms, and consider how this differs from **functional programming** (**FP**) paradigms.

- Implement a pedestrian tracker that combines KNN background subtraction, MeanShift, and Kalman filtering.

If you have been reading this book sequentially, then, by the end of this chapter, you will know a lot of ways to describe, detect, classify, and track objects in 2D. At that point, you should be ready to pursue 3D tracking in Chapter 9, *Camera Models and Augmented Reality*.

Technical requirements

This chapter uses Python, OpenCV, and NumPy. Please refer to Chapter 1, *Setting Up OpenCV*, for installation instructions.

The complete code and sample videos for this chapter can be found in this book's GitHub repository, https://github.com/PacktPublishing/Learning-OpenCV-4-Computer-Vision-with-Python-Third-Edition, in the chapter08 folder.

Detecting moving objects with background subtraction

To track anything in a video, first, we must identify the regions of a video frame that correspond to moving objects. Many motion detection techniques are based on the simple concept of **background subtraction**. For example, suppose that we have a stationary camera viewing a scene that is also mostly stationary. In addition to this, suppose that the camera's exposure and the lighting conditions in the scene are stable so that frames do not vary much in terms of brightness. Under these conditions, we can easily capture a reference image that represents the background or, in other words, the stationary components of the scene. Then, any time the camera captures a new frame, we can subtract the frame from the reference image, and take the absolute value of this difference in order to obtain a measurement of motion at each pixel location in the frame. If any region of the frame is very different from the reference image, we conclude that the given region is a moving object.

Background subtraction techniques, in general, have the following limitations:

- Any camera motion, change in exposure, or change in lighting conditions can cause a change in pixel values throughout the entire scene all at once; therefore, the entire background model (or reference image) becomes outdated.

- A piece of the background model can become outdated if an object enters the scene and then just stays there for a long period of time. For example, suppose our scene is a hallway. Someone enters the hallway, puts a poster on the wall, and leaves the poster there. For all practical purposes, the poster is now just another part of the stationary background; however, it was not part of our reference image, so our background model has become partly outdated.

These problems point to a need to dynamically update the background model based on a series of new frames. Advanced background subtraction techniques attempt to address this need in a variety of ways.

Another general limitation is that shadows and solid objects can affect a background subtractor in similar ways. For instance, we might get an inaccurate picture of a moving object's size and shape because we cannot differentiate the object from its shadow. However, advanced background subtraction techniques do attempt to distinguish between shadow regions and solid objects using various means.

Background subtractors generally have yet another limitation: they do not offer fine-grained control over the kind of motion that they detect. For example, if a scene shows a subway car that is continuously shaking as it travels on its track, this repetitive motion will affect the background subtractor. For practical purposes, we might consider the subway car's vibrations to be normal variations in a semi-stationary background. We might even know the frequency of these vibrations. However, a background subtractor does not embed any information about frequencies of motion, so it does not offer a convenient or precise way in which to filter out such predictable motions. To compensate for such shortcomings, we can apply preprocessing steps such as blurring the reference image and also blurring each new frame; in this way, certain frequencies are suppressed, albeit in a manner that is not very intuitive, efficient, or precise.

Analyzing the frequencies of motion is beyond the scope of this book. However, for an introduction to this topic in a computer vision context, see Joseph Howse's book, *OpenCV 4 for Secret Agents* (Packt Publishing, 2019), specifically *Chapter 7, Seeing a Heartbeat with a Motion-Amplifying Camera*.

Now that we have taken an overview of background subtraction and understood some of the obstacles that it faces, let's investigate how several implementations of it fare in action. We will start with a simple but not robust implementation that we can handcraft in a few lines of code, and then progress to more sophisticated alternatives that OpenCV provides for us.

Implementing a basic background subtractor

To implement a basic background subtractor, let's take the following approach:

1. Start capturing frames from a camera.
2. Discard nine frames so that the camera has time to properly adjust its autoexposure to suit the lighting conditions in the scene.
3. Take the 10th frame, convert it to grayscale, blur it, and use this blurred image as the reference image of the background.
4. For each subsequent frame, blur the frame, convert it to grayscale, and compute the absolute difference between this blurred frame and the reference image of the background. Perform thresholding, smoothing, and contour detection on the differenced image. Draw and show the bounding boxes of the major contours.

 The use of a Gaussian blur should make our background subtractor less susceptible to small vibrations, as well as digital noise. The morphological operations also offer these benefits.

To blur images, we will use the Gaussian blur algorithm, which we originally discussed in Chapter 3, *Processing Images with OpenCV*, specifically in the *HPFs and LPFs* section. To smoothen thresholded images, we will use morphological erosion and dilation, which we originally discussed in Chapter 4, *Depth Estimation and Segmentation*, specifically in the *Image segmentation with the Watershed algorithm* section. Contour detection and bounding boxes are also among the topics we introduced in Chapter 3, *Processing Images with OpenCV*, specifically in the *Contour detection* section.

Expanding the preceding list into smaller steps, we can consider our script's implementation in eight sequential blocks of code:

1. Let's begin by importing OpenCV and defining the size of our kernels for the blur, erode, and dilate operations:

```
import cv2

BLUR_RADIUS = 21
erode_kernel = cv2.getStructuringElement(cv2.MORPH_ELLIPSE, (5, 5))
dilate_kernel = cv2.getStructuringElement(
    cv2.MORPH_ELLIPSE, (9, 9))
```

2. Now, let's try to capture 10 frames from a camera:

```
cap = cv2.VideoCapture(0)

# Capture several frames to allow the camera's autoexposure to
adjust.
for i in range(10):
    success, frame = cap.read()
if not success:
    exit(1)
```

3. If we were unable to capture 10 frames, we exit. Otherwise, we proceed to convert the 10th frame to grayscale and blur it:

```
gray_background = cv2.cvtColor(frame, cv2.COLOR_BGR2GRAY)
gray_background = cv2.GaussianBlur(gray_background,
                                   (BLUR_RADIUS, BLUR_RADIUS), 0)
```

4. At this stage, we have our reference image of the background. Now, let's proceed to capture more frames, in which we may detect motion. Our processing of each frame begins with grayscale conversion and a Gaussian blur operation:

```
success, frame = cap.read()
while success:

    gray_frame = cv2.cvtColor(frame, cv2.COLOR_BGR2GRAY)
    gray_frame = cv2.GaussianBlur(gray_frame,
                                  (BLUR_RADIUS, BLUR_RADIUS), 0)
```

5. Now, we can compare the blurred, grayscale version of the current frame to the blurred, grayscale version of the background image. Specifically, we will use OpenCV's `cv2.absdiff` function to find the absolute value (or the magnitude) of the difference between these two images. Then, we will apply a threshold to obtain a pure black-and-white image, and morphological operations to smoothen the thresholded image. Here is the relevant code:

```
diff = cv2.absdiff(gray_background, gray_frame)
_, thresh = cv2.threshold(diff, 40, 255, cv2.THRESH_BINARY)
cv2.erode(thresh, erode_kernel, thresh, iterations=2)
cv2.dilate(thresh, dilate_kernel, thresh, iterations=2)
```

6. At this point, if our technique has worked well, our thresholded image should contain white blobs wherever there is a moving object. Now, we want to find the contours of the white blobs and draw bounding boxes around them. As a further means of filtering out small changes that are probably not real objects, we will apply a threshold based on the area of the contour. If the contour is too small, we conclude that it is not a real moving object. (Of course, the definition of *too small* may vary depending on your camera's resolution and your application; in some circumstances, you might not wish to apply this test at all.) Here is the code to detect contours and draw bounding boxes:

```
_, contours, hier = cv2.findContours(thresh, cv2.RETR_EXTERNAL,
                                      cv2.CHAIN_APPROX_SIMPLE)

for c in contours:
    if cv2.contourArea(c) > 4000:
        x, y, w, h = cv2.boundingRect(c)
        cv2.rectangle(frame, (x, y), (x+w, y+h), (255, 255, 0), 2)
```

7. Now, let's show the differenced image, the thresholded image, and the detection result with the bounding rectangles:

```
cv2.imshow('diff', diff)
cv2.imshow('thresh', thresh)
cv2.imshow('detection', frame)
```

8. We will continue reading frames until the user presses the *Esc* key to quit:

```
k = cv2.waitKey(1)
if k == 27: # Escape
    break

success, frame = cap.read()
```

There you have it: a basic motion detector that draws rectangles around moving objects. The final result is something like this:

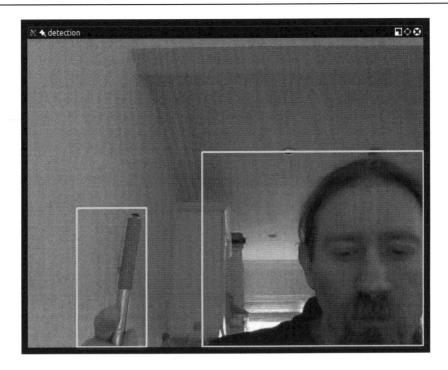

To obtain good results with this script, make sure that you (and other moving objects) do not enter the camera's field of view until after the background image has been initialized.

For such a simple technique, this result is quite promising. However, our script makes no effort to update the background image dynamically, so it will quickly become outdated if the camera moves or the lighting changes. Thus, we should move on to more flexible and intelligent background subtractors. Fortunately, OpenCV provides several ready-made background subtractors for us to use. We will start with the one that implements the MOG algorithm.

Using a MOG background subtractor

OpenCV provides a class called `cv2.BackgroundSubtractor`, which has various subclasses that implement various background subtraction algorithms.

You may recall that we previously used OpenCV's implementation of the GrabCut algorithm to perform foreground/background segmentation in `Chapter 4`, *Depth Estimation and Segmentation*, specifically in the *Foreground detection with the GrabCut algorithm* section. Like `cv2.grabCut`, the various subclass implementations of `cv2.BackgroundSubtractor` can produce a mask that assigns different values to different segments of the image. Specifically, a background subtractor can mark foreground segments as white (that is, an 8-bit grayscale value of 255), background segments as black (0), and (in some implementations) shadow segments as gray (127). Moreover, unlike GrabCut, the background subtractors update the foreground/background model over time, typically by applying machine learning to a series of frames. Many of the background subtractors are named after the statistical clustering technique on which they base their approach to machine learning. So, we will begin by looking at a background subtractor based on the MOG clustering technique.

OpenCV has two implementations of a MOG background subtractor. Perhaps not surprisingly, they are named `cv2.BackgroundSubtractorMOG` and `cv2.BackgroundSubtractorMOG2`. The latter is a more recent and improved implementation, which adds support for shadow detection, so we will use it.

As a starting point, let's take our basic background subtraction script from the previous section. We will make the following modifications to it:

1. Replace our basic background subtraction model with a MOG background subtractor.
2. As input, use a video file instead of a camera.
3. Remove the use of Gaussian blur.
4. Adjust the parameters used in the thresholding, morphology, and contour analysis steps.

These modifications affect a few lines of code, which are scattered throughout the script. Near the top of the script, let's initialize the MOG background subtractor and modify the size of the morphology kernels, as shown in bold in the following code block:

```
import cv2

bg_subtractor = cv2.createBackgroundSubtractorMOG2(detectShadows=True)

erode_kernel = cv2.getStructuringElement(cv2.MORPH_ELLIPSE, (3, 3))
dilate_kernel = cv2.getStructuringElement(cv2.MORPH_ELLIPSE, (7, 7))
```

Note that OpenCV provides a function, `cv2.createBackgroundSubtractorMOG2`, to create an instance of `cv2.BackgroundSubtractorMOG2`. The function accepts a parameter, `detectShadows`, which we set to `True` so that the shadow regions will be marked as such and not marked as part of the foreground.

The remaining changes, including the use of the MOG background subtractor to obtain a foreground/shadow/background mask, are marked in bold in the following code block:

```
cap = cv2.VideoCapture('hallway.mpg')
success, frame = cap.read()
while success:

    fg_mask = bg_subtractor.apply(frame)

    _, thresh = cv2.threshold(fg_mask, 244, 255, cv2.THRESH_BINARY)
    cv2.erode(thresh, erode_kernel, thresh, iterations=2)
    cv2.dilate(thresh, dilate_kernel, thresh, iterations=2)

    contours, hier = cv2.findContours(thresh, cv2.RETR_EXTERNAL,
                                      cv2.CHAIN_APPROX_SIMPLE)

    for c in contours:
        if cv2.contourArea(c) > 1000:
            x, y, w, h = cv2.boundingRect(c)
            cv2.rectangle(frame, (x, y), (x+w, y+h), (255, 255, 0), 2)

    cv2.imshow('mog', fg_mask)
    cv2.imshow('thresh', thresh)
    cv2.imshow('detection', frame)

    k = cv2.waitKey(30)
    if k == 27:  # Escape
        break

    success, frame = cap.read()
```

When we pass a frame to the background subtractor's `apply` method, the subtractor updates its internal model of the background and then returns a mask. As we previously discussed, the mask is white (255) for foreground segments, gray (127) for shadow segments, and black (0) for background segments. For our purposes, we treat shadows as the background, so we apply a nearly white threshold (244) to the mask.

The following set of screenshots shows a mask from the MOG detector (the top-left photograph), a thresholded and morphed version of this mask (the top-right photograph), and the detection result (the bottom photograph):

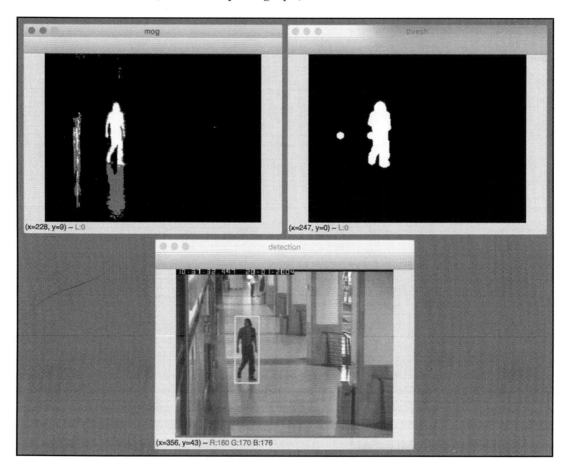

For comparison, if we disabled shadow detection by setting `detectShadows=False`, we would get results such as the following set of screenshots:

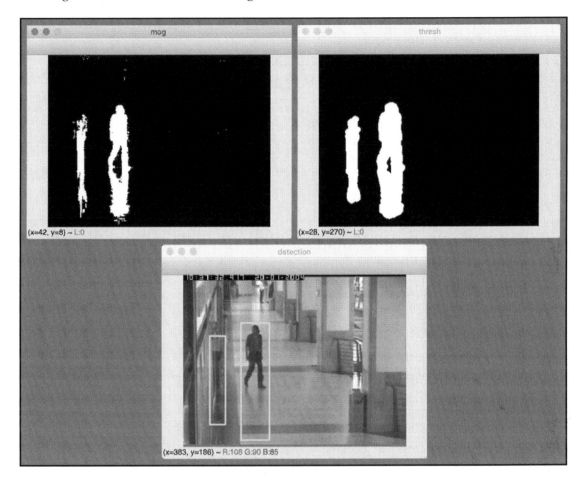

This scene contains not only shadows but also reflections, due to the polished floor and wall. When shadow detection is enabled, we are able to use a threshold to remove the shadows and reflections from our mask, leaving us with an accurate detection rectangle around the man in the hall. However, when shadow detection is disabled, we have two detections, which are both, arguably, inaccurate. One detection covers the man, his shadow, and his reflection on the floor. The second detection covers the man's reflection on the wall. These are, *arguably*, inaccurate detections because the man's shadow and reflections are not really moving objects, even though they are visual artifacts of a moving object.

So far, we have seen that a background subtraction script can be very concise and that a few small changes can drastically change the algorithm and the results, for better or for worse. Continuing in the same vein, let's see how easily we can adapt our code to use another of OpenCV's advanced background subtractors to find another kind of moving object.

Using a KNN background subtractor

By modifying just five lines of code in our MOG background subtraction script, we can use a different background subtraction algorithm, different morphology parameters, and a different video as input. Thanks to the high-level interface that OpenCV provides, even such simple changes enable us to successfully handle a wide variety of background subtraction tasks.

Just by replacing cv2.createBackgroundSubtractorMOG2 with cv2.createBackgroundSubtractorKNN, we can we use a background subtractor based on KNN clustering instead of MOG clustering:

```
bg_subtractor = cv2.createBackgroundSubtractorKNN(detectShadows=True)
```

Note that despite the change in algorithm, the detectShadows parameter is still supported. Additionally, the apply method is still supported, so we do not need to change anything related to the use of the background subtractor later in the script.

 Remember that cv2.createBackgroundSubtractorMOG2 returns a new instance of the cv2.BackgroundSubtractorMOG2 class. Similarly, cv2.createBackgroundSubtractorKNN returns a new instance of the cv2.BackgroundSubtractorKNN class. Both of these classes are subclasses of cv2.BackgroundSubtractor, which defines common methods such as apply.

With the following changes, we can use morphology kernels that are slightly better adapted to a horizontally elongated object (in this case, a car), and we can use a video of traffic as input:

```
erode_kernel = cv2.getStructuringElement(cv2.MORPH_ELLIPSE, (7, 5))
dilate_kernel = cv2.getStructuringElement(cv2.MORPH_ELLIPSE, (17, 11))

cap = cv2.VideoCapture('traffic.flv')
```

To reflect the change in algorithm, let's change the title of the mask's window from `'mog'` to `'knn'`:

```
cv2.imshow('knn', fg_mask)
```

The following set of screenshots shows the result of motion detection:

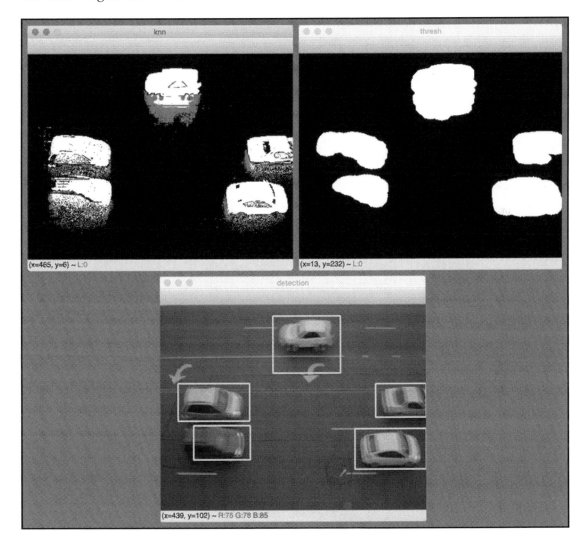

The KNN background subtractor, along with its ability to differentiate between objects and shadows, has worked quite well here. All cars have been individually detected; even though some cars are close to each other, they have not been merged into one detection. For three out of the five cars, the detection rectangles are accurate. For the dark car in the bottom-left part of the video frame, the background subtractor has failed to fully differentiate the rear of the car from the asphalt. For the white car in the top-center part of the frame, the background subtractor has failed to fully differentiate the car and its shadow from the white markings on the road. Nonetheless, overall, this is a useful detection result that could enable us to count the number of cars traveling in each lane.

As we have seen, a few simple variations on a script can produce very different background subtraction results. Let's consider how we could further explore this observation.

Using GMG and other background subtractors

You are free to experiment with your own modifications to our background subtraction script. If you have obtained OpenCV with the optional `opencv_contrib` modules, as described in Chapter 1, *Setting Up OpenCV*, then several more background subtractors are available to you in the `cv2.bgsegm` module. They can be created using the following functions:

- `cv2.bgsegm.createBackgroundSubtractorCNT`
- `cv2.bgsegm.createBackgroundSubtractorGMG`
- `cv2.bgsegm.createBackgroundSubtractorGSOC`
- `cv2.bgsegm.createBackgroundSubtractorLSBP`
- `cv2.bgsegm.createBackgroundSubtractorMOG`
- `cv2.bgsegm.createSyntheticSequenceGenerator`

These functions do not support the `detectShadows` parameter, and they create background subtractors that do not support shadow detection. However, all the background subtractors support the `apply` method.

As an example of how to modify our background subtraction sample to use one of the `cv2.bgsegm` subtractors in the preceding list, let's use a GMG background subtractor. The relevant modifications are highlighted in bold in the following block of code:

```
import cv2

bg_subtractor = cv2.bgsegm.createBackgroundSubtractorGMG()

erode_kernel = cv2.getStructuringElement(cv2.MORPH_ELLIPSE, (13, 9))
```

```
dilate_kernel = cv2.getStructuringElement(cv2.MORPH_ELLIPSE, (17, 11))

cap = cv2.VideoCapture('traffic.flv')
success, frame = cap.read()
while success:

    fg_mask = bg_subtractor.apply(frame)

    _, thresh = cv2.threshold(fg_mask, 244, 255, cv2.THRESH_BINARY)
    cv2.erode(thresh, erode_kernel, thresh, iterations=2)
    cv2.dilate(thresh, dilate_kernel, thresh, iterations=2)

    contours, hier = cv2.findContours(thresh, cv2.RETR_EXTERNAL,
                                      cv2.CHAIN_APPROX_SIMPLE)

    for c in contours:
        if cv2.contourArea(c) > 1000:
            x, y, w, h = cv2.boundingRect(c)
            cv2.rectangle(frame, (x, y), (x+w, y+h), (255, 255, 0), 2)

    cv2.imshow('gmg', fg_mask)
    cv2.imshow('thresh', thresh)
    cv2.imshow('detection', frame)

    k = cv2.waitKey(30)
    if k == 27: # Escape
        break

    success, frame = cap.read()
```

Note the modifications are similar to the ones we saw in the previous section, *Using a KNN background subtractor*. We simply use a different function to create the GMG subtractor, we adjust the morphology kernels' sizes to values that work better for this algorithm, and we change one of the window titles to 'gmg'.

The GMG algorithm is named after its authors, Andrew B. Godbehere, Akihiro Matsukawa, and Ken Goldberg. They describe it in their paper, *Visual Tracking of Human Visitors under Variable-Lighting Conditions for a Responsive Audio Art Installation* (ACC, 2012), which is available at https://ieeexplore.ieee.org/document/6315174. The GMG background subtractor takes a few frames to initialize itself before it starts producing a mask with white (object) regions.

Compared to the KNN background subtractor, the GMG background subtractor produces worse results with our sample video of traffic. This is partly because OpenCV's implementation of GMG does not differentiate between shadows and solid objects, so the detection rectangles are elongated in the direction of the cars' shadows or reflections. Here is a sample of the output:

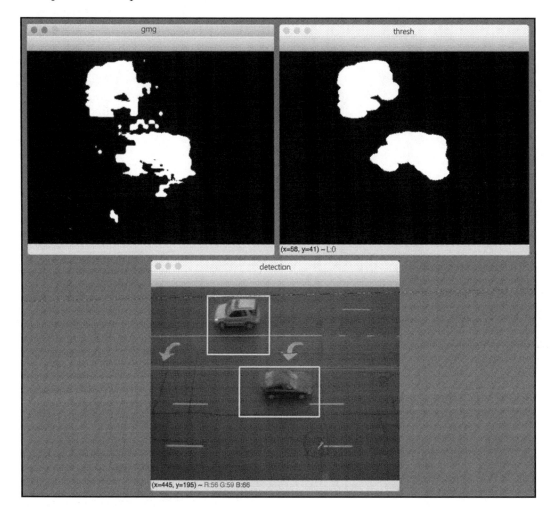

When you are finished experimenting with background subtractors, let's proceed to examine other tracking techniques that rely on a template of an object we are trying to track, rather than a template of the background.

Tracking colorful objects using MeanShift and CamShift

We have seen that background subtraction can be an effective technique for detecting moving objects; however, we know that it has some inherent limitations. Notably, it assumes that the current background can be predicted based on past frames. This assumption is fragile. For example, if the camera moves, the entire background model could suddenly become outdated. Thus, in a robust tracking system, it is important to build some kind of model of foreground objects rather than just the background.

We have already seen various ways of detecting objects in Chapter 5, *Detecting and Recognizing Faces*, Chapter 6, *Retrieving Images and Searching Using Image Descriptors*, and Chapter 7, *Building Custom Object Detectors*. For object *detection*, we favored algorithms that could deal with a lot of variation within a class of objects, so that our car detector was not too particular about what shape or color of car it would detect. For object *tracking*, our needs are a bit different. If we were tracking cars, we would want a different model for each car in the scene so that a red car and a blue car would not get mixed up. We would want to track the motion of each car separately.

Once we have detected a moving object (by background subtraction or other means), we would like to describe the object in a way that distinguishes it from other moving objects. In this way, we can continue to identify and track the object even if it crosses paths with another moving object. A **color histogram** may serve as a sufficiently unique description. Essentially, an object's color histogram is an estimate of the probability distribution of pixel colors in the object. For example, the histogram could indicate that each pixel in the object is 10% likely to be blue. The histogram is based on the actual colors observed in the object's region of a reference image. For example, the reference image could be the video frame in which we first detected the moving object.

Compared to other ways of describing an object, a color histogram has some properties that are particularly appealing in the context of motion tracking. The histogram serves as a lookup table that directly maps pixel values to probabilities, so it enables us to use every pixel as a feature, at a low computational cost. In this way, we can afford to perform tracking with very fine spatial resolution in real time. To find the most likely location of an object that we are tracking, we just have to find the region of interest where the pixel values map to the maximum probability, according to the histogram.

Naturally, this approach is leveraged by an algorithm with a catchy name: MeanShift. For each frame in a video, the MeanShift algorithm performs tracking iteratively by computing a centroid based on probability values in the current tracking rectangle, shifting the rectangle's center to this centroid, recomputing the centroid based on values in the new rectangle, shifting the rectangle again, and so on. This process continues until **convergence** is achieved (meaning that the centroid ceases to move or nearly ceases to move) or until a maximum number of iterations is reached. Essentially, MeanShift is a clustering algorithm, with applications that extend beyond computer vision. The algorithm was first described in a paper entitled *The estimation of the gradient of a density function, with applications in pattern recognition* (IEEE, 1975), by K. Fukunaga and L. Hostetler. The paper is available to IEEE subscribers at `https://ieeexplore.ieee.org/document/1055330`.

Before delving into a sample script, let's consider the type of tracking result we want to achieve with MeanShift, and let's learn more about OpenCV's functionality pertaining to color histograms.

Planning our MeanShift sample

For our first demonstration of MeanShift, we are not concerned with the approach to the initial detection of moving objects. We will use a naive approach that simply chooses the central part of the first video frame as our initial region of interest. (The user must ensure that an object of interest is initially located in the center of the video.) We will calculate a histogram of this initial region of interest. Then, in subsequent frames, we will use this histogram and the MeanShift algorithm to track the object.

Visually, the MeanShift demo will resemble many of the object detection samples that we have previously written. For every frame, we will draw a blue outline around the tracking rectangle, as shown here:

Here, the toy phone has a lilac color that is not present in any other object in the scene. Thus, the phone has a distinctive histogram, making it easy to track. Next, let's consider how such a histogram is calculated and then used as a lookup table of probabilities.

Calculating and back-projecting color histograms

To calculate a color histogram, OpenCV provides a function called `cv2.calcHist`. To apply a histogram as a lookup table, OpenCV provides another function called `cv2.calcBackProject`. The latter operation is known as **histogram back-projection**, and it transforms a given image into a probability map based on a given histogram. Let's first visualize the output of these two functions, and then examine their parameters.

A histogram can use any color model, such as **blue-green-red (BGR)**, **hue-saturation-value (HSV)**, or grayscale. (For an introduction to color models, refer to Chapter 3, *Processing Images with OpenCV*, specifically the *Converting images between different color models* section.) For our samples, we will use the histograms of only the hue (H) channel of the HSV color model. The following diagram is a visualization of a hue histogram:

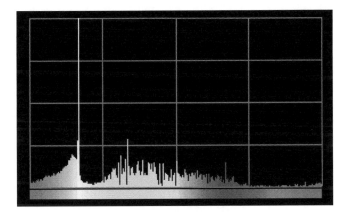

 This histogram visualization is a sample of the output from an image-viewing application called DPEx (http://www.rysys.co.jp/en/).

On the *x* axis of this plot, we have the hue, and on the *y* axis, we have the hue's estimated probability or, in other words, the proportion of pixels in the image that have the given hue. If you are reading the e-book edition of this book, you will see that the plot is color-coded according to hue. From left to right, the plot progresses through the hues of the color wheel: red, yellow, green, cyan, blue, magenta, and, finally, back to red. This particular histogram seems to represent an object with a lot of yellow in it.

OpenCV represents H values with a range from 0 to 179. Some other systems use a range from 0 to 359 (like the degrees of a circle) or from 0 to 255.

 Some caution is required in interpreting hue histograms because pure black and pure white pixels do not have a meaningful hue; however, their hue is usually represented as 0 (red).

When we use cv2.calcHist to generate a hue histogram, it returns a 1D array that is conceptually similar to the preceding plot. Alternatively, depending on the parameters we provide, we could use cv2.calcHist to generate a histogram of a different channel or of two channels at once. In the latter case, cv2.calcHist would return a 2D array.

Once we have a histogram, we can back-project the histogram onto any image. cv2.calcBackProject produces a back-projection in the format of an 8-bit grayscale image, with pixel values that potentially range from 0 (indicating a low probability) to 255 (indicating a high probability), depending on how we scale the values. For example, consider the following pair of photographs, showing a back-projection and then a visualization of the MeanShift tracking result:

Here, we are tracking a small object whose main colors are yellow, red, and brown. The back-projection is brightest in regions that are actually part of the object. The back-projection is also somewhat bright in other regions of similar color, such as Joseph Howse's brown beard, the yellow rims of his glasses, and the red border of one of the posters in the background.

Now that we have visualized the outputs of `cv2.calcHist` and `cv2.calcBackProject`, let's examine the parameters that these functions accept.

Understanding the parameters of cv2.calcHist

The `cv2.calcHist` function has the following signature:

```
calcHist(images, channels, mask, histSize, ranges[, hist[,
        accumulate]]) -> hist
```

The following table contains descriptions of the parameters (adapted from the official OpenCV documentation):

Parameter	Description
images	This parameter is a list of one or more source images. They should all have the same bit depth (8-bit, 16-bit, or 32-bit) and the same size.
channels	This parameter is a list of the indices of the channels used to compute the histogram. For example, channels=[0] means that only the first channel (that is, the channel with index 0) is used to compute the histogram.
mask	This parameter is a mask. If it is None, no masking is performed; every region of the images is used in the histogram calculation. If it is not None, then it must be an 8-bit array of the same size as each image in images. The mask's nonzero elements mark the regions of the images that should be used in the histogram calculation.
histSize	This parameter is a list of the number of histogram bins to use for each channel. The length of the histSize list must be the same as the length of the channels list. For example, if channels=[0] and histSize=[180], the histogram has 180 bins for the first channel (and any other channels are unused).

ranges	This parameter is a list that specifies the ranges (inclusive lower bound and exclusive upper bound) of values to use for each channel. The length of the `ranges` list must be twice the length of the `channels` list. For example, if `channels=[0]`, `histSize=[180]`, and `ranges=[0, 180]`, the histogram has 180 bins for the first channel, and these bins are based on values in the range from 0 to 179; in other words, there is one input value per bin.
hist	This optional parameter is the output histogram. If it is `None` (the default), a new array will be returned as the output histogram.
accumulate	This optional parameter is the `accumulate` flag. By default, it is `False`. If it is `True`, then the original content of `hist` is not cleared; instead, the new histogram is added to the original content of `hist`. This feature enables you to compute a single histogram from several lists of images, or to update the histogram over time.

In our samples, we will calculate the hue histogram of a region of interest like so:

```
roi_hist = cv2.calcHist([hsv_roi], [0], mask, [180], [0, 180])
```

Next, let's consider the parameters of `cv2.calcBackProject`.

Understanding the parameters of cv2.calcBackProject

The `cv2.calcBackProject` function has the following signature:

```
calcBackProject(images, channels, hist, ranges,
                scale[, dst]) -> dst
```

The following table contains descriptions of the parameters (adapted from the official OpenCV documentation):

Parameter	Description
images	This parameter is a list of one or more source images. They all should have the same bit depth (8-bit, 16-bit, or 32-bit) and the same size.
channels	This parameter must be the same as the `channels` parameter used in `calcHist`.
hist	This parameter is the histogram.
ranges	This parameter must be the same as the `ranges` parameter used in `calcHist`.
scale	This parameter is a scale factor. The back-projection is multiplied by this scale factor.

dst	This optional parameter is the output back-projection. If it is `None` (the default), a new array will be returned as the back-projection.

In our samples, we will use code similar to the following line to back-project a hue histogram on to an HSV image:

```
back_proj = cv2.calcBackProject([hsv], [0], roi_hist, [0, 180], 1)
```

Having examined the `cv2.calcHist` and `cv2.calcBackProject` functions in detail, let's now put them into action in a script that performs tracking with MeanShift.

Implementing the MeanShift example

Let's go sequentially through the implementation of our MeanShift example:

1. Like our basic background subtraction example, our MeanShift example begins by capturing (and discarding) several frames from a camera so that the autoexposure can adjust:

```python
import cv2

cap = cv2.VideoCapture(0)

# Capture several frames to allow the camera's autoexposure to
# adjust.
for i in range(10):
    success, frame = cap.read()
if not success:
    exit(1)
```

2. By the 10th frame, we assume that the exposure is good; therefore, we can extract an accurate histogram of a region of interest. The following code defines the bounds of the **region of interest (ROI)**:

```python
# Define an initial tracking window in the center of the frame.
frame_h, frame_w = frame.shape[:2]
w = frame_w//8
h = frame_h//8
x = frame_w//2 - w//2
y = frame_h//2 - h//2
track_window = (x, y, w, h)
```

3. Then, the following code selects the ROI's pixels and converts them to HSV color space:

```
roi = frame[y:y+h, x:x+w]
hsv_roi = cv2.cvtColor(roi, cv2.COLOR_BGR2HSV)
```

4. Next, we calculate the hue histogram of the ROI:

```
mask = None
roi_hist = cv2.calcHist([hsv_roi], [0], mask, [180], [0, 180])
```

5. After the histogram is calculated, we normalize the values to a range from 0 to 255:

```
cv2.normalize(roi_hist, roi_hist, 0, 255, cv2.NORM_MINMAX)
```

6. Remember that MeanShift performs a number of iterations before reaching convergence; however, this convergence is not assured. Thus, OpenCV allows us to specify the so-called termination criteria. Let's define the termination criteria as follows:

```
# Define the termination criteria:
# 10 iterations or convergence within 1-pixel radius.
term_crit = \
    (cv2.TERM_CRITERIA_COUNT | cv2.TERM_CRITERIA_FPS, 10, 1)
```

Based on these criteria, MeanShift will stop calculating the centroid shift after 10 iterations (the **count** criterion) or when the shift is no longer larger than 1 pixel (the **epsilon** criterion). The combination of flags (cv2.TERM_CRITERIA_COUNT | cv2.TERM_CRITERIA_EPS) indicates that we are using both of these criteria.

7. Now that we have calculated a histogram and defined MeanShift's termination criteria, let's start our usual loop in which we capture and process frames from the camera. With each frame, the first thing we do is convert it to the HSV color space:

```
success, frame = cap.read()
while success:

    hsv = cv2.cvtColor(frame, cv2.COLOR_BGR2HSV)
```

8. Now that we have an HSV image, we can perform the long-awaited operation of histogram back-projection:

```
back_proj = cv2.calcBackProject(
    [hsv], [0], roi_hist, [0, 180], 1)
```

9. The back-projection, the tracking window, and the termination criteria can be passed to `cv2.meanShift`, which is OpenCV's implementation of the MeanShift algorithm. Here is the function call:

```
# Perform tracking with MeanShift.
num_iters, track_window = cv2.meanShift(
    back_proj, track_window, term_crit)
```

Note that MeanShift returns the number of iterations that it ran, as well as the new tracking window that it found. Optionally, we could compare the number of iterations to our termination criteria in order to determine whether the result converged. (If the actual number of iterations is less than the maximum, the result must have converged.)

10. Finally, we draw and show the updated tracking rectangle:

```
# Draw the tracking window.
x, y, w, h = track_window
cv2.rectangle(
    frame, (x, y), (x+w, y+h), (255, 0, 0), 2)

cv2.imshow('back-projection', back_proj)
cv2.imshow('meanshift', frame)
```

That is the whole example. If you run the program, it should produce an output that is similar to the screenshots we saw earlier, in the *Calculating and back-projecting color histograms* section.

By now, you should have a good idea of how color histograms, back-projections, and MeanShift work. However, the preceding program (and MeanShift in general) has a limitation: the size of the window does not change with the size of the object in the frames being tracked.

Gary Bradski – one of the founders of the OpenCV project – published a paper in 1988 to improve the accuracy of MeanShift. He described a new algorithm called **Continuously Adaptive MeanShift (CAMShift** or **CamShift)**, which is very similar to MeanShift but also adapts the size of the tracking window when MeanShift reaches convergence. Let's take a look at an example of CamShift next.

Using CamShift

Although CamShift is a more complex algorithm than MeanShift, OpenCV provides a very similar interface for the two algorithms. The main difference is that a call to `cv2.CamShift` returns a rectangle with a particular rotation that follows the rotation of the object being tracked. With just a few modifications to the preceding MeanShift example, we can instead use CamShift and draw a rotated tracking rectangle. All of the necessary changes are highlighted in bold in the following excerpt:

```python
import cv2
import numpy as np

# ... Initialize the tracking window and histogram as previously ...

success, frame = cap.read()
while success:

    # Perform back-projection of the HSV histogram onto the frame.
    hsv = cv2.cvtColor(frame, cv2.COLOR_BGR2HSV)
    back_proj = cv2.calcBackProject([hsv], [0], roi_hist, [0, 180], 1)

    # Perform tracking with CamShift.
    rotated_rect, track_window = cv2.CamShift(
        back_proj, track_window, term_crit)

    # Draw the tracking window.
    box_points = cv2.boxPoints(rotated_rect)
    box_points = np.int0(box_points)
    cv2.polylines(frame, [box_points], True, (255, 0, 0), 2)

    cv2.imshow('back-projection', back_proj)
    cv2.imshow('camshift', frame)

    k = cv2.waitKey(1)
    if k == 27: # Escape
        break

    success, frame = cap.read()
```

The arguments to `cv2.CamShift` are unchanged; they have the same meanings and the same values as the arguments to `cv2.meanShift` in our previous example.

We use the `cv2.boxPoints` function to find the vertices of the rotated tracking rectangle. Then, we use the `cv2.polylines` function to draw the lines connecting these vertices. The following screenshot shows the result:

By now, you should be familiar with two families of tracking techniques. The first family uses background subtraction. The second uses histogram back-projection, combined with either MeanShift or CamShift. Now, let's meet the Kalman filter, which exemplifies a third family; it finds trends or, in other words, predicts future motion based on past motion.

Finding trends in motion using the Kalman filter

The Kalman filter is an algorithm developed mainly (but not exclusively) by Rudolf Kalman in the late 1950s. It has found practical applications in many fields, particularly navigation systems for all sorts of vehicles from nuclear submarines to aircraft.

The Kalman filter operates recursively on a stream of noisy input data to produce a statistically optimal estimate of the underlying system state. In the context of computer vision, the Kalman filter can smoothen the estimate of a tracked object's position.

Let's consider a simple example. Think of a small red ball on a table and imagine you have a camera pointing at the scene. You identify the ball as the subject to be tracked, and flick it with your fingers. The ball will start rolling on the table in accordance with the laws of motion.

If the ball is rolling at a speed of 1 meter per second in a particular direction, it is easy to estimate where the ball will be in 1 second's time: it will be 1 meter away. The Kalman filter applies laws such as this to predict an object's position in the current video frame based on tracking results gathered in previous frames. The Kalman filter itself is not gathering these tracking results, but it is updating its model of the object's motion based on the tracking results derived from another algorithm, such as MeanShift. Naturally, the Kalman filter cannot foresee new forces acting on the ball – such as a collision with a pencil lying on the table – but it can update its model of the motion after the fact, based on new tracking results. Through the use of the Kalman filter, we can obtain estimates that are more stable and more consistent with the laws of motion than the tracking results alone.

Understanding the predict and update phases

From the preceding description, we gather that the Kalman filter's algorithm has two phases:

- **Predict**: In the first phase, the Kalman filter uses the covariance calculated up to the current point in time to estimate the object's new position.
- **Update**: In the second phase, the Kalman filter records the object's position and adjusts the covariance for the next cycle of calculations.

The update phase is – in OpenCV's terms – a **correction**. Thus, OpenCV provides a `cv2.KalmanFilter` class with the following methods:

```
predict([, control]) -> retval
correct(measurement) -> retval
```

For the purpose of smoothly tracking objects, we will call the `predict` method to estimate the position of an object, and then use the `correct` method to instruct the Kalman filter to adjust its calculations based on a new tracking result from another algorithm such as MeanShift. However, before we combine the Kalman filter with a computer vision algorithm, let's examine how it performs with position data from a simple motion sensor.

Tracking a mouse cursor

Motion sensors have been commonplace in user interfaces for a long time. A computer's mouse senses its own motion relative to a surface such as a table. The mouse is a real, physical object, so it is reasonable to apply the laws of motion in order to predict changes in mouse coordinates. We are going to do exactly this as a demo of the Kalman filter.

Our demo will implement the following sequence of operations:

1. Start by initializing a black image and a Kalman filter. Show the black image in a window.
2. Every time the windowed application processes input events, use the Kalman filter to predict the mouse's position. Then, correct the Kalman filter's model based on the actual mouse coordinates. On top of the black image, draw a red line from the old predicted position to the new predicted position, and then draw a green line from the old actual position to the new actual position. Show the drawing in the window.
3. When the user hits the *Esc* key, exit and save the drawing to a file.

To begin the script, the following code initializes an 800 x 800 black image:

```
import cv2
import numpy as np

# Create a black image.
img = np.zeros((800, 800, 3), np.uint8)
```

Now, let's initialize the Kalman filter:

```
# Initialize the Kalman filter.
kalman = cv2.KalmanFilter(4, 2)
kalman.measurementMatrix = np.array(
    [[1, 0, 0, 0],
     [0, 1, 0, 0]], np.float32)
kalman.transitionMatrix = np.array(
    [[1, 0, 1, 0],
     [0, 1, 0, 1],
     [0, 0, 1, 0],
     [0, 0, 0, 1]], np.float32)
kalman.processNoiseCov = np.array(
    [[1, 0, 0, 0],
     [0, 1, 0, 0],
     [0, 0, 1, 0],
     [0, 0, 0, 1]], np.float32) * 0.03
```

Based on the preceding initialization, our Kalman filter will track a 2D object's position and velocity. We will take a deeper look at the process of initializing a Kalman filter in `Chapter 9`, *Camera Models and Augmented Reality*, where we will track a 3D object's position, velocity, acceleration, rotation, angular velocity, and angular acceleration. For now, let's just take note of the two parameters in `cv2.KalmanFilter(4, 2)`. The first parameter is the number of variables tracked (or predicted) by the Kalman filter, in this case, 4: the *x* position, the *y* position, the *x* velocity, and the *y* velocity. The second parameter is the number of variables provided to the Kalman filter as measurements, in this case, 2: the *x* position and the *y* position. We also initialize several matrices that describe the relationships among all these variables.

Having initialized the image and the Kalman filter, we also have to declare variables to hold the actual (measured) and predicted mouse coordinates. Initially, we have no coordinates, so we will assign `None` to these variables:

```
last_measurement = None
last_prediction = None
```

Then, we declare a callback function that handles mouse movement. This function is going to update the state of the Kalman filter, and draw a visualization of both the unfiltered mouse movement and the Kalman-filtered mouse movement. The first time we receive mouse coordinates, we initialize the Kalman filter's state so that its initial prediction is the same as the actual initial mouse coordinates. (If we did not do this, the Kalman filter would assume that the initial mouse position was `(0, 0)`.) Subsequently, whenever we receive new mouse coordinates, we correct the Kalman filter with the current measurement, calculate the Kalman prediction, and, finally, draw two lines: a green line from the last measurement to the current measurement and a red line from the last prediction to the current prediction. Here is the callback function's implementation:

```
def on_mouse_moved(event, x, y, flags, param):
    global img, kalman, last_measurement, last_prediction

    measurement = np.array([[x], [y]], np.float32)
    if last_measurement is None:
        # This is the first measurement.
        # Update the Kalman filter's state to match the measurement.
        kalman.statePre = np.array(
            [[x], [y], [0], [0]], np.float32)
        kalman.statePost = np.array(
            [[x], [y], [0], [0]], np.float32)
        prediction = measurement
    else:
        kalman.correct(measurement)
        prediction = kalman.predict()  # Gets a reference, not a copy
```

```
        # Trace the path of the measurement in green.
        cv2.line(img, (last_measurement[0], last_measurement[1]),
                (measurement[0], measurement[1]), (0, 255, 0))

        # Trace the path of the prediction in red.
        cv2.line(img, (last_prediction[0], last_prediction[1]),
                (prediction[0], prediction[1]), (0, 0, 255))

    last_prediction = prediction.copy()
    last_measurement = measurement
```

The next step is to initialize the window and pass our callback function to
the cv2.setMouseCallback function:

```
cv2.namedWindow('kalman_tracker')
cv2.setMouseCallback('kalman_tracker', on_mouse_moved)
```

Since most of the program's logic is in the mouse callback, the implementation of the main
loop is simple. We just continually show the updated image until the user hits the *Esc* key:

```
while True:
    cv2.imshow('kalman_tracker', img)
    k = cv2.waitKey(1)
    if k == 27:  # Escape
        cv2.imwrite('kalman.png', img)
        break
```

Run the program and move your mouse around. If you make a sudden turn at high speed,
you will notice that the prediction line (in red) will trace a wider curve than the
measurement line (in green). This is because the prediction is following the momentum of
the mouse's movement up to that time. Here is a sample result:

Perhaps the preceding diagram will give us inspiration for our next sample application, in which we track pedestrians.

Tracking pedestrians

Up to this point, we have familiarized ourselves with the concepts of motion detection, object detection, and object tracking. You are probably anxious to put this newfound knowledge to good use in a real-life scenario. Let's do just that by tracking pedestrians in a video from a surveillance camera.

 You can find a surveillance video inside the OpenCV repository at `samples/data/vtest.avi`. A copy of this video is located inside this book's GitHub repository at `chapter08/pedestrians.avi`.

Let's lay out a plan and then implement the application!

Planning the flow of the application

The application will adhere to the following logic:

1. Capture frames from a video file.
2. Use the first 20 frames to populate the history of a background subtractor.
3. Based on background subtraction, use the 21st frame to identify moving foreground objects. We will treat these as pedestrians. For each pedestrian, assign an ID and an initial tracking window, and then calculate a histogram.
4. For each subsequent frame, track each pedestrian using a Kalman filter and MeanShift.

If this were a real-world application, you would probably store a record of each pedestrian's route through the scene so that a user could analyze it later. However, this type of record-keeping is beyond the remit of this example.

Additionally, in a real-world application, you would make sure to identify new pedestrians entering the scene; however, for now, we will focus on tracking only those objects that are in the scene near the start of the video.

You will find the code for this application inside the book's GitHub repository at `chapter08/track_pedestrians.py`. Before examining the implementation, let's briefly digress to consider programming paradigms and how they relate to our use of OpenCV.

Comparing the object-oriented and functional paradigms

Although most programmers are either familiar (or work on a constant basis) with OOP, another paradigm called FP has, for many years, been gaining support among programmers who favor a purer mathematical foundation.

 The works of Samuel Howse demonstrate a specification of a programming language with a pure mathematical foundation. You can find his doctoral thesis, *NummSquared 2006a0 Explained,* at `https://nummist.com/poohbist/NummSquared2006a0Explained.pdf`, and his paper, *NummSquared: a New Foundation for Formal Methods,* at `https://nummist.com/poohbist/NummSquaredFormalMethods.pdf`.

FP treats programs as the evaluation of mathematical functions, allows functions to return functions, and permits functions as arguments in a function. The strength of FP resides not only in what it can do, but also in what it can avoid, or aims at avoiding: for example, side effects and changing states. If the topic of FP has sparked an interest, make sure that you take a look at languages such as Haskell, Clojure, or **Meta Language** (**ML**).

 So, what is a side effect in programming terms? A function is said to have side effects if it produces any changes that are accessible outside its local scope, except for its return values. Python, like many other languages, is susceptible to side effects because it allows you to gain access to member variables and global variables – and, sometimes, this access can be accidental!

In languages that are not purely functional, a function's output can vary even when we pass it the same parameters repeatedly. For example, if a function takes an object as an argument, and the computation relies on the internal state of that object, the function will return different results according to changes in the object's state. This is a common occurrence in OOP with languages such as Python and C++.

So, why this digression? Well, it is a good occasion to consider the paradigms used in our own samples and in OpenCV, and how they differ from a purer mathematical approach. Throughout this book, we have often used global variables or object-oriented classes with member variables. The next program is another example of OOP. OpenCV, too, contains many functions with side effects and many object-oriented classes.

For example, any OpenCV drawing function, such as `cv2.rectangle` or `cv2.circle`, modifies the image that we pass to it as an argument. This approach contravenes one of FP's cardinal rules: avoid side effects and changes in state.

As a brief exercise, let's wrap `cv2.rectangle` in another Python function to perform a drawing in an FP style, without any side effects. The following implementation relies on making a copy of the input image, rather than modifying the original:

```
def draw_rect(img, top_left, bottom_right, color,
              thickness, fill=cv2.LINE_AA):
    new_img = img.copy()
    cv2.rectangle(new_img, top_left, bottom_right, color,
                  thickness, fill)
    return new_img
```

This approach – while computationally more expensive due to the `copy` operation – allows for code such as the following to run without side effects:

```
frame = camera.read()
frame_with_rect = draw_rect(
    frame, (0, 0), (10, 10), (0, 255, 0), 1)
```

Here, `frame` and `frame_with_rect` are references to two different NumPy arrays containing different values. If we had used `cv2.rectangle` instead of our FP-inspired `draw_rect` wrapper, then `frame` and `frame_with_rect` would have been references to one and the same NumPy array (containing a drawing of a rectangle on top of the original image).

To conclude this digression, let's note that a variety of programming languages and paradigms can be applied successfully to computer vision problems. It is useful to know about multiple languages and paradigms so that you can choose the right tool for a given job.

Now, let's get back to our program and explore the implementation of a surveillance application, tracking moving objects in a video.

Implementing the Pedestrian class

The nature of the Kalman filter provides the main rationale for creating a `Pedestrian` class. The Kalman filter can predict the position of an object based on historical observations and can correct the prediction based on the actual data, but it can only do this for one object. As a consequence, we need one Kalman filter per object tracked.

Each `Pedestrian` object will act as a holder for a Kalman filter, a color histogram (calculated on the first detection of the object and used as a reference for the subsequent frames), and a tracking window, which will be used by the MeanShift algorithm. Furthermore, each pedestrian has an ID, which we will display so that we can easily distinguish between all of the pedestrians being tracked. Let's proceed sequentially through the class's implementation:

1. As arguments, the `Pedestrian` class's constructor takes an ID, an initial frame in HSV format, and an initial tracking window. Here are the declarations of the class and its constructor:

   ```
   import cv2
   import numpy as np

   class Pedestrian():
       """A tracked pedestrian with a state including an ID, tracking
       window, histogram, and Kalman filter.
       """

       def __init__(self, id, hsv_frame, track_window):
   ```

2. To begin the constructor's implementation, we define variables for the ID, the tracking window, and the MeanShift algorithm's termination criteria:

   ```
   self.id = id

   self.track_window = track_window
   self.term_crit = \
       (cv2.TERM_CRITERIA_COUNT | cv2.TERM_CRITERIA_EPS, 10, 1)
   ```

3. We proceed by creating a normalized hue histogram of the region of interest in the initial HSV image:

   ```
   # Initialize the histogram.
   x, y, w, h = track_window
   roi = hsv_frame[y:y+h, x:x+w]
   roi_hist = cv2.calcHist([roi], [0], None, [16], [0, 180])
   self.roi_hist = cv2.normalize(roi_hist, roi_hist, 0, 255,
                                  cv2.NORM_MINMAX)
   ```

4. Then, we initialize the Kalman filter:

```
# Initialize the Kalman filter.
self.kalman = cv2.KalmanFilter(4, 2)
self.kalman.measurementMatrix = np.array(
    [[1, 0, 0, 0],
     [0, 1, 0, 0]], np.float32)
self.kalman.transitionMatrix = np.array(
    [[1, 0, 1, 0],
     [0, 1, 0, 1],
     [0, 0, 1, 0],
     [0, 0, 0, 1]], np.float32)
self.kalman.processNoiseCov = np.array(
    [[1, 0, 0, 0],
     [0, 1, 0, 0],
     [0, 0, 1, 0],
     [0, 0, 0, 1]], np.float32) * 0.03
cx = x+w/2
cy = y+h/2
self.kalman.statePre = np.array(
    [[cx], [cy], [0], [0]], np.float32)
self.kalman.statePost = np.array(
    [[cx], [cy], [0], [0]], np.float32)
```

Like in our mouse tracking example, we are configuring the Kalman filter to predict the motion of a 2D point. As the initial point, we use the center of the initial tracking window. This concludes the implementation of the constructor.

5. The `Pedestrian` class also has an `update` method, which we will call once per frame. As arguments, the `update` method takes a BGR frame (to use when we draw a visualization of the tracking result) and an HSV version of the same frame (to use for histogram back-projection). The implementation of the `update` method begins with familiar code for histogram back-projection and MeanShift, as displayed in the following lines:

```
def update(self, frame, hsv_frame):

    back_proj = cv2.calcBackProject(
        [hsv_frame], [0], self.roi_hist, [0, 180], 1)

    ret, self.track_window = cv2.meanShift(
        back_proj, self.track_window, self.term_crit)
    x, y, w, h = self.track_window
    center = np.array([x+w/2, y+h/2], np.float32)
```

6. Note that we have extracted the tracking window's center coordinates because we want to perform Kalman filtering on them. We proceed to do exactly this, and then we update the tracking window so that it is centered on the corrected coordinates:

```
prediction = self.kalman.predict()
estimate = self.kalman.correct(center)
center_offset = estimate[:,0][:2] - center
self.track_window = (x + int(center_offset[0]),
                     y + int(center_offset[1]), w, h)
x, y, w, h = self.track_window
```

7. To conclude the `update` method, we draw the Kalman filter's prediction as a blue circle, the corrected tracking window as a cyan rectangle, and the pedestrian's ID as blue text above the rectangle:

```
# Draw the predicted center position as a circle.
cv2.circle(frame, (int(prediction[0]), int(prediction[1])),
           4, (255, 0, 0), -1)

# Draw the corrected tracking window as a rectangle.
cv2.rectangle(frame, (x,y), (x+w, y+h), (255, 255, 0), 2)

# Draw the ID above the rectangle.
cv2.putText(frame, 'ID: %d' % self.id, (x, y-5),
            cv2.FONT_HERSHEY_SIMPLEX, 0.6, (255, 0, 0),
            1, cv2.LINE_AA)
```

This is all the functionality and data that we need to associate with an individual pedestrian. Next, we need to implement a program that provides the necessary video frames to create and update `Pedestrian` objects.

Implementing the main function

Now that we have a `Pedestrian` class to maintain data about the tracking of each pedestrian, let's implement our program's `main` function. We will look at the parts of the implementation sequentially:

1. We begin by loading a video file, initializing a background subtractor, and setting the background subtractor's history length (that is, the number of frames affecting the background model):

```
def main():
```

```
cap = cv2.VideoCapture('pedestrians.avi')

# Create the KNN background subtractor.
bg_subtractor = cv2.createBackgroundSubtractorKNN()
history_length = 20
bg_subtractor.setHistory(history_length)
```

2. Then, we define morphology kernels:

```
erode_kernel = cv2.getStructuringElement(
    cv2.MORPH_ELLIPSE, (3, 3))
dilate_kernel = cv2.getStructuringElement(
    cv2.MORPH_ELLIPSE, (8, 3))
```

3. We define a list called `pedestrians`, which is initially empty. A little later, we will add `Pedestrian` objects to this list. We also set up a frame counter, which we will use to determine whether enough frames have elapsed to fill the background subtractor's history. Here are the relevant definitions of the variables:

```
pedestrians = []
num_history_frames_populated = 0
```

4. Now, we start a loop. At the start of each iteration, we try to read a video frame. If this fails (for instance, at the end of the video file), we exit the loop:

```
while True:
    grabbed, frame = cap.read()
    if (grabbed is False):
        break
```

5. Proceeding with the body of the loop, we update the background subtractor based on the newly captured frame. If the background subtractor's history is not yet full, we simply continue to the next iteration of the loop. Here is the relevant code:

```
# Apply the KNN background subtractor.
fg_mask = bg_subtractor.apply(frame)

# Let the background subtractor build up a history.
if num_history_frames_populated < history_length:
    num_history_frames_populated += 1
    continue
```

6. Once the background subtractor's history is full, we do more processing on each newly captured frame. Specifically, we apply the same approach we used with background subtractors earlier in this chapter: we perform thresholding, erosion, and dilation on the foreground mask; and then we detect contours, which might be moving objects:

```
# Create the thresholded image.
_, thresh = cv2.threshold(fg_mask, 127, 255,
                          cv2.THRESH_BINARY)
cv2.erode(thresh, erode_kernel, thresh, iterations=2)
cv2.dilate(thresh, dilate_kernel, thresh, iterations=2)

# Detect contours in the thresholded image.
contours, hier = cv2.findContours(
    thresh, cv2.RETR_EXTERNAL, cv2.CHAIN_APPROX_SIMPLE)
```

7. We also convert the frame to HSV format because we intend to use histograms in this format for MeanShift. The following line of code performs the conversion:

```
hsv_frame = cv2.cvtColor(frame, cv2.COLOR_BGR2HSV)
```

8. Once we have contours and an HSV version of the frame, we are ready to detect and track moving objects. We find and draw a bounding rectangle for each contour that is large enough to be a pedestrian. Moreover, if we have not yet populated the pedestrians list, we do so now by adding a new Pedestrian object based on each bounding rectangle (and the corresponding region of the HSV image). Here is the subloop that handles the contours in the manner we have just described:

```
# Draw rectangles around large contours.
# Also, if no pedestrians are being tracked yet, create
some.
should_initialize_pedestrians = len(pedestrians) == 0
id = 0
for c in contours:
    if cv2.contourArea(c) > 500:
        (x, y, w, h) = cv2.boundingRect(c)
        cv2.rectangle(frame, (x, y), (x+w, y+h),
                      (0, 255, 0), 1)
        if should_initialize_pedestrians:
            pedestrians.append(
                Pedestrian(id, frame, hsv_frame,
                           (x, y, w, h)))
    id += 1
```

9. By now, we have a list of pedestrians whom we are tracking. We call each `Pedestrian` object's `update` method, to which we pass the original BGR frame (for use in drawing) and the HSV frame (for use in tracking with MeanShift). Remember that each `Pedestrian` object is responsible for drawing its own information (text, the tracking rectangle, and the Kalman filter's prediction). Here is the subloop that updates the `pedestrians` list:

```
# Update the tracking of each pedestrian.
for pedestrian in pedestrians:
    pedestrian.update(frame, hsv_frame)
```

10. Finally, we display the tracking results in a window, and we allow the user to exit the program at any time by pressing the *Esc* key:

```
cv2.imshow('Pedestrians Tracked', frame)

k = cv2.waitKey(110)
if k == 27:  # Escape
    break

if __name__ == "__main__":
    main()
```

There you have it: MeanShift working in tandem with the Kalman filter to track moving objects. All being well, you should see tracking results visualized in the following manner:

In this cropped screenshot, the green rectangle with the thin border is the detected contour, the cyan rectangle with the thick border is the Kalman-corrected MeanShift tracking rectangle, and the blue dot is the center position predicted by the Kalman filter.

As usual, feel free to experiment with the script. You may want to adjust the parameters, try a MOG background subtractor instead of KNN, or try CamShift instead of MeanShift. These changes should affect just a few lines of code. When you have finished, next, we will consider other possible modifications that might have a larger effect on the structure of the script.

Considering the next steps

The preceding program can be expanded and improved in various ways, depending on the requirements of a particular application. Consider the following examples:

- You could remove a `Pedestrian` object from the `pedestrians` list (and thereby destroy the `Pedestrian` object) if the Kalman filter predicts the pedestrian's position to be outside the frame.
- You could check whether each detected moving object corresponds to an existing `Pedestrian` instance in the `pedestrians` list, and, if not, add a new object to the list so that it will be tracked in subsequent frames.
- You could train a **support vector machine (SVM)** and use it to classify each moving object. Using these means, you could establish whether or not the moving object is something you intend to track. For instance, a dog might enter the scene but your application might require the tracking of humans only. For more information on training an SVM, refer to `Chapter 7`, *Building Custom Object Detectors*.

Whatever your needs, hopefully, this chapter has provided you with the necessary knowledge to build 2D tracking applications that satisfy your requirements.

Summary

This chapter has dealt with video analysis and, in particular, a selection of useful techniques for tracking objects.

We began by learning about background subtraction with a basic motion detection technique that calculates frame differences. Then, we moved on to more complex and efficient background subtraction algorithms – namely, MOG and KNN – which are implemented in OpenCV's `cv2.BackgroundSubtractor` class.

We then proceeded to explore the MeanShift and CamShift tracking algorithms. In the course of this, we talked about color histograms and back-projections. We also familiarized ourselves with the Kalman filter and its usefulness in smoothing the results of a tracking algorithm. Finally, we put all of our knowledge together in a sample surveillance application, which is capable of tracking pedestrians (or other moving objects) in a video.

By now, our foundation in OpenCV, computer vision, and machine learning are solidifying. We can look forward to a couple of advanced topics in the remaining two chapters of this book. We will extend our knowledge of tracking into 3D space in Chapter 9, *Camera Models and Augmented Reality*. Then, we will tackle **artificial neural networks** (**ANNs**) and dive deeper into artificial intelligence in Chapter 10, *Introduction to Neural Networks with OpenCV*.

9
Camera Models and Augmented Reality

If you like geometry, photography, or 3D graphics, then this chapter's topics should especially appeal to you. We will learn about the relationship between 3D space and a 2D projection. We will model this relationship in terms of the basic optical parameters of a camera and lens. Finally, we will apply the same relationship to the task of drawing 3D shapes in an accurate perspective projection. Throughout all of this, we will integrate our previous knowledge of image matching and object tracking in order to track 3D motion of a real-world object whose 2D projection is captured by a camera in real time.

On a practical level, we will build an augmented reality application that uses information about a camera, an object, and motion in order to superimpose 3D graphics on top of a tracked object in real time. To achieve this, we will conquer the following technical challenges:

- Modeling the parameters of a camera and lens
- Modeling a 3D object using 2D and 3D keypoints
- Detecting the object by matching keypoints
- Finding the object's 3D pose using the `cv2.solvePnPRansac` function
- Smoothing the 3D pose using a Kalman filter
- Drawing graphics atop the object

Over the course of this chapter, you will acquire skills that will serve you well if you go on to build your own augmented reality engine or any other system that relies on 3D tracking, such as a robotic navigation system.

Technical requirements

This chapter uses Python, OpenCV, and NumPy. Please refer back to Chapter 1, *Setting Up OpenCV*, for installation instructions.

The completed code and sample videos for this chapter can be found in this book's GitHub repository, https://github.com/PacktPublishing/Learning-OpenCV-4-Computer-Vision-with-Python-Third-Edition, in the chapter09 folder.

 This chapter's code contains excerpts from an open source demo project called *Visualizing the Invisible*, by Joseph Howse (one of this book's authors). To learn more about this project, please visit its repository at https://github.com/JoeHowse/VisualizingTheInvisible/.

Understanding 3D image tracking and augmented reality

We have already solved problems involving image matching in Chapter 6, *Retrieving Images and Searching Using Image Descriptors*. Moreover, we have solved problems involving continuous tracking in Chapter 8, *Tracking Objects*. Therefore, we are familiar with many of the components of an image tracking system, though we have not yet tackled any 3D tracking problems.

So, what exactly is **3D tracking**? Well, it is the process of continually updating an estimate of an object's pose in a 3D space, typically, in terms of six variables: three variables to represent the object's 3D **translation** (that is, position) and the other three variables to represent its 3D rotation.

 A more technical term for 3D tracking is **6DOF tracking** – that is, tracking with **6 degrees of freedom**, meaning the 6 variables we just mentioned.

There are several different ways of representing the 3D rotation as three variables. Elsewhere, you might have encountered various kinds of Euler angle representations, which describe the 3D rotation in terms of three separate 2D rotations around the x, y, and z axes in a particular order. OpenCV does not use Euler angles to represent 3D rotation; instead, it uses a representation called the **Rodrigues rotation vector**. Specifically, OpenCV uses the following six variables to represent the 6DOF pose:

1. t_x: This is the object's translation along the x axis.
2. t_y: This is the object's translation along the y axis.
3. t_z: This is the object's translation along the z axis.
4. r_x: This is the first element of the object's Rodrigues rotation vector.
5. r_y: This is the second element of the object's Rodrigues rotation vector.
6. r_z: This is the third element of the object's Rodrigues rotation vector.

Unfortunately, in the Rodrigues representation, there is no easy way to interpret r_x, r_y, and r_z separately from each other. Taken together, as the vector r, they encode both an axis of rotation and an angle of rotation about this axis. Specifically, the following formulas define the relationship among the r vector; an angle, θ; a normalized axis vector, $\hat{r}$; and a 3 x 3 rotation matrix, R:

$$\theta = |r|$$

$$\hat{r} = r/\theta$$

$$R = cos(\theta)I + (1 - cos\theta)\hat{r}\hat{r}^T + sin(\theta)\begin{bmatrix} 0 & -\hat{r}_z & \hat{r}_y \\ \hat{r}_z & 0 & -\hat{r}_x \\ -\hat{r}_y & \hat{r}_x & 0 \end{bmatrix}$$

As OpenCV programmers, we are not obliged to compute or interpret any of these variables directly. OpenCV provides functions that give us a Rodrigues rotation vector as a return value, and we can pass this rotation vector to other OpenCV functions as an argument – without ever needing to manipulate its contents for ourselves.

For our purposes (and, indeed, for many problems in computer vision), the camera is the origin of the 3D coordinate system. Therefore, in any given frame, the camera's current t_x, t_y, t_z, r_x, r_y, and r_z values are all defined to be 0. We will endeavor to track other objects relative to the camera's current pose.

Of course, for our edification, we will want to visualize the 3D tracking results. This brings us into the territory of **augmented reality (AR)**. Broadly speaking, AR is the process of continually tracking relationships between real-world objects and applying these relationships to virtual objects, in such a way that a user perceives the virtual objects as being anchored to something in the real world. Typically, visual AR is based on relationships in terms of 3D space and perspective projection. Indeed, our case is typical; we want to visualize a 3D tracking result by drawing a projection of some 3D graphics atop the object we tracked in the frame.

We will return to the concept of perspective projection in a few moments. Meanwhile, let's take an overview of a typical set of steps involved in 3D image tracking and visual AR:

1. Define the parameters of the camera and lens. We will introduce this topic in this chapter.
2. Initialize a Kalman filter that we will use to stabilize the 6DOF tracking results. For more information about Kalman filtering, refer back to `Chapter 8`, *Tracking Objects*.
3. Choose a reference image, representing the surface of the object we want to track. For our demo, the object will be a plane, such as a piece of paper on which the image is printed.
4. Create a list of 3D points, representing the vertices of the object. The coordinates can be in any unit, such as meters, millimeters, or something arbitrary. For example, you could arbitrarily define 1 unit to be equal to the object's height.
5. Extract feature descriptors from the reference image. For 3D tracking applications, ORB is a popular choice of descriptor since it can be computed in real time, even on modest hardware such as smartphones. Our demo will use ORB. For more information about ORB, refer back to `Chapter 6`, *Retrieving Images and Searching Using Image Descriptors*.
6. Convert the feature descriptors from pixel coordinates to 3D coordinates, using the same mapping that we used in *step 4*.
7. Start capturing frames from the camera. For each frame, perform the following steps:
    1. Extract feature descriptors, and attempt to find good matches between the reference image and the frame. Our demo will use FLANN-based matching with a ratio test. For more information about these approaches for matching descriptors, refer back to `Chapter 6`, *Retrieving Images and Searching Using Image Descriptors*.
    2. If an insufficient number of good matches were found, continue to the next frame. Otherwise, proceed with the remaining steps.

3. Attempt to find a good estimate of the tracked object's 6DOF pose based on the camera and lens parameters, the matches, and the 3D model of the reference object. For this, we will use the `cv2.solvePnPRansac` function.

4. Apply the Kalman filter to stabilize the 6DOF pose so that it does not jitter too much from frame to frame.

5. Based on the camera and lens parameters, and the 6DOF tracking results, draw a projection of some 3D graphics atop the tracked object in the frame.

Before proceeding to our demo's code, let's discuss two aspects of this outline a bit further: first, the parameters of the camera and lens; and second, the role of the mysterious function, `cv2.solvePnPRansac`.

Understanding camera and lens parameters

Typically, when we capture an image, at least three objects are involved:

- The **subject** is something we want to capture in the image. Typically, it is an object that reflects light, and we want this object to appear in focus (sharp) in the image.
- The **lens** transmits light and focuses any reflected light from the **focal plane** onto the **image plane**. The focal plane is a circular slice of space that includes the subject (as defined previously). The image plane is a circular slice of space that includes the image sensor (as defined later). Typically, these planes are perpendicular to the lens's main (lengthwise) axis. The lens has an **optical center**, which is the point where incoming light from the focal plane converges before being projected back toward the image plane. The **focal distance** (that is, the distance between the optical center and the focal plane) varies depending on the distance between the optical center and the image plane. If we move the optical center closer to the image plane, the focal distance increases; conversely, if we move the optical center farther from the image plane, the focal distance decreases (typically, in a camera system, the focus is adjusted by a mechanism that simply moves the lens back and forth). The **focal length** is defined as the distance between the optical center and the image plane when the focal distance is infinity.

- The **image sensor** is a photosensitive surface that receives light and records it as an image, in either an analog medium (such as film) or a digital medium. Typically, the image sensor is rectangular. Therefore, it does not cover the corners of the circular image plane. The image's diagonal **field of view** (**FOV**: the angular extent of the 3D space being imaged) bears a trigonometric relationship to the focal length, the image sensor's width, and the image sensor's height. We shall explore this relationship soon.

Here is a diagram to illustrate the preceding definitions:

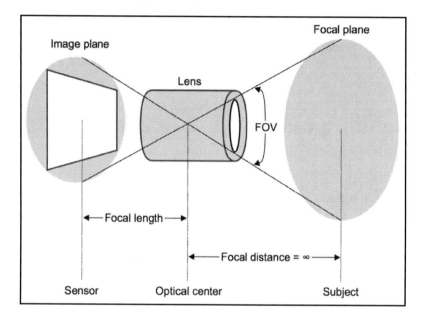

For computer vision, we typically use a lens with a fixed focal length that is optimal for a given application. However, a lens can have a variable focal length; such a lens is called a **zoom lens**. **Zooming in** means increasing the focal length, while **zooming out** means decreasing the focal length. Mechanically, a zoom lens achieves this by moving the optical elements inside the lens.

Let's use the variable *f* to represent the focal length, and the variables (c_x, c_y) to represent the image sensor's center point within the image plane. OpenCV uses the following matrix, which it calls a **camera matrix**, to represent the basic parameters of a camera and lens:

f	0	c_x
0	*f*	c_y
0	0	1

Assuming that the image sensor is centered in the image plane (as it normally should be), we can calculate c_x and c_y based on the image sensor's width, *w*, and height, *h*, as follows:

$$c_x = w/2$$

$$c_y = h/2$$

If we know the diagonal FOV, θ, we can calculate the focal length using the following trigonometric formula:

$$f = \frac{\sqrt{w^2 + h^2}}{2(\tan\frac{\theta}{2})}$$

Alternatively, if we do not know the diagonal FOV, but we know the horizontal FOV, ϕ, and the vertical FOV, ψ, we can calculate the focal length as follows:

$$f = \frac{\sqrt{w^2 + h^2}}{2\sqrt{(\tan\frac{\phi}{2})^2 + (\tan\frac{\psi}{2})^2}}$$

You might be wondering how we obtain values for any of these variables as starting points. Sometimes, the manufacturer of a camera or lens provides data on the sensor size, focal length, or FOV in the product's specification sheet. For example, the specification sheet might list the sensor size and focal length in millimeters and the FOV in degrees. However, if the specification sheet is not so informative, we have other ways of obtaining the necessary data. Importantly, the sensor size and focal length do not need to be expressed in real-world units such as millimeters. We can express them in arbitrary units, such as **pixel-equivalent units**.

You may well ask, what is a pixel-equivalent unit? Well, when we capture a frame from a camera, each pixel in the image corresponds to some region of the image sensor, and this region has a real-world width (and a real-world height, which is normally the same as the width). Therefore, if we are capturing frames with a resolution of 1280 x 720, we can say that the image sensor's width, w, is 1280 pixel-equivalent units and its height, h, is 720 pixel-equivalent units. These units are not comparable across different real-world sensor sizes or different resolutions; however, for a given camera and resolution, they allow us to make internally consistent measurements without needing to know the real-world scale of these measurements.

This trick gets us as far as being able to define w and h for any image sensor (since we can always check the pixel dimensions of a captured frame). Now, to be able to calculate the focal length, we just need one more type of data: the FOV. We can measure this using a simple experiment. Take a piece of paper and tape it to a wall (or another vertical surface). Position the camera and lens so that they are directly facing the piece of paper and the paper fills the frame diagonally. (If the paper's aspect ratio does not match the frame's aspect ratio, cut the paper to match.) Measure the diagonal size, s, from one corner of the paper to the diagonally opposite corner. Additionally, measure the distance, d, from the paper to a point halfway down the barrel of the lens. Then, calculate the diagonal FOV, θ, by trigonometry:

$$\theta = 2(atan\frac{s}{2d})$$

Let's suppose that with this experiment, we determine that a given camera and lens have a diagonal FOV of 70 degrees. If we know that we are capturing frames at a resolution of 1280 x 720, then we can calculate the focal length in pixel-equivalent units as follows:

$$f = \frac{\sqrt{w^2 + h^2}}{2(tan\frac{\theta}{2})} = \frac{\sqrt{1280^2 + 720^2}}{2\sqrt{tan(70 * \pi/180/2)}} = 1048.7$$

In addition to this, we can calculate the image sensor's center coordinates:

$$c_x = w/2 = 1280/2 = 640$$

$$c_y = h/2 = 720/2 = 360$$

Therefore, we have the following camera matrix:

1048.7	0	640
0	1048.7	360
0	0	1

The preceding parameters are necessary for 3D tracking, and they correctly represent an ideal camera and lens. However, real equipment may deviate noticeably from this ideal, and the camera matrix alone cannot represent all the possible types of deviations. **Distortion coefficients** are a set of additional parameters that can represent the following kinds of deviations from the ideal model:

- **Radial distortion**: This means that the lens does not magnify all parts of the image equally; thus, it makes straight edges appear curvy or wavy. For radial distortion coefficients, variable names such as k_n (for example, k_1, k_2, k_3, and so forth) are typically used. If $k_1<0$, this usually implies that the lens suffers from **barrel distortion**, meaning that straight edges appear to bend outward toward the borders of the image. Conversely, $k_1>0$ usually implies that the lens suffers from **pincushion distortion**, meaning that straight edges appear to bend inward toward the center of the image. If the sign alternates across the series (for example, $k_1>0$, $k_2<0$, and $k_3>0$), this might imply that the lens suffers from **mustache distortion**, meaning that straight edges appear wavy.
- **Tangential distortion**: This means that the lens's main (lengthwise) axis is not perpendicular to the image sensor; thus, the perspective is skewed, and the angles between the straight edges appear to be different than in a normal perspective projection. For tangential distortion coefficients, variable names such as p_n (for example, p_1, p_2, and so forth) are typically used. The sign of the coefficient depends on the direction of the lens's tilt relative to the image sensor.

The following diagram illustrates some types of radial distortion:

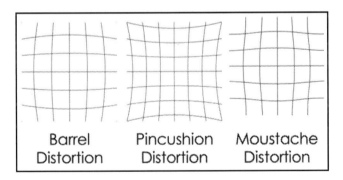

Barrel Distortion   Pincushion Distortion   Moustache Distortion

OpenCV provides functions to work with as many as five distortion coefficients: k_1, k_2, p_1, p_2, and k_3. (OpenCV expects them in this order, as elements of an array.) Rarely, you might be able to obtain official data about distortion coefficients from the vendor of a camera or lens. Alternatively, you can estimate the distortion coefficients, along with the camera matrix, using OpenCV's chessboard calibration process. This involves capturing a series of images of a printed a chessboard pattern, viewed from various positions and angles. For further details, you can refer to the official tutorial at `https://docs.opencv.org/master/dc/dbb/tutorial_py_calibration.html`.

For our demo's purposes, we will simply assume that all the distortion coefficients are 0, meaning there is no distortion. Of course, we do not really believe that our webcam lenses are distortion-less masterpieces of optical engineering; we just believe that the distortion is not bad enough to noticeably affect our demo of 3D tracking and AR. If we were trying to build a precise measurement device instead of a visual demo, we would be more concerned about the effects of distortion.

Compared to the chessboard calibration process, the formulas and assumptions that we have outlined in this section produce a more constrained or idealistic model. However, our approach has the advantages of being simpler and more easily reproducible. The chessboard calibration process is more laborious, and each user might execute it differently, producing different (and, sometimes, erroneous) results.

Having absorbed this background information on camera and lens parameters, let's now examine an OpenCV function that uses these parameters as part of a solution to the 6DOF tracking problem.

Understanding cv2.solvePnPRansac

The `cv2.solvePnPRansac` function implements a solver for the so-called **Perspective-*n*-Point (PnP)** problem. Given a set of *n* unique matches between 3D and 2D points, along with the parameters of the camera and lens that generated this 2D projection of the 3D points, the solver attempts to estimate the 6DOF pose of the 3D object relative to the camera. This problem is somewhat similar to finding the homography for a set of 2D-to-2D keypoint matches, as we did in `Chapter 6`, *Retrieving Images and Searching Using Image Descriptors*. However, in the PnP problem, we have enough additional information to estimate a more specific spatial relationship – the DOF pose – as opposed to the homography, which just tells us a projective relationship.

So, how does `cv2.solvePnPRansac` work? As the function's name suggests, it implements a Ransac algorithm, which is a general-purpose iterative approach designed to deal with a set of inputs that may contain outliers – in our case, bad matches. Each Ransac iteration finds a potential solution that minimizes a measurement of mean error for the inputs. Then, before the next iteration, any inputs with an unacceptably large error are marked as outliers and discarded. This process continues until the solution converges, meaning that no new outliers are found and the mean error is acceptably low.

For the PnP problem, the error is measured in terms of **reprojection error**, meaning the distance between the observed position of a 2D point and the predicted position according to the camera and lens parameters, and the 6DOF pose that we are currently considering as the potential solution. At the end of the process, we hope to obtain a 6DOF pose that is consistent with most of the 3D-to-2D keypoint matches. Additionally, we want to know which of the matches are inliers for this solution.

Let's consider the function signature of `cv2.solvePnPRansac`:

```
retval, rvec, tvec, inliers = cv.solvePnPRansac(
    objectPoints,
    imagePoints,
    cameraMatrix,
    distCoeffs,
    rvec=None,
    tvec=None,
    useExtrinsicGuess=False
    iterationsCount=100,
    reprojectionError=8.0,
    confidence=0.98,
    inliers=None,
    flags=cv2.SOLVEPNP_ITERATIVE)
```

As we can see, the function has four return values:

- `retval`: This is `True` if the solver converged on a solution; otherwise, it is `False`.
- `rvec`: This array contains r_x, r_y, and r_z – the three rotational degrees of freedom in the 6DOF pose.
- `tvec`: This array contains t_x, t_y, and t_z – the three translational (positional) degrees of freedom in the 6DOF pose.
- `inliers`: If the solver converged on a solution, this vector contains the indices of the input points (in `objectPoints` and `imagePoints`) that are congruous with the solution.

The function also has 12 arguments:

- `objectPoints`: This is an array of 3D points that represent the object's keypoints when there is no translation and no rotation – in other words, when the 6DOF pose variables are all 0.
- `imagePoints`: This is an array of 2D points that represent the object's keypoint matches in the image. Specifically, `imagePoints[i]` is believed to be a match for `objectPoints[i]`.
- `cameraMatrix`: This 2D array is the camera matrix, which we can derive in the manner described in the previous *Understanding camera and lens parameters* section.
- `distCoeffs`: This is the array of distortion coefficients. If we do not know them, we can assume (for simplicity) that they are all 0, as mentioned in the previous section.
- `rvec`: If the solver converges on a solution, it will put the solution's r_x, r_y, and r_z values in this array.
- `tvec`: If the solver converges on a solution, it will put the solution's t_x, t_y, and t_z values in this array.
- `useExtrinsicGuess`: If this is `True`, the solver treats the values in the `rvec` and `tvec` arguments as an initial guess, and then it tries to find a solution that is close to these. Otherwise, the solver takes an unbiased approach in its search for a solution.
- `iterationsCount`: This is the maximum number of iterations that the solver should attempt. If it does not converge on a solution after this number of iterations, it gives up.
- `reprojectionError`: This is the maximum reprojection error that the solver will accept; if a point has a greater reprojection error than this, the solver treats it as an outlier.
- `confidence`: The solver attempts to converge on a solution that has a confidence score greater than or equal to this value.
- `inliers`: If the solver converges on a solution, it will put the indices of the solution's inlier points in this array.
- `flags`: The flags specify the solver's algorithm. The default, `cv2.SOLVEPNP_ITERATIVE`, is an approach that minimizes reprojection error and has no special restrictions, so it is generally the best choice. A useful alternative is `cv2.SOLVEPNP_IPPE` (**IPPE**, short for **Infinitesimal Plane-Based Pose Estimation**), but it is restricted to planar objects.

Although this function involves a lot of variables, we will see that its usage is a natural extension of the keypoint matching problems we have covered in Chapter 6, *Retrieving Images and Searching Using Image Descriptors*, and the 3D and projective problems we are introducing in this chapter. With this in mind, let's begin to explore this chapter's sample code.

Implementing the demo application

We are going to implement our demo in a single script, ImageTrackingDemo.py, which will contain the following components:

1. Import statements
2. A helper function for a custom grayscale conversion
3. Helper functions to convert keypoints from 2D to 3D space
4. An application class, ImageTrackingDemo, which will encapsulate a model of the camera and lens, a model of the reference image, a Kalman filter, 6DOF tracking results, and an application loop that will track the image and draw a simple AR visualization
5. A main function to launch the application

The script will depend on one other file, reference_image.png, which will represent the image that we want to track.

Without further ado, let's dive into the script's implementation.

Importing modules

From the Python standard library, we will use the math module for trigonometric calculations, and the timeit module for accurate time measurement (which will enable us to use a Kalman filter more effectively). As usual, we will also use NumPy and OpenCV. Thus, our implementation of ImageTrackingDemo.py begins with the following import statements:

```
import math
import timeit

import cv2
import numpy
```

Now, let's proceed to the implementation of the helper functions.

Performing grayscale conversion

Throughout this book, we have performed grayscale conversions using code such as the following:

```
gray_img = cv2.cvtColor(bgr_img, cv2.COLOR_BGR2GRAY)
```

Perhaps a question is long overdue: how exactly does this function map BGR values to grayscale values? The answer is that each output pixel's grayscale value is a weighted average of the corresponding input pixel's B, G, and R values, as follows:

```
gray = (0.114 * blue) + (0.587 * green) + (0.299 * red)
```

These weights are widely used. They come from a telecommunications industry standard called CCIR 601, which was issued in 1982. They are loosely consistent with a characteristic of human vision; when we see a brightly lit scene, our eyes are most sensitive to yellowish-green light. Moreover, these weights should produce high contrast in scenes with yellowish light and blueish shadows, such as an outdoor scene on a sunny day. Are these good reasons for us to use the CCIR 601 weights? No, they are not; there is no scientific evidence that the CCIR 601 conversion weights yield optimal grayscale input for any particular purpose in computer vision.

Indeed, for the purpose of image tracking, there is evidence in favor of other grayscale conversion algorithms. Samuel Macêdo, Givânio Melo, and Judith Kelner address this topic in their paper, *A comparative study of grayscale conversion techniques applied to SIFT descriptors* (SBC Journal on Interactive Systems, vol. 6, no. 2, 2015). They test a variety of conversion algorithms, including the following types:

- A weighted-average conversion, `gray = (0.07 * blue) + (0.71 * green) + (0.21 * red)`, which is somewhat similar to CCIR 601
- An unweighted-average conversion, `gray = (blue + green + red) / 3`
- Conversions based on only a single color channel, such as `gray = green`
- Gamma-corrected conversions, such as `gray = 255 * (green / 255) ^ (1/2.2)`, in which the grayscale value varies exponentially (not linearly) with the inputs

According to the paper, the weighted-average conversion produces results that are relatively unstable – good for finding matches and homography with some images, but bad with others. The unweighted-average conversion and the single-channel conversions yield more consistent results. For some images, the gamma-corrected conversions yield the best results, but these conversions are computationally more expensive.

For our demo's purposes, we will perform grayscale conversion by taking the simple (unweighted) average of each pixel's B, G, and R values. This approach is computationally cheap (which is desirable in real-time tracking), and we expect that it leads to more consistent tracking results than the default weighted-average conversion in OpenCV. Here is our implementation of a helper function to perform the custom conversion:

```
def convert_to_gray(src, dst=None):
    weight = 1.0 / 3.0
    m = numpy.array([[weight, weight, weight]], numpy.float32)
    return cv2.transform(src, m, dst)
```

Note the use of the `cv2.transform` function. This is a well-optimized, general-purpose matrix transformation function, provided by OpenCV. We can use it to perform operations where the values of a pixel's output channels are a linear combination of the values of the input channels. In the case of our BGR-to-grayscale conversion, we have one output channel and three input channels, so our transformation matrix, `m`, has one row and three columns.

Having written our helper function for grayscale conversions, let's go on to consider helper functions for conversions from 2D to 3D space.

Performing 2D-to-3D spatial conversions

Remember that we have a reference image, `reference_image.png`, and we want our AR application to track a print copy of this image. For the purpose of 3D tracking, we can represent this printed image as a plane in 3D space. Let's define the local coordinate system by saying that, normally (when the elements of the 6DOF pose are all 0), this planar object stands upright like a picture hanging on a wall; its front is the side with the image on it, and its origin is the center of the image.

Now, let's suppose that we want to map a given pixel from the reference image onto this 3D plane. Given the 2D pixel coordinates, the image's pixel dimensions, and a scaling factor to convert from pixels to some unit of measurement we want to use in 3D space, we can use the following helper function to map a pixel onto the plane:

```
def map_point_onto_plane(point_2D, image_size, image_scale):
    x, y = point_2D
    w, h = image_size
    return (image_scale * (x - 0.5 * w),
            image_scale * (y - 0.5 * h),
            0.0)
```

The scaling factor depends on the real-world size of the printed image and our choice of unit. For example, we might know that our printed image is 20 cm tall – or we might not care about the absolute scale, in which case we could define an arbitrary unit such that the printed image is one unit tall. Anyway, given a list of 2D pixel coordinates, the reference image's size, and the reference image's real-world height in any unit (absolute or relative), we can use the following helper function to obtain a list of the corresponding 3D coordinates on the plane:

```python
def map_points_to_plane(points_2D, image_size, image_real_height):

    w, h = image_size
    image_scale = image_real_height / h

    points_3D = [map_point_onto_plane(
                    point_2D, image_size, image_scale)
                for point_2D in points_2D]
    return numpy.array(points_3D, numpy.float32)
```

Note that we have a helper function for multiple points, `map_points_to_plane`, and it calls a helper function for every single point, `map_point_to_plane`.

Later, in the *Initializing the tracker* section, we will generate ORB keypoint descriptors for the reference image, and we will use our `map_points_to_plane` helper function in order to convert the keypoint coordinates from 2D to 3D. We will also convert the image's four 2D vertices (that is, its top-left, top-right, bottom-right, and bottom-left corners) to obtain the four 3D vertices of the plane. We will use these vertices when we perform our AR drawing – specifically, in the *Drawing the tracking results* section. Drawing-related functions (in OpenCV and many other frameworks) expect the vertices to be specified in clockwise order (from a frontal perspective) for each face of the 3D shape. To deal with this requirement, let's implement another helper function that is specific to mapping vertices; here it is:

```python
def map_vertices_to_plane(image_size, image_real_height):

    w, h = image_size

    vertices_2D = [(0, 0), (w, 0), (w, h), (0, h)]
    vertex_indices_by_face = [[0, 1, 2, 3]]

    vertices_3D = map_points_to_plane(
        vertices_2D, image_size, image_real_height)
    return vertices_3D, vertex_indices_by_face
```

Note that our vertex-mapping helper function, `map_vertices_to_plane`, calls our `map_points_to_plane` helper function, which, in turn, calls `map_point_to_plane`. Therefore, all our mapping functionality shares a common core.

 Of course, 2D-to-3D keypoint mapping and vertex mapping can be applied to other kinds of 3D shapes besides planes. To learn how our approach can extend to 3D cuboids and 3D cylinders, please refer to the *Visualizing the Invisible* demo project, by Joseph Howse, which is available at `https://github.com/JoeHowse/VisualizingTheInvisible/`.

We have finished implementing the helper functions. Now, let's proceed to the object-oriented part of the code.

Implementing the application class

We will implement our application in a class named `ImageTrackingDemo`, which will have the following methods:

- `__init__(self, capture, diagonal_fov_degrees, target_fps, reference_image_path, reference_image_real_height)`: The initializer will set up a capture device, a camera matrix, a Kalman filter, and 2D and 3D keypoints for the reference image.
- `run(self)`: This method will run the application's main loop, which captures, processes, and displays frames until the user quits by hitting the *Esc* key. The processing of each frame is performed with the help of other methods, which are mentioned next in this list.
- `_track_object(self)`: This method will perform 6DOF tracking and draw an AR visualization of the tracking result.
- `_init_kalman_transition_matrix(self, fps)`: This method will configure the Kalman filter to ensure that acceleration and velocity are simulated properly for the specified frame rate.
- `_apply_kalman(self)`: This method will stabilize the 6DOF tracking result by applying the Kalman filter.

Let's walk through the methods' implementations one by one, starting with `__init__`.

Initializing the tracker

The __init__ method involves a lot of steps to initialize the camera matrix, the ORB descriptor extractor, the Kalman filter, the reference image's 2D and 3D keypoints, and other variables related to our tracking algorithm:

1. To begin, let's look at the arguments that __init__ accepts. These include a cv2.VideoCapture object, called capture (the camera); the camera's diagonal FOV, in degrees; the expected frame rate in **frames per second** (**FPS**); a path to a file containing the reference image; and a measurement of the reference image's real-world height (in any unit):

```
class ImageTrackingDemo():
```

```
    def __init__(self, capture, diagonal_fov_degrees=70.0,
                 target_fps=25.0,
                 reference_image_path='reference_image.png',
                 reference_image_real_height=1.0):
```

2. We attempt to capture a frame from the camera in order to determine its pixel dimensions; failing that, we get the dimensions from the camera's properties:

```
self._capture = capture
success, trial_image = capture.read()
if success:
    # Use the actual image dimensions.
    h, w = trial_image.shape[:2]
else:
    # Use the nominal image dimensions.
    w = capture.get(cv2.CAP_PROP_FRAME_WIDTH)
    h = capture.get(cv2.CAP_PROP_FRAME_HEIGHT)
self._image_size = (w, h)
```

3. Now, given the frame's dimensions in pixels, and the FOV of the camera and lens, we can use trigonometry to calculate the focal length in pixel-equivalent units. (The formula is the one we derived earlier in this chapter, in the *Understanding camera and lens parameters* section.) Moreover, using the focal length and the frame's center point, we can construct the camera matrix. Here is the relevant code:

```
diagonal_image_size = (w ** 2.0 + h ** 2.0) ** 0.5
diagonal_fov_radians = \
    diagonal_fov_degrees * math.pi / 180.0
focal_length = 0.5 * diagonal_image_size / math.tan(
    0.5 * diagonal_fov_radians)
```

```
self._camera_matrix = numpy.array(
    [[focal_length, 0.0, 0.5 * w],
     [0.0, focal_length, 0.5 * h],
     [0.0, 0.0, 1.0]], numpy.float32)
```

4. For the sake of simplicity, we assume that the lens does not suffer from any distortion whatsoever:

```
self._distortion_coefficients = None
```

5. Initially, we are not tracking the object, so we have no estimate of its rotation and position; we just define the relevant variables as None:

```
self._rotation_vector = None
self._translation_vector = None
```

6. Now, let's set up a Kalman filter:

```
self._kalman = cv2.KalmanFilter(18, 6)

self._kalman.processNoiseCov = numpy.identity(
    18, numpy.float32) * 1e-5
self._kalman.measurementNoiseCov = numpy.identity(
    6, numpy.float32) * 1e-2
self._kalman.errorCovPost = numpy.identity(
    18, numpy.float32)

self._kalman.measurementMatrix = numpy.array(
    [[1.0, 0.0, 0.0, 0.0, 0.0, 0.0, 0.0, 0.0, 0.0,
      0.0, 0.0, 0.0, 0.0, 0.0, 0.0, 0.0, 0.0, 0.0],
     [0.0, 1.0, 0.0, 0.0, 0.0, 0.0, 0.0, 0.0, 0.0,
      0.0, 0.0, 0.0, 0.0, 0.0, 0.0, 0.0, 0.0, 0.0],
     [0.0, 0.0, 1.0, 0.0, 0.0, 0.0, 0.0, 0.0, 0.0,
      0.0, 0.0, 0.0, 0.0, 0.0, 0.0, 0.0, 0.0, 0.0],
     [0.0, 0.0, 0.0, 0.0, 0.0, 0.0, 0.0, 0.0, 0.0,
      1.0, 0.0, 0.0, 0.0, 0.0, 0.0, 0.0, 0.0, 0.0],
     [0.0, 0.0, 0.0, 0.0, 0.0, 0.0, 0.0, 0.0, 0.0,
      0.0, 1.0, 0.0, 0.0, 0.0, 0.0, 0.0, 0.0, 0.0],
     [0.0, 0.0, 0.0, 0.0, 0.0, 0.0, 0.0, 0.0, 0.0,
      0.0, 0.0, 1.0, 0.0, 0.0, 0.0, 0.0, 0.0, 0.0]],
    numpy.float32)

self._init_kalman_transition_matrix(target_fps)
```

As indicated by the preceding code, `cv2.KalmanFilter(18, 6)`, this Kalman filter will track 18 output variables (or predictions), based on 6 input variables (or measurements). Specifically, the input variables are the elements of the 6DOF tracking result: t_x, t_y, t_z, r_x, r_y, and r_z. The output variables are the elements of the stabilized 6DOF tracking result, plus their first-order derivatives (velocity) and their second-order derivatives (acceleration), in the following order: t_x, t_y, t_z, t_x', t_y', t_z', t_x'', t_y'', t_z'', r_x, r_y, r_z, r_x', r_y', r_z', r_x'', r_y'', and r_z''. The Kalman filter's measurement matrix has 18 columns (representing the output variables) and 6 rows (representing the input variables). Within each row, we put 1.0 in the index that corresponds to the matching output variable; elsewhere, we put 0.0. We also initialize a transition matrix, which defines the relationships among the output variables over time. This part of the initialization is handled by a helper method, `_init_kalman_transition_matrix(target_fps)`, which we will examine later, in the *Initializing and applying the Kalman filter* section.

> Not all of the Kalman filter's matrices are initialized by our `__init__` method. The transition matrix is updated every frame during tracking because the actual frame rate (and, thus, the time step) may change. The state matrices are initialized every time we start tracking an object. We will cover these aspects of the Kalman filter's usage in due course, in the *Initializing and applying the Kalman filter* section.

7. We need a Boolean variable (initially, `False`) to indicate whether we successfully tracked the object in the previous frame:

```
self._was_tracking = False
```

8. We need to define the vertices of some 3D graphics that we will draw every frame as part of our AR visualization. Specifically, the graphics will be a set of arrows representing the object's *X*, *Y*, and *Z* axes. The scale of these graphics will relate to the scale of the real object – that is, the printed image that we intend to track. Remember that, as one of its arguments, the `__init__` method takes the image's scale – specifically, its height – and that this measurement may be in any unit. Let's define the length of the 3D axis arrows to be half the height of the printed image:

```
self._reference_image_real_height = \
    reference_image_real_height
reference_axis_length = 0.5 * reference_image_real_height
```

9. Using the length that we have just defined, let's define the vertices of the axis arrows relative to the printed image's center, [0.0, 0.0, 0.0]:

```
self._reference_axis_points_3D = numpy.array(
    [[0.0, 0.0, 0.0],
    [-reference_axis_length, 0.0, 0.0],
    [0.0, -reference_axis_length, 0.0],
    [0.0, 0.0, -reference_axis_length]], numpy.float32)
```

Note that OpenCV's coordinate system has nonstandard axis directions, as follows:

- +*X* (the positive X direction) is the object's left-hand direction, or the viewer's right-hand direction in a frontal view of the object.
- +*Y* is down.
- +*Z* is the object's backward direction, or the viewer's frontward direction in a frontal view of the object.

We must negate all of the preceding directions in order to obtain the following standard right-handed coordinate system, like the one used in many 3D graphics frameworks such as OpenGL:

- +*X* is the object's right-hand direction, or the viewer's left-hand direction in a frontal view of the object.
- +*Y* is up.
- +*Z* is the object's forward direction, or the viewer's backward direction in a frontal view of the object.

For the purposes of this book, we use OpenCV to draw 3D graphics, so we could simply adhere to OpenCV's nonstandard axis directions, even when we draw visualizations. However, if you do further AR work in the future, you will likely need to integrate your computer vision code with OpenGL and other 3D graphics frameworks using a right-handed coordinate system. To better prepare you for this eventuality, we will convert the axis directions in our OpenCV-centric demo.

10. We will use three arrays to hold three kinds of images: the BGR video frame (where we will do our AR drawing), the grayscale version of the frame (which we will use for keypoint matching), and the mask (where we will draw a silhouette of the tracked object). Initially, these arrays are all None:

```
self._bgr_image = None
self._gray_image = None
self._mask = None
```

11. We will use a `cv2.ORB` object to detect keypoints and compute descriptors for the reference image and, later, for camera frames. We initialize the `cv2.ORB` object as follows:

```
# Create and configure the feature detector.
patchSize = 31
self._feature_detector = cv2.ORB_create(
    nfeatures=250, scaleFactor=1.2, nlevels=16,
    edgeThreshold=patchSize, patchSize=patchSize)
```

 For a refresher on the ORB algorithm and its usage in OpenCV, refer back to Chapter 6, *Retrieving Images and Searching Using Image Descriptors*, specifically to the *Using ORB with FAST features and BRIEF descriptors* section.

Here, we have specified several optional parameters for the constructor of `cv2.ORB`. The diameter covered by a descriptor is 31 pixels, our image pyramid has 16 levels with a scale factor of 1.2 between consecutive levels, and we want, at most, 250 keypoints and descriptors per detection attempt.

12. Now, we load the reference image from a file, resize it, convert it to grayscale, and create an empty mask for it:

```
bgr_reference_image = cv2.imread(
    reference_image_path, cv2.IMREAD_COLOR)
reference_image_h, reference_image_w = \
    bgr_reference_image.shape[:2]
reference_image_resize_factor = \
    (2.0 * h) / reference_image_h
bgr_reference_image = cv2.resize(
    bgr_reference_image, (0, 0), None,
    reference_image_resize_factor,
    reference_image_resize_factor, cv2.INTER_CUBIC)
gray_reference_image = convert_to_gray(bgr_reference_image)
reference_mask = numpy.empty_like(gray_reference_image)
```

When resizing the reference image, we have chosen to make it twice as high as the camera frame. The exact number is arbitrary; however, the idea is that we want to perform keypoint detection and description with an image pyramid that covers a useful range of magnifications. The base of the pyramid (that is, the resized reference image) should be larger than the camera frame so that we can match keypoints at an appropriate scale even when the target object is so close to the camera that it cannot all fit into the frame. Conversely, the top level of the pyramid should be smaller than the camera frame so that we can match keypoints at an appropriate scale even when the target object is too far away to fill the whole frame.

Let's consider an example. Suppose that our original reference image is 4000 x 3000 pixels and that our camera frame is 1280 x 720 pixels. We resize the reference image to 1920 x 1440 pixels (twice the height of the frame, and the same aspect ratio as the original reference image). Thus, the base of our image pyramid is also 1920 x 1440 pixels. Since our `cv2.ORB` object is configured to use 16 pyramid levels and a scale factor of 1.2, the top of the image pyramid has a width of $1920/(1.2^{16-1})=124$ pixels and a height of $1440/(1.2^{16-1})=93$ pixels; in other words, it is 124 x 93 pixels. Therefore, we can potentially match keypoints and track the object even if it is so far away that it fills just 10% of the frame's width or height. Realistically, to perform useful keypoint matching at this scale, we would need a good lens, the object would need to be in focus, and the lighting would need to be good as well.

13. At this stage, we have an appropriately sized reference image in BGR color and in grayscale, and we have an empty mask for this image. We are going to partition the image into 36 equally-sized regions of interest (in a 6 x 6 grid), and for each region, we will attempt to generate as many as 250 keypoints and descriptors (since our `cv2.ORB` object is configured to use this maximum number of keypoints and descriptors). This partitioning scheme helps to ensure that we have some keypoints and descriptors in every region, so we can potentially match keypoints and track the object even if most parts of the object are not visible in a given frame. The following code block shows how we iterate over the regions of interest and, for each region, create a mask, perform keypoint detection and descriptor extraction, and append the keypoints and descriptors to master lists:

```
# Find keypoints and descriptors for multiple segments of
# the reference image.
reference_keypoints = []
self._reference_descriptors = numpy.empty(
    (0, 32), numpy.uint8)
num_segments_y = 6
```

```
num_segments_x = 6
for segment_y, segment_x in numpy.ndindex(
        (num_segments_y, num_segments_x)):
    y0 = reference_image_h * \
        segment_y // num_segments_y - patchSize
    x0 = reference_image_w * \
        segment_x // num_segments_x - patchSize
    y1 = reference_image_h * \
        (segment_y + 1) // num_segments_y + patchSize
    x1 = reference_image_w * \
        (segment_x + 1) // num_segments_x + patchSize
    reference_mask.fill(0)
    cv2.rectangle(
        reference_mask, (x0, y0), (x1, y1), 255, cv2.FILLED)
    more_reference_keypoints, more_reference_descriptors = \
        self._feature_detector.detectAndCompute(
            gray_reference_image, reference_mask)
    if more_reference_descriptors is None:
        # No keypoints were found for this segment.
        continue
    reference_keypoints += more_reference_keypoints
    self._reference_descriptors = numpy.vstack(
        (self._reference_descriptors,
         more_reference_descriptors))
```

14. Now, we draw a visualization of the keypoints atop the grayscale reference image:

```
cv2.drawKeypoints(
    gray_reference_image, reference_keypoints,
    bgr_reference_image,
    flags=cv2.DRAW_MATCHES_FLAGS_DRAW_RICH_KEYPOINTS)
```

15. Next, we save the visualization to a file with `_keypoints` appended to the name. For example, if the filename of the reference image was `reference_image.png`, we save the visualization as `reference_image_keypoints.png`. Here is the relevant code:

```
ext_i = reference_image_path.rfind('.')
reference_image_keypoints_path = \
    reference_image_path[:ext_i] + '_keypoints' + \
    reference_image_path[ext_i:]
cv2.imwrite(
    reference_image_keypoints_path, bgr_reference_image)
```

16. We proceed to initialize the FLANN-based matcher with custom parameters:

```
FLANN_INDEX_LSH = 6
index_params = dict(algorithm=FLANN_INDEX_LSH,
                    table_number=6, key_size=12,
                    multi_probe_level=1)
search_params = dict()
self._descriptor_matcher = cv2.FlannBasedMatcher(
    index_params, search_params)
```

These parameters specify that we are using a multi-probe LSH (locality-sensitive hashing) indexing algorithm with 6 hash tables, a hash key size of 12 bits, and 1 multi-probe level.

 For a description of the multi-probe LSH algorithm, refer to the paper *Multi-Probe LSH: Efficient Indexing for High-Dimensional Similarity Search* (VLDB, 2007), by Qin Lv, William Josephson, Zhe Wang, Moses Charikar, and Kai Li. An electronic version is available at `https://www.cs.princeton.edu/cass/papers/mplsh_vldb07.pdf`.

17. We train the matcher by feeding the reference descriptors to it:

```
self._descriptor_matcher.add([self._reference_descriptors])
```

18. We take the 2D coordinates of the keypoints, and we feed these to our `map_points_to_plane` helper function in order to obtain equivalent 3D coordinates on the surface of the object's plane:

```
reference_points_2D = [keypoint.pt
                       for keypoint in reference_keypoints]
self._reference_points_3D = map_points_to_plane(
    reference_points_2D, gray_reference_image.shape[::-1],
    reference_image_real_height)
```

19. Similarly, we call our `map_vertices_to_plane` function in order to obtain the 3D vertices and 3D face of the plane:

```
(self._reference_vertices_3D,
 self._reference_vertex_indices_by_face) = \
    map_vertices_to_plane(
            gray_reference_image.shape[::-1],
            reference_image_real_height)
```

This concludes the implementation of the __init__ method. Next, let's take a look at the run method, which represents the application's main loop.

Implementing the main loop

As usual, our main loop's primary role is to capture and process frames, until the user hits the *Esc* key. The processing of each frame – including 3D tracking and AR drawing – is delegated to a helper method called _track_object, which we will examine later, in the *Tracking the image in 3D* section. The main loop also has a secondary role: that is, to perform timekeeping by measuring the frame rate and updating the Kalman filter's transition matrix accordingly. This update is delegated to another helper method, _init_kalman_transition_matrix, which we will examine in the *Initializing and applying the Kalman filter* section. With these roles in mind, we can implement the main loop in the run method as follows:

```
def run(self):

    num_images_captured = 0
    start_time = timeit.default_timer()

    while cv2.waitKey(1) != 27:  # Escape
        success, self._bgr_image = self._capture.read(
            self._bgr_image)
        if success:
            num_images_captured += 1
            self._track_object()
            cv2.imshow('Image Tracking', self._bgr_image)
        delta_time = timeit.default_timer() - start_time
        if delta_time > 0.0:
            fps = num_images_captured / delta_time
            self._init_kalman_transition_matrix(fps)
```

Note the use of the timeit.default_timer function from Python's standard library. This function provides a precise measurement of the current system time in seconds (as a floating-point number, so fractions of seconds can be expressed). As the name timeit suggests, this module contains useful functionality for situations where you have time-sensitive code and you want to *time it*.

Let's move on to the implementation of _track_object, since this helper performs the largest part of the application's work on behalf of run.

Tracking the image in 3D

The _track_object method is directly responsible for keypoint matching, keypoint visualizations, and solving the PnP problem. Additionally, it calls other methods to deal with Kalman filtering, AR drawing, and masking the tracked object:

1. To begin _track_object's implementation, we call our convert_to_gray helper function to convert the frame to grayscale:

```
def _track_object(self):

    self._gray_image = convert_to_gray(
        self._bgr_image, self._gray_image)
```

2. Now, we use our cv2.ORB object to detect keypoints and compute descriptors in a masked region of the grayscale image:

```
if self._mask is None:
    self._mask = numpy.full_like(self._gray_image, 255)

keypoints, descriptors = \
    self._feature_detector.detectAndCompute(
        self._gray_image, self._mask)
```

If we were already tracking the object in the previous frame, the mask covers the region where we previously found the object. Otherwise, the mask covers the whole frame because we have no idea where the object might be. We will see how the mask is created later, in the *Drawing the tracking results and masking the tracked object* section.

3. Next, we use our FLANN matcher to find matches between the reference image's keypoints and the frame's keypoints, and we filter these matches according to the ratio test:

```
# Find the 2 best matches for each descriptor.
matches = self._descriptor_matcher.knnMatch(descriptors, 2)

# Filter the matches based on the distance ratio test.
good_matches = [
    match[0] for match in matches
    if len(match) > 1 and \
    match[0].distance < 0.6 * match[1].distance
]
```

For details about FLANN matching and the ratio test, refer back to `Chapter 6`, *Retrieving Images and Searching Using Image Descriptors.*

4. At this stage, we have a list of good matches that passed the ratio test. Let's select the subset of the frame's keypoints that correspond to these good matches, and let's draw red circles on the frame to visualize these keypoints:

```
# Select the good keypoints and draw them in red.
good_keypoints = [keypoints[match.queryIdx]
                  for match in good_matches]
cv2.drawKeypoints(self._gray_image, good_keypoints,
                  self._bgr_image, (0, 0, 255))
```

5. Having found the good matches, we obviously know how many of them there are. If the count is small, then, overall, the set of matches can be considered doubtful and inadequate for tracking. We define two different thresholds for the minimum number of good matches: a higher threshold if we are just starting tracking (that is, we were not tracking the object in the previous frame), and a lower threshold if we are continuing tracking (after already tracking the object in the previous frame):

```
min_good_matches_to_start_tracking = 8
min_good_matches_to_continue_tracking = 6
num_good_matches = len(good_matches)
```

5. If we fail to meet even the lower threshold, then we note that we did not track the object in this frame, and we reset the mask so that it covers the whole frame:

```
if num_good_matches < min_good_matches_to_continue_tracking:
    self._was_tracking = False
    self._mask.fill(255)
```

6. On the other hand, if we have enough matches to satisfy the applicable threshold, we proceed to try to track the object. The first step in this is to select the good matches' 2D coordinates in the frame and their 3D coordinates in the model of the `reference` object:

```
elif num_good_matches >= \
        min_good_matches_to_start_tracking or \
            self._was_tracking:

    # Select the 2D coordinates of the good matches.
    # They must be in an array of shape (N, 1, 2).
    good_points_2D = numpy.array(
```

```
        [[keypoint.pt] for keypoint in good_keypoints],
        numpy.float32)

    # Select the 3D coordinates of the good matches.
    # They must be in an array of shape (N, 1, 3).
    good_points_3D = numpy.array(
        [[self._reference_points_3D[match.trainIdx]]
         for match in good_matches],
        numpy.float32)
```

7. Now, we are ready to call `cv2.solvePnPRansac` using the kinds of arguments we described near the start of this chapter, in the *Understanding* `cv2.solvePnPRansac` section. Notably, we use the 3D reference keypoints and the 2D scene keypoints from only the good matches:

```
    # Solve for the pose and find the inlier indices.
    (success, self._rotation_vector,
     self._translation_vector, inlier_indices) = \
        cv2.solvePnPRansac(good_points_3D, good_points_2D,
                           self._camera_matrix,
                           self._distortion_coefficients,
                           self._rotation_vector,
                           self._translation_vector,
                           useExtrinsicGuess=False,
                           iterationsCount=100,
                           reprojectionError=8.0,
                           confidence=0.99,
                           flags=cv2.SOLVEPNP_ITERATIVE)
```

8. The solver may or may not have converged on a solution to the PnP problem. If it did not converge, we do nothing further in this method. If it did converge, the next thing we do is to check whether we were already tracking the object in the previous frame. If we were not already tracking it – in other words, if we are starting to track the object afresh in this frame – then we reinitialize the Kalman filter by calling a helper method, `_init_kalman_state_matrices`:

```
    if success:

        if not self._was_tracking:
            self._init_kalman_state_matrices()
```

9. Now, in any case, we are tracking the object in this frame, so we can apply the Kalman filter by calling another helper method, _apply_kalman:

```
self._was_tracking = True

self._apply_kalman()
```

10. At this stage, we have a Kalman-filtered 6DOF pose. We also have a list of the inlier keypoints from cv2.solvePnPRansac. To help the user visualize the result, let's draw the inlier keypoints in green:

```
# Select the inlier keypoints.
inlier_keypoints = [good_keypoints[i]
                    for i in inlier_indices.flat]

# Draw the inlier keypoints in green.
cv2.drawKeypoints(self._bgr_image, inlier_keypoints,
                  self._bgr_image, (0, 255, 0))
```

Remember that earlier in this method, we drew all the keypoints in red. Now that we have drawn over the inlier keypoints in green, only the outlier keypoints are still red.

11. Finally, we call two more helper methods: the self._draw_object axes to draw the tracked object's 3D axes, and self._make_and_draw_object_mask to make and draw a mask of the region that contains the object:

```
# Draw the axes of the tracked object.
self._draw_object_axes()

# Make and draw a mask around the tracked object.
self._make_and_draw_object_mask()
```

There ends the implementation of our _track_object method. By now, we have a mostly complete picture of our tracking algorithm's implementation, but we still need to implement helper methods relating to the Kalman filter (in the next section, *Initializing and applying the Kalman filter*), and masking and AR drawing (in the section after that, *Drawing the tracking results and masking the tracked object*).

Initializing and applying the Kalman filter

We looked at some aspects of the Kalman filter's initialization earlier, in the *Initializing the tracker* section. However, in that section, we noted that some of Kalman filter's matrices need to be initialized or reinitialized multiple times, as the application runs through various frames and various states of tracking or not tracking. Specifically, the following matrices will change:

- **The transition matrix**: This matrix expresses the temporal relationships among all the output variables. For example, this matrix can model the effects of acceleration on velocity, and of velocity on position. We will reinitialize the transition matrix every frame because the frame rate (and, therefore, the time step between frames) is variable. Effectively, this is a way of scaling the previous predictions of acceleration and velocity to match the new time step.
- **The pre-correction and post-correction state matrices**: These matrices contain the predictions of the output variables. The predictions in the pre-correction matrix only take account of the previous state and the transition matrix. The predictions in the post-correction matrix also take account of new inputs and the Kalman filter's other matrices. We will reinitialize the state matrices whenever we go from a non-tracking state to a tracking state – in other words, when we failed to track the object in the previous frame but now we succeed in tracking it in the current frame. Effectively, this is a way of clearing outdated predictions, and starting afresh from new measurements.

Let's take a look at the transition matrix first. Its initialization method will take one argument, `fps`, that is, the frame rate in frames per second. We can implement the method in three steps:

1. We begin by validating the `fps` argument. If it is not positive, we return immediately without updating the transition matrix:

```
def _init_kalman_transition_matrix(self, fps):

    if fps <= 0.0:
        return
```

2. Having determined that `fps` is positive, we proceed to calculate transition rates for velocity and acceleration. We want the velocity transition rate to be proportional to the time step (that is, the time per frame). Because `fps` (frames per second) is the inverse of the time step (that is, seconds per frame), the velocity transition rate is inversely proportional to `fps`. The acceleration transition rate is proportional to the square of the velocity transition rate (and thus, indirectly, the acceleration transition rate is inversely proportional to the square of `fps`). Choosing 1.0 as a base scale for the velocity transition rate and 0.5 as a base scale for the acceleration transition rate, we can calculate them in code as follows:

```
# Velocity transition rate
vel = 1.0 / fps

# Acceleration transition rate
acc = 0.5 * (vel ** 2.0)
```

3. Next, we populate the transition matrix. Since we have 18 output variables, the transition matrix has 18 rows and 18 columns. First, let's take a look at the content of the matrix, and, afterward, we will consider how to interpret it:

```
self._kalman.transitionMatrix = numpy.array(
    [[1.0, 0.0, 0.0, vel, 0.0, 0.0, acc, 0.0, 0.0,
      0.0, 0.0, 0.0, 0.0, 0.0, 0.0, 0.0, 0.0, 0.0],
     [0.0, 1.0, 0.0, 0.0, vel, 0.0, 0.0, acc, 0.0,
      0.0, 0.0, 0.0, 0.0, 0.0, 0.0, 0.0, 0.0, 0.0],
     [0.0, 0.0, 1.0, 0.0, 0.0, vel, 0.0, 0.0, acc,
      0.0, 0.0, 0.0, 0.0, 0.0, 0.0, 0.0, 0.0, 0.0],
     [0.0, 0.0, 0.0, 1.0, 0.0, 0.0, vel, 0.0, 0.0,
      0.0, 0.0, 0.0, 0.0, 0.0, 0.0, 0.0, 0.0, 0.0],
     [0.0, 0.0, 0.0, 0.0, 1.0, 0.0, 0.0, vel, 0.0,
      0.0, 0.0, 0.0, 0.0, 0.0, 0.0, 0.0, 0.0, 0.0],
     [0.0, 0.0, 0.0, 0.0, 0.0, 1.0, 0.0, 0.0, vel,
      0.0, 0.0, 0.0, 0.0, 0.0, 0.0, 0.0, 0.0, 0.0],
     [0.0, 0.0, 0.0, 0.0, 0.0, 0.0, 1.0, 0.0, 0.0,
      0.0, 0.0, 0.0, 0.0, 0.0, 0.0, 0.0, 0.0, 0.0],
     [0.0, 0.0, 0.0, 0.0, 0.0, 0.0, 0.0, 1.0, 0.0,
      0.0, 0.0, 0.0, 0.0, 0.0, 0.0, 0.0, 0.0, 0.0],
     [0.0, 0.0, 0.0, 0.0, 0.0, 0.0, 0.0, 0.0, 1.0,
      0.0, 0.0, 0.0, 0.0, 0.0, 0.0, 0.0, 0.0, 0.0],
     [0.0, 0.0, 0.0, 0.0, 0.0, 0.0, 0.0, 0.0, 0.0,
      1.0, 0.0, 0.0, vel, 0.0, 0.0, acc, 0.0, 0.0],
     [0.0, 0.0, 0.0, 0.0, 0.0, 0.0, 0.0, 0.0, 0.0,
      0.0, 1.0, 0.0, 0.0, vel, 0.0, 0.0, acc, 0.0],
     [0.0, 0.0, 0.0, 0.0, 0.0, 0.0, 0.0, 0.0, 0.0,
      0.0, 0.0, 1.0, 0.0, 0.0, vel, 0.0, 0.0, acc],
```

```
           [0.0, 0.0, 0.0, 0.0, 0.0, 0.0, 0.0, 0.0, 0.0,
            0.0, 0.0, 0.0, 1.0, 0.0, 0.0, vel, 0.0, 0.0],
           [0.0, 0.0, 0.0, 0.0, 0.0, 0.0, 0.0, 0.0, 0.0,
            0.0, 0.0, 0.0, 0.0, 1.0, 0.0, 0.0, vel, 0.0],
           [0.0, 0.0, 0.0, 0.0, 0.0, 0.0, 0.0, 0.0, 0.0,
            0.0, 0.0, 0.0, 0.0, 0.0, 1.0, 0.0, 0.0, vel],
           [0.0, 0.0, 0.0, 0.0, 0.0, 0.0, 0.0, 0.0, 0.0,
            0.0, 0.0, 0.0, 0.0, 0.0, 0.0, 1.0, 0.0, 0.0],
           [0.0, 0.0, 0.0, 0.0, 0.0, 0.0, 0.0, 0.0, 0.0,
            0.0, 0.0, 0.0, 0.0, 0.0, 0.0, 0.0, 1.0, 0.0],
           [0.0, 0.0, 0.0, 0.0, 0.0, 0.0, 0.0, 0.0, 0.0,
            0.0, 0.0, 0.0, 0.0, 0.0, 0.0, 0.0, 0.0, 1.0]],
       numpy.float32)
```

Each row expresses a formula for calculating a new output value based on the previous frame's output values. Let's consider the first row as an example. We can interpret it as follows:

$$t_x \leftarrow 1(t_x) + 0(t_y) + 0(t_z) + v(t'_x) + 0(t'_y) + 0(t'_z) + a(t''_x) + 0(t''_y) + 0(t''_z) = t_x + v(t'x) + a(t''x)$$

The new t_x value depends on the old t_x, t_x', and t_x'' values, along with the velocity transition rate, v, and the acceleration transition rate, a. As we saw earlier in this function, these transition rates may vary because the time step may vary.

That concludes the implementation of the helper method to initialize or update the transition matrix. Remember that we call this function every frame because the frame rate (and thus the time step) may have changed.

We also need a helper function to initialize the state matrices. Remember that we call this method whenever we transition from a non-tracking state to a tracking state. This transition is an appropriate time to clear out any previous predictions; instead, we are starting afresh with the belief that the object's 6DOF pose is exactly what the PnP solver says it is. Moreover, we assume that the object is stationary, with zero velocity and zero acceleration. Here is the helper method's implementation:

```
def _init_kalman_state_matrices(self):

    t_x, t_y, t_z = self._translation_vector.flat
    r_x, r_y, r_z = self._rotation_vector.flat

    self._kalman.statePre = numpy.array(
        [[t_x], [t_y], [t_z],
         [0.0], [0.0], [0.0],
         [0.0], [0.0], [0.0],
         [r_x], [r_y], [r_z],
         [0.0], [0.0], [0.0],
```

```
          [0.0], [0.0], [0.0]], numpy.float32)
    self._kalman.statePost = numpy.array(
        [[t_x], [t_y], [t_z],
         [0.0], [0.0], [0.0],
         [0.0], [0.0], [0.0],
         [r_x], [r_y], [r_z],
         [0.0], [0.0], [0.0],
         [0.0], [0.0], [0.0]], numpy.float32)
```

Note that the state matrices have one row and 18 columns since we have 18 output variables.

Now that we have covered the process of initializing and reinitializing the Kalman filter's matrices, let's take a look at how we apply the filter. As we have previously seen in `Chapter 8`, *Tracking Objects*, we can ask the Kalman filter to estimate the object's new pose (the pre-correction state of the output variables), then we can tell it to take account of the latest unstabilized tracking result (the input variables) in order to adjust its estimate (thereby producing the post-correction state), and, finally, we can extract variables from the adjusted estimate to use as our stabilized tracking result. Compared to our previous work, the only difference this time is that we have more input and output variables. The following code shows how we implement a method to apply the Kalman filter in the context of our 6DOF tracker:

```
def _apply_kalman(self):

    self._kalman.predict()

    t_x, t_y, t_z = self._translation_vector.flat
    r_x, r_y, r_z = self._rotation_vector.flat

    estimate = self._kalman.correct(numpy.array(
        [[t_x], [t_y], [t_z],
         [r_x], [r_y], [r_z]], numpy.float32))

    self._translation_vector = estimate[0:3]
    self._rotation_vector = estimate[9:12]
```

Here, note that `estimate[0:3]` corresponds to t_x, t_y, and t_z, while `estimate[9:12]` corresponds to r_x, r_y, and r_z. The rest of the `estimate` array corresponds to the first-order derivatives (velocity) and second-order derivatives (acceleration).

By this point, we have almost fully explored the implementation of our 3D tracking algorithm, including the use of the Kalman filter to stabilize the 6DOF pose, as well as the velocity and acceleration. Now, let's turn our attention to two final implementation details of our `ImageTrackingDemo` class: the AR drawing methods and the creation of a mask based on the tracking results.

Drawing the tracking results and masking the tracked object

We will implement one helper method, `_draw_object_axes`, to draw a visualization of the tracked object's *X*, *Y*, and *Z* axes. We will also implement another helper method, `_make_and_draw_object_mask`, to project the object's vertices from 3D to 2D, create a mask based on the object's silhouette, and tint this masked region yellow as a visualization.

Let's start with the implementation of `_draw_object_axes`. We can consider it in three stages:

1. First, we want to take a set of 3D points located along the axes, and project these points to the 2D image space. Remember that we defined the 3D axis points in our `__init__` method, in the *Initializing the tracker* section. They will simply serve as endpoints of the axis arrows that we will draw. Using the `cv2.projectPoints` function, our 6DOF tracking result, and our camera matrix, we can find the 2D projected points as follows:

   ```
   def _draw_object_axes(self):

       points_2D, jacobian = cv2.projectPoints(
           self._reference_axis_points_3D, self._rotation_vector,
           self._translation_vector, self._camera_matrix,
           self._distortion_coefficients)
   ```

    Besides returning the projected 2D points, `cv2.projectPoints` also returns the **Jacobian matrix**, which represents the partial derivatives (with respect to the input parameters) of the function used to calculate the 2D points. This information is potentially useful for camera calibration, but we do not use it in our example.

2. The projected points are in floating-point format, but we will need integers to pass to OpenCV's drawing functions. Thus, we perform the following conversions to integer format:

```
origin = (int(points_2D[0, 0, 0]), int(points_2D[0, 0, 1]))
right = (int(points_2D[1, 0, 0]), int(points_2D[1, 0, 1]))
up = (int(points_2D[2, 0, 0]), int(points_2D[2, 0, 1]))
forward = (int(points_2D[3, 0, 0]), int(points_2D[3, 0, 1]))
```

3. Having calculated the endpoints, we can now draw three arrowed lines to represent the X, Y, and Z axes:

```
# Draw the X axis in red.
cv2.arrowedLine(self._bgr_image, origin, right, (0, 0, 255))

# Draw the Y axis in green.
cv2.arrowedLine(self._bgr_image, origin, up, (0, 255, 0))

# Draw the Z axis in blue.
cv2.arrowedLine(
    self._bgr_image, origin, forward, (255, 0, 0))
```

We have finished implementing _draw_object_axes. Now, let's turn our attention to _make_and_draw_object_mask, which we can also consider in terms of three steps:

1. Like the previous function, this one begins by projecting points from 3D to 2D. This time, we are projecting the reference object's vertices, which we defined in our __init__ method, in the *Initializing the tracker* section. Here is the projection code:

```
def _make_and_draw_object_mask(self):

    # Project the object's vertices into the scene.
    vertices_2D, jacobian = cv2.projectPoints(
        self._reference_vertices_3D, self._rotation_vector,
        self._translation_vector, self._camera_matrix,
        self._distortion_coefficients)
```

2. Again, we convert the projected points from a floating-point format to an integer format (as OpenCV's drawing functions expect integers):

```
vertices_2D = vertices_2D.astype(numpy.int32)
```

3. The projected vertices form a convex polygon. We can paint the mask black (as a background), and then draw this convex polygon in white:

```
# Make a mask based on the projected vertices.
self._mask.fill(0)
for vertex_indices in \
        self._reference_vertex_indices_by_face:
    cv2.fillConvexPoly(
        self._mask, vertices_2D[vertex_indices], 255)
```

Remember that our `_track_object` method will use this mask when it processes the next frame. Specifically, `_track_object` will only look for keypoints in the masked region. Therefore, it will attempt to find the object in the region where we recently found it.

Potentially, we could improve this technique by applying a morphological dilation operation to expand the masked region. In this way, we would search for the object, not only in the region where we recently found it, but also in the surrounding region.

4. Now, in the BGR frame, let's highlight the masked region in yellow in order to visualize the shape of the tracked object. To make a region more yellow, we can subtract a value from the blue channel. The `cv2.subtract` function suits our purpose because it accepts an optional mask argument. Here is how we use it:

```
# Draw the mask in semi-transparent yellow.
cv2.subtract(
    self._bgr_image, 48, self._bgr_image, self._mask)
```

When we tell `cv2.subtract` to subtract a single scalar value such as 48 from an image, it subtracts the value only from the image's first channel – in this case (and most cases), the blue channel of a BGR image. This is arguably a bug, but it is convenient for tinting things yellow!

That was the last method in the ImageTrackingDemo class. Now, let's bring the demo to life by instantiating this class and calling its run method!

Running and testing the application

To complete the implementation of ImageTrackingDemo.py, let's write a main function that launches the application with a specified capture device, FOV, and target frame rate:

```python
def main():

    capture = cv2.VideoCapture(0)
    capture.set(cv2.CAP_PROP_FRAME_WIDTH, 1280)
    capture.set(cv2.CAP_PROP_FRAME_HEIGHT, 720)
    diagonal_fov_degrees = 70.0
    target_fps = 25.0

    demo = ImageTrackingDemo(
        capture, diagonal_fov_degrees, target_fps)
    demo.run()

if __name__ == '__main__':
    main()
```

Here, we are using a capture resolution of 1280 x 720, a diagonal FOV of 70 degrees, and a target frame rate of 25 FPS. You should choose parameters that are appropriate for your camera and lens, and for the speed of your system.

Let's suppose we run the application, and it loads the following image from reference_image.png:

This is, of course, the cover of *OpenCV 4 for Secret Agents* (Packt Publishing, 2019), a book by Joseph Howse. Not only is it a vault of secret knowledge, it is also a good target for image tracking. You should buy a print copy!

During initialization, the application saves the following visualization of the reference keypoints to a new file called `reference_image_keypoints.png`:

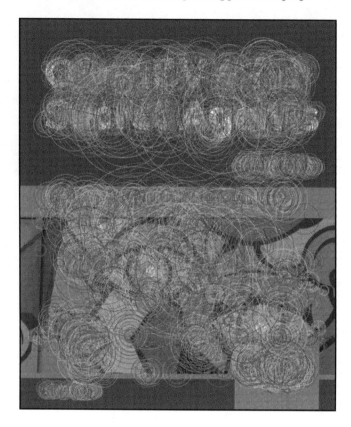

We have seen this type of visualization before in Chapter 6, *Retrieving Images and Searching Using Image Descriptors*. The large circles represent keypoints that can be matched at a small scale (for example, when we view the printed image from a large distance or with a low-resolution camera). The small circles represent keypoints that can be matched at a large scale (for example, when we view the printed image at a close distance or with a high-resolution camera). The best keypoints are the ones marked by many concentric circles, since these can be matched at various scales. Within each circle, the radial line represents the normal orientation of the keypoint.

Studying this visualization, we can infer that this image's best keypoints are concentrated in the high-contrast text (white against dark gray) in the top part of the image. Other useful keypoints are found in many regions, including the high-contrast lines (black against saturated colors) in the bottom part of the image.

Next, we see a camera feed. When we put a print of the reference image in front of the camera, we see an AR visualization of the tracking results:

Of course, the preceding screenshot shows a nearly-frontal view of the book cover. The axis directions are drawn as expected. The X axis (in red) points to the book cover's right (the viewer's left). The Y axis (in green) points up. The Z axis (in blue) points forward from the book cover (toward the viewer). As an AR effect, a semitransparent yellow highlight is superimposed atop the tracked book cover (including the part covered up by Joseph Howse's index finger and middle finger). The positions of the small green and red dots show that in this frame, the good keypoint matches are concentrated in the region of the book's title, and most of these good matches are inliers for `cv2.solvePnPRansac`.

 If you are reading the print edition of this book, the screenshots are reproduced in grayscale. To make the X, Y, and Z axes easier to distinguish in a grayscale print, text labels have been added to the screenshots manually; these text labels are not part of the program's output.

Because we took care to find good keypoints in several regions throughout the image, the tracking can succeed even when a large part of the tracked image is in shadow, covered up, or outside the frame. For example, in the following screenshot, the axis directions and highlighted region are correct, even though most of the book cover (including nearly all of the book title's, with the best keypoints) is outside the frame:

Go ahead and conduct your own experiments with various reference images, cameras, and viewing conditions. Try various resolutions for the reference image and camera. Remember to measure your camera's FOV and adjust the FOV argument accordingly. Study the keypoint visualizations and the tracking results. What kinds of input yield good (or bad) tracking results in our demo?

If you find it inconvenient to use printed images for tracking, you can instead point your camera at a screen (such as a smartphone screen) where you are displaying the image you want to track. Because a screen is backlit (and it might be glossy, too), it might not give a faithful representation of how a printed image would look in any given scene, but it typically works well for a tracker's purposes.

Once you have experimented to your heart's content, let's consider some of the ways our 3D tracker could be improved.

Improving the 3D tracking algorithm

Essentially, our 3D tracking algorithm combines three approaches:

1. Find a 6DOF pose with a PnP solver, whose inputs depend on FLANN-based matches of ORB descriptors.
2. Use a Kalman filter to stabilize the 6DOF tracking result.
3. If an object was tracked in the previous frame, use a mask to limit the search to the region where the object is now most likely to be found.

Often, commercial solutions for 3D tracking involve additional approaches. We have relied on successfully using a descriptor matcher and a PnP solver for every frame; however, a more complex algorithm may provide some alternatives as fallbacks or as cross-checking mechanisms. This is in case the descriptor matcher and PnP solver miss the object in some frames, or in case they are too computationally expensive to use for every frame. The following alternatives are widely used:

- Update the previous keypoint matches based on optical flow, and update the previous 6DOF pose based on the homography between the keypoints' old and new positions (according to the optical flow).
- Update the rotational component of the 6DOF pose based on a gyroscope and magnetometer (compass). Typically, even in consumer devices, these sensors can successfully measure small or large changes in rotation.
- Update the positional component of the 6DOF pose based on a barometer and GPS. Typically, in consumer devices, a barometer can measure changes in altitude with an accuracy of approximately 10 cm, while GPS can measure changes in longitude and latitude with an accuracy of approximately 10 m. Depending on the use case, these may or may not be usable levels of accuracy. If we are attempting to perform AR on large and distant features of a landscape – for example, if we want to draw a virtual dragon perched atop a real mountaintop – then 10 m accuracy may be fine. For detailed work – for example, if we want to draw a virtual ring on a real finger – 10 cm accuracy is unusable.
- Update the positional acceleration component of the Kalman filter based on an accelerometer. Typically, in consumer devices, accelerometers suffer from drift (a tendency for errors to exhibit runaway growth in one direction or another), so this option should be approached with caution.

These alternative techniques are beyond the scope of this book – and, indeed, some of them are not computer vision techniques – so we leave them to you for independent study.

A final word: Sometimes, significant improvements in tracking results are achievable by altering a preprocessing algorithm rather than the tracking algorithm per se. Earlier in this chapter, in the *Performing grayscale conversion* section, we mentioned Macêdo, Melo, and Kelner's paper on grayscale conversion algorithms and SIFT descriptors. You may wish to read that paper and conduct your own experiments to determine how the choice of grayscale conversion algorithm affects the number of tracking inliers when using ORB descriptors or other types of descriptors.

Summary

This chapter introduced AR, along with a robust set of approaches to the problem of tracking an image in 3D space.

We began by learning the concept of 6DOF tracking. We recognized that familiar tools such as ORB descriptors, FLANN-based matching, and Kalman filtering are useful in this kind of tracking, but that we also needed to work with camera and lens parameters in order to solve the PnP problem.

Next, we addressed practical considerations of how best to represent a reference object (such as a book cover or a photo print) in the form of a grayscale image, a set of 2D keypoints, and a set of 3D keypoints.

We proceeded to implement a class that encapsulated a demo of image tracking in 3D space, with a 3D highlighting effect as a basic form of AR. Our implementation dealt with real-time considerations, such as the need to update the Kalman filter's transition matrix based on fluctuations in the frame rate.

Finally, we considered ways to potentially improve the 3D tracking algorithm using additional computer vision techniques, or other sensor-based techniques.

Now, we are approaching the book's final chapter, which offers a different perspective on many of the problems we have tackled up to this point. We can set aside (for now) our thoughts of cameras and geometry, and instead start thinking as statisticians, because we are going to deepen our knowledge of machine learning with a look at **artificial neural networks (ANNs)**.

10
Introduction to Neural Networks with OpenCV

This chapter introduces a family of machine learning models called **artificial neural networks (ANNs)**, or sometimes just **neural networks**. A key characteristic of these models is that they attempt to learn relationships among variables in a multi-layered fashion; they learn multiple functions to predict intermediate results before combining these into a single function to predict something meaningful (such as the class of an object). Recent versions of OpenCV contain an increasing amount of functionality related to ANNs – and, in particular, ANNs with many layers, called **deep neural networks (DNNs)**. We will experiment with both shallower ANNs and DNNs in this chapter.

We have already gained some exposure to machine learning in other chapters – especially in Chapter 7, *Building Custom Object Detectors*, where we developed a car/non-car classifier using SURF descriptors, a BoW, and an SVM. With this basis for comparison, you might be wondering, what is so special about ANNs? Why are we devoting this book's final chapter to them?

ANNs aim to provide superior accuracy in the following circumstances:

- There are many input variables, which may have complex, nonlinear relationships to each other.
- There are many output variables, which may have complex, nonlinear relationships to the input variables. (Typically, the output variables in a classification problem are the confidence scores for the classes, so if there are many classes, there are many output variables.)

- There are many hidden (unspecified) variables that may have complex, nonlinear relationships to the input and output variables. DNNs even aim to model *multiple* layers of hidden variables, which are interrelated primarily to each other rather than being related primarily to input or output variables.

These circumstances exist in many – perhaps most – real-world problems. Thus, the promised advantages of ANNs and DNNs are enticing. On the other hand, ANNs and especially DNNs are notoriously opaque models, insofar as they work by predicting the existence of an arbitrary number of nameless, hidden variables that may relate to everything else.

Over the course of this chapter, we will cover the following topics:

- Understanding ANNs as a statistical model and as a tool for supervised machine learning.
- Understanding ANN topology or, in other words, the organization of an ANN into layers of interconnected neurons. Particularly, we will consider the topology that enables an ANN to act as a type of classifier known as a **multi-layer perceptron (MLP)**.
- Training and using ANNs as classifiers in OpenCV.
- Building an application that detects and recognizes handwritten digits (0 to 9). For this, we will train an ANN based on a widely used dataset called MNIST, which contains samples of handwritten digits.
- Loading and using pre-trained DNNs in OpenCV. We will cover examples of object classification, face detection, and gender classification with DNNs.

By the end of this chapter, you will be in a good position to train and use ANNs in OpenCV, to use pre-trained DNNs from a variety of sources, and to start exploring other libraries that allow you to train your own DNNs.

Technical requirements

This chapter uses Python, OpenCV, and NumPy. Please refer to `Chapter 1`, *Setting Up OpenCV*, for installation instructions.

The completed code and sample videos for this chapter can be found in this book's GitHub repository, `https://github.com/PacktPublishing/Learning-OpenCV-4-Computer-Vision-with-Python-Third-Edition`, in the `chapter10` folder.

Understanding ANNs

Let's define ANNs in terms of their basic role and components. Although much of the literature on ANNs emphasizes the idea that they are *biologically inspired* by the way neurons connect in a brain, we don't need to be biologists or neuroscientists to understand the fundamental concepts of an ANN.

First of all, an ANN is a **statistical model**. What is a statistical model? A statistical model is a pair of elements, namely the space S (a set of observations) and the probability, P, where P is a distribution that approximates S (in other words, a function that would generate a set of observations that is very similar to S).

Here are two different ways to think of P:

- P is a simplification of a complex scenario.
- P is the function that generated S in the first place, or at the very least a set of observations very similar to S.

Thus, ANNs are models that take a complex reality, simplify it, and deduce a function to (approximately) represent the statistical observations we would expect from that reality, in a mathematical form.

ANNs, like other types of machine learning models, can learn from observations in one of the following ways:

- **Supervised learning**: Under this approach, we want the model's training process to produce a function that maps a known set of input variables to a known set of output variables. We know, *a priori*, the nature of the prediction problem, and we delegate the process of finding a function that solves this problem to the ANN. To train the model, we must provide input samples along with the correct, corresponding outputs. For a classification problem, the output variables may be confidence scores for one or more classes.

- **Unsupervised learning**: Under this approach, the set of output variables is not known *a priori*. The model's training process must yield a set of output variables, as well as a function to map the input variables to these output variables. For a classification problem, unsupervised learning can lead to the discovery of previously unknown classes, such as previously unknown diseases in the context of medical data. Unsupervised learning may use techniques including (but not limited to) clustering, which we explored in the context of BoW models in `Chapter 7`, *Building Custom Object Detectors*.

- **Reinforcement learning**: This approach turns the typical prediction problem upside down. Before training the model, we already have a system that yields values for a known set of output variables when we feed it values for a known set of input variables. We know, *a priori*, a way of scoring a sequence of outputs based on their goodness (desirability) or lack thereof. However, we might not know the real function that maps inputs to outputs – or, even if we do know it, it is so complex that we cannot solve it for optimal inputs. Thus, we want the model's training process to produce a function that predicts the next-in-sequence optimal inputs, based on the last outputs. During training, the model learns from the score that eventually arises from its actions (its chosen inputs). Essentially, the model must learn to become a good decision-maker within the context of a particular system of rewards and punishments.

Throughout the remainder of this chapter, we will confine our discussions to supervised learning, as this is the most common approach to machine learning in the context of computer vision.

The next step in our journey toward comprehending ANNs is to understand how an ANN improves on the concept of a simple statistical model, and on other types of machine learning.

What if the function that generated the dataset is likely to take a large number of (unknown) inputs?

The strategy that ANNs adopt is to delegate work to a number of **neurons**, **nodes**, or **units**, each of which is capable of approximating the function that created the inputs. In mathematics, approximation is the process of defining a simpler function whose output is similar to that of a more complex function, at least for some range of inputs.

The difference between the approximate function's output and the original function's output is called the **error**. A defining characteristic of a neural network is that the neurons must be capable of approximating a nonlinear function.

Let's take a closer look at neurons.

Understanding neurons and perceptrons

Often, to solve a classification problem, an ANN is designed as a **multi-layer perceptron (MLP)**, in which each neuron acts as a kind of binary classifier called a **perceptron**. The perceptron is a concept that dates back to the 1950s. To put it simply, a perceptron is a function that takes a number of inputs and produces a single value. Each of the inputs has an associated weight that signifies its importance in an **activation function**. The activation function should have a nonlinear response; for example, a sigmoid function (sometimes called an S-curve) is a common choice. A threshold function, called a **discriminant**, is applied to the activation function's output to convert it into a binary classification of 0 or 1. Here is a visualization of this sequence, with inputs on the left, the activation function in the middle, and the discriminant on the right:

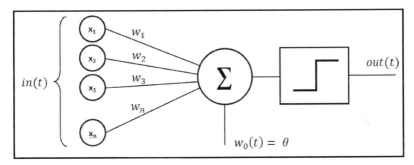

What do the input weights represent, and how are they determined?

Neurons are interconnected, insofar as one neuron's output can be an input for many other neurons. Each input weight defines the strength of the connection between two neurons. These weights are adaptive, meaning that they change in time according to a learning algorithm.

Due to the neurons' interconnectedness, the network has layers. Now, let's examine how these layers are typically organized.

Understanding the layers of a neural network

Here is a visual representation of a neural network:

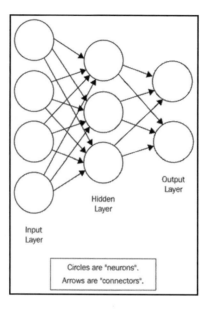

As the preceding diagram shows, there are at least three distinct layers in a neural network: the **input layer**, the **hidden layer**, and the **output layer**. There can be more than one hidden layer; however, one hidden layer is enough to resolve many real-life problems. A neural network with multiple hidden layers is sometimes called a **deep neural network (DNN)**.

 If we are using an ANN as a classifier, then each output node's output value is a confidence score for a class. For a given sample (that is, a given set of input values), we want to know which output node produces the highest output value. This highest-scoring output node corresponds to the predicted class.

How do we determine the network's topology, and how many neurons do we need to create for each layer? Let's make this determination layer by layer.

Choosing the size of the input layer

The number of nodes in the input layer is, by definition, the number of inputs into the network. For example, let's say you want to create an ANN to help you determine an animal's species based on measurements of its physical attributes. In principle, we can choose any measurable attributes. If we choose to classify animals based on weight, length, and number of teeth, that is a set of three attributes, and thus our network needs to contain three input nodes.

Are these three input nodes an adequate basis for species classification? Well, in a real-life problem, surely not – but in a toy problem, it depends on the output we are trying to achieve, and this is our next consideration.

Choosing the size of the output layer

For a classifier, the number of nodes in the output layer is, by definition, the number of classes the network can distinguish. Continuing with the preceding example of an animal classification network, we can use an output layer of four nodes if we know we are going to deal with the following animals: dog, condor, dolphin, and dragon(!). If we try to classify data for an animal that is not in one of these categories, the network will predict the class that is most likely to resemble this unrepresented animal.

Now, we come to a difficult problem – the size of the hidden layer.

Choosing the size of the hidden layer

There are no agreed-upon rules of thumb for choosing the size of the hidden layer; it must be chosen based on experimentation. For every real-world problem where you want to apply ANNs, you will need to train, test, and retrain your ANN until you find a number of hidden nodes that yield acceptable accuracy.

Of course, even when choosing a parameter's value by experimentation, you might wish for the experts to suggest a starting value, or a range of values, for your tests. Unfortunately, there is no expert consensus on these points either. Some experts offer rules of thumb based on the following broad suggestions (these should be taken with a grain of salt):

- If the input layer is large, the number of hidden neurons should be between the size of the input layer and the size of the output layer – and, typically, closer to the size of the output layer.

- On the other hand, if the input and output layers are both small, the hidden layer should be the largest layer.
- If the input layer is small but the output layer is large, the hidden layer should be closer to the size of the input layer.

Other experts suggest that the number of training samples also needs to be taken into account; a greater number of training samples implies that a greater number of hidden nodes might be useful.

One critical factor to keep in mind is **overfitting**. Overfitting occurs when there is such an inordinate amount of pseudo-information contained in the hidden layer, compared to the information actually provided by the training data, that the classification is not very meaningful. The larger the hidden layer, the more training data it requires in order for it to learn properly. Of course, as the size of the training dataset grows, so does the training time.

For some of the ANN sample projects in this chapter, we will use a hidden layer size of 60 as a starting point. Given a large training set, 60 hidden nodes can yield decent accuracy for a variety of classification problems.

Now that we have a general idea of what ANNs are, let's see how OpenCV implements them, and how to put them to good use. We will start with a minimal code example. Then, we will flesh out the animal-themed classifier that we discussed in the previous two sections. Finally, we will work our way up to a more realistic application, in which we will classify handwritten digits based on image data.

Training a basic ANN in OpenCV

OpenCV provides a class, `cv2.ml_ANN_MLP`, that implements an ANN as a **multi-layer perceptron (MLP)**. This is exactly the kind of model we described earlier, in the *Understanding neurons and perceptrons* section.

To create an instance of `cv2.ml_ANN_MLP`, and to format data for this ANN's training and use, we rely on functionality in OpenCV's machine learning module, `cv2.ml`. As you may recall, this is the same module that we used for SVM-related functionality in Chapter 7, *Building Custom Object Detectors*. Moreover, `cv2.ml_ANN_MLP` and `cv2.ml_SVM` share a common base class called `cv2.ml_StatModel`. Therefore, you will find that OpenCV provides similar APIs for ANNs and SVMs.

Let's examine a dummy example as a gentle introduction to ANNs. This example will use completely meaningless data, but it will show us the basic API for training and using an ANN in OpenCV:

1. To begin, we import OpenCV and NumPy as usual:

```
import cv2
import numpy as np
```

2. Now, we create an untrained ANN:

```
ann = cv2.ml.ANN_MLP_create()
```

3. After creating the ANN, we need to configure its number of layers and nodes:

```
ann.setLayerSizes(np.array([9, 15, 9], np.uint8))
```

The layer sizes are defined by the NumPy array that we pass to the setLayerSizes method. The first element is the size of the input layer, the last element is the size of the output layer, and all the in-between elements define the sizes of the hidden layers. For example, [9, 15, 9] specifies 9 input nodes, 9 output nodes, and a single hidden layer with 15 nodes. If we changed this to [9, 15, 13, 9], it would specify two hidden layers with 15 and 13 nodes, respectively.

4. We can also configure the activation function, the training method, and the training termination criteria, as follows:

```
ann.setActivationFunction(cv2.ml.ANN_MLP_SIGMOID_SYM, 0.6, 1.0)
ann.setTrainMethod(cv2.ml.ANN_MLP_BACKPROP, 0.1, 0.1)
ann.setTermCriteria(
    (cv2.TERM_CRITERIA_MAX_ITER | cv2.TERM_CRITERIA_EPS, 100, 1.0))
```

Here, we are using a symmetrical sigmoid activation function (cv2.ml.ANN_MLP_SIGMOID_SYM) and a backpropagation training method (cv2.ml.ANN_MLP_BACKPROP). Backpropagation is an algorithm that calculates errors of predictions at the output layer, traces the sources of the errors backward through previous layers, and updates the weights in order to reduce errors.

5. Let's train the ANN. We need to specify training inputs (or `samples`, in OpenCV's terminology), the corresponding correct outputs (or `responses`), and whether the data's format (or `layout`) is one row per sample or one column per sample. Here is an example of how we train the model with a single sample:

```
training_samples = np.array(
    [[1.2, 1.3, 1.9, 2.2, 2.3, 2.9, 3.0, 3.2, 3.3]], np.float32)
layout = cv2.ml.ROW_SAMPLE
training_responses = np.array(
    [[0.0, 0.0, 0.0, 0.0, 0.0, 1.0, 0.0, 0.0, 0.0]], np.float32)
data = cv2.ml.TrainData_create(
    training_samples, layout, training_responses)
ann.train(data)
```

Realistically, we would want to train any ANN with a larger dataset that contains far more than one sample. We could do this by extending `training_samples` and `training_responses` so that they contain multiple rows, representing multiple samples and their corresponding responses. Alternatively, we could call the ANN's `train` method multiple times, with new data each time. The latter approach requires some additional arguments for the `train` method, and it is demonstrated in the next section, *Training an ANN- classifier in multiple epochs*.

Note that in this case, we are training the ANN as a classifier. Each response is a confidence score for a class, and in this case, there are nine classes. We will refer to them by their 0-based indices, as classes 0 to 8. Our training sample in this case has a response of `[0.0, 0.0, 0.0, 0.0, 0.0, 1.0, 0.0, 0.0, 0.0]`, meaning that it is an instance of class 5 (with confidence 1.0), and it is definitely not an instance of any other class (as the confidence is 0.0 for every other class).

6. To complete our minimal tour of the ANN's API, let's make another sample, classify it, and print the result:

```
test_samples = np.array(
    [[1.4, 1.5, 1.2, 2.0, 2.5, 2.8, 3.0, 3.1, 3.8]], np.float32)
prediction = ann.predict(test_samples)
print(prediction)
```

This will print the following result:

```
(5.0, array([[-0.08763029, -0.01616517, 0.13196233, 0.0402631 , 0.05711843,
        1.1642447 , 0.18130444, 0.1857026 , -0.07486832]],
      dtype=float32))
```

This means that the provided input was classified as belonging to class 5. Again, this is only a dummy example and the classification is pretty meaningless; however, the network behaved correctly. In the preceding code, we only provided one training record, which was a sample of class 5, so the network classified a new input as belonging to class 5. (As far as our woefully limited training dataset suggests, other classes besides 5 might never occur.)

As you may have guessed, the output of a prediction is a tuple, with the first value being the class and the second being an array containing the probabilities for each class. The predicted class will have the highest value.

Let's move on to a slightly more believable example – animal classification.

Training an ANN classifier in multiple epochs

Let's create an ANN that attempts to classify animals based on three measurements: weight, length, and number of teeth. This is, of course, a mock scenario. Realistically, no one would describe an animal with just these three statistics. However, our intent is to improve our understanding of ANNs before we start applying them to image data.

Compared to the minimal example in the previous section, our animal classification mock-up will be more sophisticated in the following ways:

- We will increase the number of neurons in the hidden layer.
- We will use a larger training dataset. For convenience, we will generate this dataset pseudorandomly.
- We will train the ANN in multiple epochs, meaning that we will train and retrain it multiple times with the same dataset each time.

The number of neurons in the hidden layer is an important parameter that needs to be tested in order to optimize the accuracy of any ANN. You will find that a larger hidden layer may improve accuracy up to a point, and then it will overfit, unless you start compensating with an enormous training dataset. Likewise, up to a point, a greater number of epochs may improve accuracy, but too many will result in overfitting.

Let's go through the implementation step by step:

1. First, we import OpenCV and NumPy as usual. Then, from the Python standard library, we import the `randint` function to generate pseudorandom integers and the `uniform` function to generate pseudorandom floating-point numbers:

```
import cv2
import numpy as np
from random import randint, uniform
```

2. Next, we create and configure the ANN. This time, we use a three-neuron input layer, a 50-neuron hidden layer, and a four-neuron output layer, as highlighted **in bold** in the following code:

```
animals_net = cv2.ml.ANN_MLP_create()
animals_net.setLayerSizes(np.array([3, 50, 4]))
animals_net.setActivationFunction(cv2.ml.ANN_MLP_SIGMOID_SYM, 0.6,
1.0)
animals_net.setTrainMethod(cv2.ml.ANN_MLP_BACKPROP, 0.1, 0.1)
animals_net.setTermCriteria(
    (cv2.TERM_CRITERIA_MAX_ITER | cv2.TERM_CRITERIA_EPS, 100, 1.0))
```

3. Now, we need some data. We aren't really interested in representing animals accurately; we just require a bunch of records to be used as training data. Thus, we define four functions in order to generate random samples of different classes, along with another four functions to generate the correct classification results for training purposes:

```
"""Input arrays
weight, length, teeth
"""

"""Output arrays
dog, condor, dolphin, dragon
"""

def dog_sample():
    return [uniform(10.0, 20.0), uniform(1.0, 1.5),
```

```
        randint(38, 42)]

def dog_class():
    return [1, 0, 0, 0]

def condor_sample():
    return [uniform(3.0, 10.0), randint(3.0, 5.0), 0]

def condor_class():
    return [0, 1, 0, 0]

def dolphin_sample():
    return [uniform(30.0, 190.0), uniform(5.0, 15.0),
        randint(80, 100)]

def dolphin_class():
    return [0, 0, 1, 0]

def dragon_sample():
    return [uniform(1200.0, 1800.0), uniform(30.0, 40.0),
        randint(160, 180)]

def dragon_class():
    return [0, 0, 0, 1]
```

4. We also define the following helper function in order to convert a sample and classification into a pair of NumPy arrays:

```
def record(sample, classification):
    return (np.array([sample], np.float32),
            np.array([classification], np.float32))
```

5. Let's proceed with the creation of our fake animal data. We will create 20,000 samples per class:

```
RECORDS = 20000
records = []
for x in range(0, RECORDS):
    records.append(record(dog_sample(), dog_class()))
    records.append(record(condor_sample(), condor_class()))
    records.append(record(dolphin_sample(), dolphin_class()))
    records.append(record(dragon_sample(), dragon_class()))
```

6. Now, let's train the ANN. As we discussed at the start of this section, we will use multiple training epochs. Each epoch is an iteration of a loop, as shown in the following code:

```
EPOCHS = 10
for e in range(0, EPOCHS):
    print("epoch: %d" % e)
    for t, c in records:
        data = cv2.ml.TrainData_create(t, cv2.ml.ROW_SAMPLE, c)
        if animals_net.isTrained():
            animals_net.train(data, cv2.ml.ANN_MLP_UPDATE_WEIGHTS |
cv2.ml.ANN_MLP_NO_INPUT_SCALE | cv2.ml.ANN_MLP_NO_OUTPUT_SCALE)
        else:
            animals_net.train(data, cv2.ml.ANN_MLP_NO_INPUT_SCALE |
cv2.ml.ANN_MLP_NO_OUTPUT_SCALE)
```

For real-world problems with large and diverse training datasets, an ANN can potentially benefit from hundreds of training epochs. For the best results, you may wish to keep training and testing an ANN until you reach convergence, which means that further epochs no longer produce a noticeable improvement in the accuracy of the results.

Note that we must pass the `cv2.ml.ANN_MLP_UPDATE_WEIGHTS` flag to the ANN's `train` function to update the previously trained model rather than training a new model from scratch. This is a critical point to remember whenever you are training a model incrementally, as we are doing here.

7. Having trained our ANN, we should test it. For each class, let's generate 100 new random samples, classify them using the ANN, and keep track of the number of correct classifications:

```
TESTS = 100

dog_results = 0
for x in range(0, TESTS):
    clas = int(animals_net.predict(
        np.array([dog_sample()], np.float32))[0])
    print("class: %d" % clas)
    if clas == 0:
        dog_results += 1

condor_results = 0
for x in range(0, TESTS):
    clas = int(animals_net.predict(
        np.array([condor_sample()], np.float32))[0])
    print("class: %d" % clas)
```

```
        if clas == 1:
            condor_results += 1

    dolphin_results = 0
    for x in range(0, TESTS):
        clas = int(animals_net.predict(
            np.array([dolphin_sample()], np.float32))[0])
        print("class: %d" % clas)
        if clas == 2:
            dolphin_results += 1

    dragon_results = 0
    for x in range(0, TESTS):
        clas = int(animals_net.predict(
            np.array([dragon_sample()], np.float32))[0])
        print("class: %d" % clas)
        if clas == 3:
            dragon_results += 1
```

8. Finally, let's print the accuracy statistics:

```
    print("dog accuracy: %.2f%%" % (100.0 * dog_results / TESTS))
    print("condor accuracy: %.2f%%" % (100.0 * condor_results / TESTS))
    print("dolphin accuracy: %.2f%%" % \
        (100.0 * dolphin_results / TESTS))
    print("dragon accuracy: %.2f%%" % (100.0 * dragon_results / TESTS))
```

When we run the script, the preceding code block should produce the following output:

```
dog accuracy: 100.00%
condor accuracy: 100.00%
dolphin accuracy: 100.00%
dragon accuracy: 100.00%
```

Since we are dealing with random data, the results may vary each time you run the script. Typically, the accuracy should be high or even perfect because we have set up a simple classification problem with non-overlapping ranges of input data. (The range of random weight values for a dog does not overlap with the range for a dragon, and so forth.)

You may wish to take some time to experiment with the following modifications (one at a time) so that you can see how the ANN's accuracy is affected:

- Change the number of training samples by modifying the value of the RECORDS variable.
- Change the number of training epochs by modifying the value of the EPOCHS variable.

- Make the ranges of input data partially overlapping by editing the parameters of the `uniform` and `randint` function calls in our `dog_sample`, `condor_sample`, `dolphin_sample`, and `dragon_sample` functions.

When you are ready, we will proceed with an example containing real-life image data. With this, we will train an ANN to recognize handwritten digits.

Recognizing handwritten digits with an ANN

A handwritten digit is any of the 10 Arabic numerals (0 to 9), written manually with a pen or pencil, as opposed to being printed by a machine. The appearance of handwritten digits can vary significantly. Different people have different handwriting, and – with the possible exception of a skilled calligrapher – a person does not produce identical digits every time he or she writes. This variability means that the visual recognition of handwritten digits is a non-trivial problem for machine learning. Indeed, students and researchers in machine learning often test their skills and new algorithms by attempting to train an accurate recognizer for handwritten digits. We will approach this challenge in the following manner:

1. Load data from a Python-friendly version of the MNIST database. This is a widely used database containing images of handwritten digits.
2. Using the MNIST data, train an ANN in multiple epochs.
3. Load an image of a sheet of paper with many handwritten digits on it.
4. Based on contour analysis, detect the individual digits on the paper.
5. Use our ANN to classify the detected digits.
6. Review the results in order to determine the accuracy of our detector and our ANN-based classifier.

Before we delve into the implementation, let's review some information about the MNIST database.

Understanding the MNIST database of handwritten digits

The **MNIST** database (or **Modified National Institute of Standards and Technology** database) is publicly available at `http://yann.lecun.com/exdb/mnist/`. The database includes a training set of 60,000 images of handwritten digits. Half of these were written by employees of the United States Census Bureau, while the other half were written by high school students in the United States.

The database also includes a test set of 10,000 images, gathered from the same writers. All the training and test images are in grayscale format, with dimensions of 28 x 28 pixels. The digits are white (or shades of gray) on a black background. For example, here are three of the MNIST training samples:

 As an alternative to using MNIST, you could, of course, build a similar database yourself. This would involve collecting a large number of images of handwritten digits, converting the images into grayscale, cropping them so that each image contains a single digit in a standardized position, and scaling the images so that they are all the same size. You would also need to label the images so that a program could read the correct classification for the purpose of training and testing a classifier.

Many authors provide examples of how to use the MNIST database with various machine learning libraries and algorithms – not just OpenCV and not just ANNs. Michael Nielsen, the author of the free online book *Neural Networks and Deep Learning*, devotes a chapter to MNIST and ANNs here: `http://neuralnetworksanddeeplearning.com/chap1.html`. He shows how to implement an ANN almost from scratch, using only NumPy, and this is excellent reading if you want to deepen your understanding beyond the kind of high-level functionality that OpenCV exposes. His code is freely available on GitHub at `https://github.com/mnielsen/neural-networks-and-deep-learning`.

Nielsen provides a version of MNIST as a `PKL.GZ` (gzip-compressed Pickle) file, which can be easily loaded into Python. For the purposes of our book's OpenCV sample, we (the authors) have taken Nielsen's `PKL.GZ` version of MNIST, reorganized it for our purposes, and placed it inside this book's GitHub repository at `chapter10/digits_data/mnist.pkl.gz`.

Now that we know something about the MNIST database, let's consider what ANN parameters are appropriate for this training set.

Choosing training parameters for the MNIST database

Each MNIST sample is an image containing 784 pixels (that is, 28 x 28 pixels). Thus, our ANN's input layer will have 784 nodes. The output layer will have 10 nodes because there are 10 classes of digits (0 to 9).

We are free to choose the values of other parameters, such as the number of nodes in the hidden layer, the number of training samples to use, and the number of training epochs. As usual, experimentation can help us find values that offer acceptable training time and accuracy, without overfitting the model to the training data. Based on some experimentation that the authors of this book have done, we will use 60 hidden nodes, 50,000 training samples, and 10 epochs. These parameters will be good enough for a preliminary test, keeping the training time down to a few minutes (depending on the processing power of your machine).

Implementing a module to train the ANN

Training an ANN based on MNIST is something you might want to do in future projects as well. To make our code more reusable, we can write a Python module that is solely dedicated to this training process. Then (in the next section, *Implementing the main module*), we will import this training module into a main module, where we will implement our demonstration of digit detection and classification.

Let's implement the training module in a file called `digits_ann.py`:

1. To begin, we will import the `gzip` and `pickle` modules from the Python standard library. As usual, we will also import OpenCV and NumPy:

   ```
   import gzip
   import pickle

   import cv2
   import numpy as np
   ```

   We will use the `gzip` and `pickle` modules to decompress and load the MNIST data from the `mnist.pkl.gz` file. We briefly mentioned this file earlier, in the *Understanding the MNIST database of handwritten digits* section. It contains the MNIST data in nested tuples, in the following format:

   ```
   ((training_images, training_ids),
    (test_images, test_ids))
   ```

In turn, the elements of these tuples are in the following format:

- `training_images` is a NumPy array of 60,000 images, where each image is a vector of 784-pixel values (flattened from an original shape of 28 x 28 pixels). The pixel values are floating-point numbers in the range 0.0 (black) to 1.0 (white), inclusive.
- `training_ids` is a NumPy array of 60,000 digit IDs, where each ID is a number in the range 0 to 9, inclusive. `training_ids[i]` corresponds to `training_images[i]`.
- `test_images` is a NumPy array of 10,000 images, where each image is a vector of 784-pixel values (flattened from an original shape of 28 x 28 pixels). The pixel values are floating-point numbers in the range 0.0 (black) to 1.0 (white), inclusive.
- `test_ids` is a NumPy array of 10,000 digit IDs, where each ID is a number in the range 0 to 9, inclusive. `test_ids[i]` corresponds to `test_images[i]`.

2. Let's write the following helper function to decompress and load the contents of `mnist.pkl.gz`:

```
def load_data():
    mnist = gzip.open('./digits_data/mnist.pkl.gz', 'rb')
    training_data, test_data = pickle.load(mnist)
    mnist.close()
    return (training_data, test_data)
```

Note that in the preceding code, `training_data` is a tuple, equivalent to `(training_images, training_ids)`, and `test_data` is also a tuple, equivalent to `(test_images, test_ids)`.

3. We must reformat the raw data in order to match the format that OpenCV expects. Specifically, when we provide sample output to train the ANN, it must be a vector with 10 elements (for 10 classes of digits), rather than a single digit ID. For convenience, we will also apply Python's built-in `zip` function to reorganize the data in such a way that we can iterate over matching pairs of input and output vectors as tuples. Let's write the following helper function to reformat the data:

```
def wrap_data():
    tr_d, te_d = load_data()
    training_inputs = tr_d[0]
    training_results = [vectorized_result(y) for y in tr_d[1]]
```

```
training_data = zip(training_inputs, training_results)
test_data = zip(te_d[0], te_d[1])
return (training_data, test_data)
```

4. Note that the preceding code calls `load_data` and another helper function,
   `vectorized_result`. The latter function converts an ID into a classification
   vector, as follows:

```
def vectorized_result(j):
    e = np.zeros((10,), np.float32)
    e[j] = 1.0
    return e
```

For example, the ID `1` is converted into a NumPy array containing the values
`[0.0, 1.0, 0.0, 0.0, 0.0, 0.0, 0.0, 0.0, 0.0. 0.0]`. This 10-element
array, as you may have guessed, corresponds to the ANN's output layer, and we
can use it as a sample of correct output when we train the ANN.

The preceding functions – `load_data`, `wrap_data`, and
`vectorized_result` – have been adapted from Nielsen's code for
loading his version of `mnist.pkl.gz`. For more information about
Nielsen's work, refer to the *Understanding the MNIST database of
handwritten digits* section of this chapter.

5. So far, we have written functions that load and reformat MNIST data. Now, let's
   write a function that will create an untrained ANN:

```
def create_ann(hidden_nodes=60):
    ann = cv2.ml.ANN_MLP_create()
    ann.setLayerSizes(np.array([784, hidden_nodes, 10]))
    ann.setActivationFunction(cv2.ml.ANN_MLP_SIGMOID_SYM, 0.6, 1.0)
    ann.setTrainMethod(cv2.ml.ANN_MLP_BACKPROP, 0.1, 0.1)
    ann.setTermCriteria(
        (cv2.TERM_CRITERIA_MAX_ITER | cv2.TERM_CRITERIA_EPS,
        100, 1.0))
    return ann
```

Note that we have hardcoded the sizes of the input and output layers, based on
the nature of the MNIST data. However, we have allowed the caller of this
function to specify the number of nodes in the hidden layer.

For further discussion of parameters, refer to the *Choosing training
parameters for the MNIST database* section of this chapter.

6. Now, we need a training function that allows the caller to specify the number of MNIST training samples and the number of epochs. Much of the training functionality should be familiar from our previous ANN samples, so let's look at the implementation in its entirety and then discuss some details afterward:

```python
def train(ann, samples=50000, epochs=10):

    tr, test = wrap_data()

    # Convert iterator to list so that we can iterate multiple
    # times in multiple epochs.
    tr = list(tr)

    for epoch in range(epochs):
        print("Completed %d/%d epochs" % (epoch, epochs))
        counter = 0
        for img in tr:
            if (counter > samples):
                break
            if (counter % 1000 == 0):
                print("Epoch %d: Trained on %d/%d samples" % \
                    (epoch, counter, samples))
            counter += 1
            sample, response = img
            data = cv2.ml.TrainData_create(
                np.array([sample], dtype=np.float32),
                cv2.ml.ROW_SAMPLE,
                np.array([response], dtype=np.float32))
            if ann.isTrained():
                ann.train(data, cv2.ml.ANN_MLP_UPDATE_WEIGHTS |
cv2.ml.ANN_MLP_NO_INPUT_SCALE | cv2.ml.ANN_MLP_NO_OUTPUT_SCALE)
            else:
                ann.train(data, cv2.ml.ANN_MLP_NO_INPUT_SCALE |
cv2.ml.ANN_MLP_NO_OUTPUT_SCALE)
    print("Completed all epochs!")

    return ann, test
```

Note that we load the data and then train the ANN incrementally by iterating over a specified number of training epochs, with a specified number of samples in each epoch. For every 1,000 training samples that we process, we print a message about the progress of the training. Finally, we return both the trained ANN and the MNIST test data. We could have just returned the ANN, but having the test data on hand is useful in case we want to check the ANN's accuracy.

7. Of course, the purpose of a trained ANN is to make predictions, so we will provide the following `predict` function in order to wrap the ANN's own `predict` method:

```
def predict(ann, sample):
    if sample.shape != (784,):
        if sample.shape != (28, 28):
            sample = cv2.resize(sample, (28, 28),
                            interpolation=cv2.INTER_LINEAR)
        sample = sample.reshape(784,)
    return ann.predict(np.array([sample], dtype=np.float32))
```

This function takes a trained ANN and a sample image; it performs a minimal amount of data sanitization by making sure the sample image is 28 x 28 and by resizing it if it isn't. Then, it flattens the image data into a vector before giving it to the ANN for classification.

That's all the ANN-related functionality we will need to support our demo application. However, let's also implement a `test` function that measures a trained ANN's accuracy by classifying a given set of test data, such as the MNIST test data. Here is the relevant code:

```
def test(ann, test_data):
    num_tests = 0
    num_correct = 0
    for img in test_data:
        num_tests += 1
        sample, correct_digit_class = img
        digit_class = predict(ann, sample)[0]
        if digit_class == correct_digit_class:
            num_correct += 1
    print('Accuracy: %.2f%%' % (100.0 * num_correct / num_tests))
```

Now, let's take a short detour and write a minimal test that leverages all the preceding code and the MNIST dataset. After that, we will proceed to implement the main module of our demo application.

Implementing a minimal test module

Let's make another script, `test_digits_ann.py`, in order to test the functions from our `digits_ann` module. The test script is quite trivial; here it is:

```
from digits_ann import create_ann, train, test


ann, test_data = train(create_ann())
test(ann, test_data)
```

Note that we haven't specified the number of hidden nodes, so `create_ann` will use its default parameter value: 60 hidden nodes. Similarly, `train` will use its default parameter values: 50,000 samples and 10 epochs.

When we run this script, it should print training and test information similar to the following:

```
Completed 0/10 epochs
Epoch 0: Trained on 0/50000 samples
Epoch 0: Trained on 1000/50000 samples
... [more reports on progress of training] ...
Completed all epochs!
Accuracy: 95.39%
```

Here, we can see that the ANN achieved 95.39% accuracy when classifying the 10,000 test samples in the MNIST dataset. This is an encouraging result, but let's see how well the ANN can generalize. Can it accurately classify data from an entirely different source, unrelated to MNIST? Our main application, which detects digits from our own image of a sheet of paper, will provide this kind of challenge to the classifier.

Implementing the main module

Our demo's main script takes everything we have learned in this chapter about ANNs and MNIST and combines it with some of the object detection techniques that we studied in previous chapters. Thus, in many ways, this is a capstone project for us.

Let's implement the main script in a new file called `detect_and_classify_digits.py`:

1. To begin, we will import OpenCV, NumPy, and our `digits_ann` module:

```
import cv2
import numpy as np

import digits_ann
```

2. Now, let's write a couple of helper functions to analyze and adjust the bounding rectangles of digits and other contours. As we have seen in previous chapters, overlapping detections are a common problem. The following function, called `inside`, will help us determine whether one bounding rectangle is entirely contained inside another:

```
def inside(r1, r2):
    x1, y1, w1, h1 = r1
    x2, y2, w2, h2 = r2
    return (x1 > x2) and (y1 > y2) and (x1+w1 < x2+w2) and \
            (y1+h1 < y2+h2)
```

With the help of the `inside` function, we will be able to easily choose only the outermost bounding rectangle for each digit. This is important because we do not want our detector to miss any extremities of a digit; such a mistake in detection could make the classifier's job impossible. For example, if we detected only the bottom half of a digit, 8, the classifier might reasonably see this region as a 0.

To further ensure that the bounding rectangles meet the classifier's needs, we will use another helper function, called `wrap_digit`, to convert a tightly-fitting bounding rectangle into a square with padding around the digit. Remember that the MNIST data contains 28 x 28 pixel square images of digits, so we must rescale any region of interest to this size before we attempt to classify it with our MNIST-trained ANN. By using a padded bounding square instead of a tightly-fitting bounding rectangle, we ensure that skinny digits (such as a 1) and fat digits (such as a 0) are not stretched differently.

3. Let's look at the implementation of `wrap_digit` in multiple stages. First, we modify the rectangle's smaller dimension (be it width or height) so that it equals the larger dimension, and we modify the rectangle's x or y position so that the center remains unchanged:

```
def wrap_digit(rect, img_w, img_h):

    x, y, w, h = rect
```

```
x_center = x + w//2
y_center = y + h//2
if (h > w):
    w = h
    x = x_center - (w//2)
else:
    h = w
    y = y_center - (h//2)
```

4. Next, we add 5-pixel padding on all sides:

```
padding = 5
x -= padding
y -= padding
w += 2 * padding
h += 2 * padding
```

At this point, our modified rectangle could possibly extend outside the image.

5. To avoid out of bounds problems, we crop the rectangle so that it lies entirely within the image. This could leave us with non-square rectangles in these edge cases, but this is an acceptable compromise; we would prefer to use a non-square region of interest rather than having to entirely throw out a detected digit just because it is at the edge of the image. Here is the code for bounds-checking and cropping the rectangle:

```
if x < 0:
    x = 0
elif x > img_w:
    x = img_w

if y < 0:
    y = 0
elif y > img_h:
    y = img_h

if x+w > img_w:
    w = img_w - x

if y+h > img_h:
    h = img_h - y
```

6. Finally, we return the modified rectangle's coordinates:

```
return x, y, w, h
```

This concludes the implementation of the `wrap_digit` helper function.

7. Now, let's proceed to the main part of the program. Here, we start by creating an ANN and training it on MNIST data:

```
ann, test_data = digits_ann.train(
    digits_ann.create_ann(60), 50000, 10)
```

Note that we are using the `create_ann` and `train` functions from our `digits_ann` module. As we mentioned earlier (in the *Choosing parameters for the MNIST database* section), we are using 60 hidden nodes, 50,000 training samples, and 10 epochs. Although these are the default parameter values for our functions, we specify them here anyway so that they are easier to see and modify later, in case we want to experiment with other values.

8. Now, let's load a test image that contains many handwritten digits on a white sheet of paper:

```
img_path = "./digit_images/digits_0.jpg"
img = cv2.imread(img_path, cv2.IMREAD_COLOR)
```

We are using the following image of Joe Minichino's handwriting (but, of course, you could substitute another image if you prefer):

9. Let's convert the image into grayscale and blur it in order to remove noise and make the darkness of the ink more uniform:

```
gray = cv2.cvtColor(img, cv2.COLOR_BGR2GRAY)
cv2.GaussianBlur(gray, (7, 7), 0, gray)
```

10. Now that we have a smoothened grayscale image, we can apply a threshold and some morphology operations to ensure that the numbers stand out from the background and that the contours are relatively free of irregularities, which might throw off the prediction. Here is the relevant code:

```
ret, thresh = cv2.threshold(gray, 127, 255, cv2.THRESH_BINARY_INV)
erode_kernel = np.ones((2, 2), np.uint8)
thresh = cv2.erode(thresh, erode_kernel, thresh, iterations=2)
```

Note the threshold flag, `cv2.THRESH_BINARY_INV`, which is for an inverse binary threshold. Since the samples in the MNIST database are white on black (and not black on white), we turn the image into a black background with white numbers. We use the thresholded image for both detection and classification.

11. After the morphology operation, we need to separately detect each digit in the picture. As a step toward this, first, we need to find the contours:

```
contours, hier = cv2.findContours(thresh, cv2.RETR_TREE,
                                  cv2.CHAIN_APPROX_SIMPLE)
```

12. Then, we iterate through the contours and find their bounding rectangles. We discard any rectangles that we deem too large or too small to be digits. We also discard any rectangles that are entirely contained in other rectangles. The remaining rectangles are appended to a list of good rectangles, which (we believe) contain individual digits. Let's look at the following code snippet:

```
rectangles = []

img_h, img_w = img.shape[:2]
img_area = img_w * img_h
for c in contours:

    a = cv2.contourArea(c)
    if a >= 0.98 * img_area or a <= 0.0001 * img_area:
        continue

    r = cv2.boundingRect(c)
    is_inside = False
    for q in rectangles:
        if inside(r, q):
            is_inside = True
            break
    if not is_inside:
        rectangles.append(r)
```

13. Now that we have a list of good rectangles, we can iterate through them, sanitize them using our `wrap_digit` function, and classify the image data inside them:

```
for r in rectangles:
    x, y, w, h = wrap_digit(r, img_w, img_h)
    roi = thresh[y:y+h, x:x+w]
    digit_class = int(digits_ann.predict(ann, roi)[0])
```

14. Moreover, after classifying each digit, we draw the sanitized bounding rectangle and the classification result:

```
cv2.rectangle(img, (x,y), (x+w, y+h), (0, 255, 0), 2)
cv2.putText(img, "%d" % digit_class, (x, y-5),
            cv2.FONT_HERSHEY_SIMPLEX, 1, (255, 0, 0), 2)
```

15. After processing all the regions of interest, we save the thresholded image and the fully annotated image and display them until the user hits any key to end the program:

```
cv2.imwrite("detected_and_classified_digits_thresh.png", thresh)
cv2.imwrite("detected_and_classified_digits.png", img)
cv2.imshow("thresh", thresh)
cv2.imshow("detected and classified digits", img)
cv2.waitKey()
```

That is the end of the script. When running it, we should see the thresholded image as well as a visualization of detection and classification results. (The two windows may overlap initially, so you might need to move one to see the other.) Here is the thresholded image:

Here is the visualization of the results:

This image contains 110 sample digits: 10 digits in the single-digit numbers from 0 to 9, plus 100 digits in the double-digit numbers from 10 to 59. Out of these 110 samples, the bounds are correctly detected for 108 samples, meaning that the detector's accuracy is 98.18%. Then, out of these 108 correctly detected samples, the classification result is correct for 80 samples, meaning that the ANN classifier's accuracy is 74.07%. This is a lot better than a random classifier, which would correctly classify a digit only 10% of the time.

Thus, the ANN is evidently capable of learning to classify handwritten digits in general, not just the ones in the MNIST training and test datasets. Let's consider some ways to improve its learning.

Trying to improve the ANN's training

We could apply a number of potential improvements to the problem of training our ANN. We have already mentioned some of these potential improvements, but let's review them here:

- You could experiment with the size of your training dataset, the number of hidden nodes, and the number of epochs until you find a peak level of accuracy.
- You could modify our `digits_ann.create_ann` function so that it supports more than one hidden layer.

- You could also try different activation functions. We have used `cv2.ml.ANN_MLP_SIGMOID_SYM`, but it isn't the only option; the others include `cv2.ml.ANN_MLP_IDENTITY`, `cv2.ml.ANN_MLP_GAUSSIAN`, `cv2.ml.ANN_MLP_RELU`, and `cv2.ml.ANN_MLP_LEAKYRELU`.
- Similarly, you could try different training methods. We have used `cv2.ml.ANN_MLP_BACKPROP`. The other options include `cv2.ml.ANN_MLP_RPROP` and `cv2.ml.ANN_MLP_ANNEAL`.

For more information about ANN-related parameters in OpenCV, refer to the official documentation at `https://docs.opencv.org/master/d0/dce/classcv_1_1ml_1_1ANN__MLP.html`.

Aside from experimenting with parameters, think carefully about your application requirements. For example, where and by whom will your classifier be used? Not everyone draws digits the same way. Indeed, people in different countries tend to draw numbers in slightly different ways.

The MNIST database was compiled in the United States, where the digit 7 is handwritten like the typewritten character 7. However, in Europe, the digit 7 is often handwritten with a small horizontal line halfway through the diagonal portion of the number. This stroke was introduced to help distinguish the handwritten digit 7 from the handwritten digit 1.

For a more detailed overview of regional handwriting variations, check the Wikipedia article on the subject, which is a good introduction, available at `https://en.wikipedia.org/wiki/Regional_handwriting_variation`.

This variation means that an ANN trained on the MNIST database may be less accurate when applied to the classification of European handwritten digits. To avoid such an outcome, you may choose to create your own training dataset instead. In almost all circumstances, it is preferable to utilize training data that belongs to the current application domain.

Finally, remember that once you are happy with the accuracy of your classifier, you can always save it and reload it later so that it can be utilized in applications without having to train the ANN every time.

The interface for this is just like the interface we saw in the *Saving and loading a trained SVM* section, near the end of Chapter 7, *Building Custom Object Detectors*. Specifically, you can use code such as the following to save a trained ANN to an XML file:

```
ann = cv2.ml.ANN_MLP_create()
data = cv2.ml.TrainData_create(
    training_samples, layout, training_responses)
ann.train(data)
ann.save('my_ann.xml')
```

Subsequently, you can reload the trained ANN using code such as the following:

```
ann = cv2.ml.ANN_MLP_create()
ann.load('my_ann.xml')
```

Now that we have learned how to create a reusable ANN for handwritten digit classification, let's think about the use cases for such a classifier.

Finding other potential applications

The preceding demonstration is only the foundation of a handwriting recognition application. You could readily extend the approach to videos and detect handwritten digits in real-time, or you could train your ANN to recognize the entire alphabet for a full-blown **optical character recognition** (**OCR**) system.

Detection and recognition of car registration plates would be another useful extension of the lessons we have learned up to this point. The characters on registration plates have a consistent appearance (at least, within a given country), and this should be a simplifying factor in the OCR part of the problem.

You could also try applying ANNs to problems where we have previously used SVMs, or vice versa. This way, you could see how their accuracy compares for different kinds of data. Recall that in Chapter 7, *Building Custom Object Detectors*, we used SIFT descriptors as inputs for SVMs. Likewise, ANNs are capable of handling high-level descriptors and not just plain old pixel data.

As we have seen, the cv2.ml_ANN_MLP class is quite versatile, but in truth, it covers only a small subset of the ways an ANN can be designed. Next, we will learn about OpenCV's support for more complex **deep neural networks** (**DNNs**) that can be trained with a variety of other frameworks.

Using DNNs from other frameworks in OpenCV

OpenCV can load and use DNNs that have been trained in any of the following frameworks:

- Caffe (http://caffe.berkeleyvision.org/)
- TensorFlow (https://www.tensorflow.org/)
- Torch (http://torch.ch/)
- Darknet (https://pjreddie.com/darknet/)
- ONNX (https://onnx.ai/)
- DLDT (https://github.com/opencv/dldt/)

> The **Deep Learning Deployment Toolkit (DLDT)** is part of Intel's OpenVINO Toolkit (https://software.intel.com/openvino-toolkit/) for computer vision. DLDT provides tools for optimizing DNNs from other frameworks and for converting them into a common format. A collection of DLDT-compatible models is freely available in a repository called the Open Model Zoo (https://github.com/opencv/open_model_zoo/). DLDT, the Open Model Zoo, and OpenCV have some of the same people on their development teams; all three of these projects are sponsored by Intel.

These frameworks use various file formats to store trained DNNs. Several of these frameworks use a combination of a pair of file formats: a text file to describe the model's parameters, plus a binary file to store the model itself. The following code snippet shows the file types and OpenCV functions that are relevant to loading a model from each framework:

```
caffe_model = cv2.dnn.readNetFromCaffe(
    'my_model_description.protext', 'my_model.caffemodel')

tensor_flow_model = cv2.dnn.readNetFromTensorflow(
    'my_model.pb', 'my_model_description.pbtxt')

# Some Torch models use the .t7 extension and others use
# the .net extension.
torch_model_0 = cv2.dnn.readNetFromTorch('my_model.t7')
torch_model_1 = cv2.dnn.readNetFromTorch('my_model.net')

darknet_model = cv2.dnn.readNetFromDarket(
    'my_model_description.cfg', 'my_model.weights')
```

```
onnx_model = cv2.dnn.readNetFromONNX('my_model.onnx')

dldt_model = cv2.dnn.readNetFromModelOptimizer(
    'my_model_description.xml', 'my_model.bin')
```

After we load a model, we need to preprocess the data we will use with the model. The necessary preprocessing is specific to the way the given DNN was designed and trained, so any time we use a third-party DNN, we must read about how that DNN was designed and trained. OpenCV provides a function, `cv2.dnn.blobFromImage`, that can perform some common preprocessing steps, depending on the parameters we pass to it. We can perform other preprocessing steps manually before passing data to this function.

 A neural network's input vector is sometimes called a **tensor** or **blob** – hence the function's name, `cv2.dnn.blobFromImage`.

Let's proceed to a practical example where we'll see a third-party DNN in action.

Detecting and classifying objects with third-party DNNs

For this demo, we are going to capture frames from a webcam in real-time and use a DNN to detect and classify 20 kinds of objects that may be in any given frame. Yes, a single DNN can do all this in real-time on a typical laptop that a programmer might use!

Before delving into the code, let's introduce the DNN that we will use. It is a Caffe version of a model called MobileNet-SSD, which uses a hybrid of a framework from Google called **MobileNet** and another framework called **Single Shot Detector** (SSD) MultiBox. The latter framework has a GitHub repository at `https://github.com/weiliu89/caffe/tree/ssd/`. The training technique for the Caffe version of MobileNet-SSD is provided by a project on GitHub at `https://github.com/chuanqi305/MobileNet-SSD/`. Copies of the following MobileNet-SSD files can be found in this book's repository, in the `chapter10/objects_data` folder:

- `MobileNetSSD_deploy.caffemodel`: This is the model.
- `MobileNetSSD_deploy.prototxt`: This is the text file that describes the model's parameters.

This model's capabilities and proper usage will soon become clear as we progress through our sample code:

1. As usual, we begin by importing OpenCV and NumPy:

```
import cv2
import numpy as np
```

2. We proceed to load the Caffe model with OpenCV in the same manner that we described in the previous section:

```
model = cv2.dnn.readNetFromCaffe(
    'objects_data/MobileNetSSD_deploy.prototxt',
    'objects_data/MobileNetSSD_deploy.caffemodel')
```

3. We need to define some preprocessing parameters that are specific to this model. It expects the input image to be 300 pixels high. Also, it expects the pixel values in the image to be on a scale from -1.0 to 1.0. This means that, relative to the usual scale from 0 to 255, it is necessary to subtract 127.5 and then divide by 127.5. We define the parameters as follows:

```
blob_height = 300
color_scale = 1.0/127.5
average_color = (127.5, 127.5, 127.5)
```

4. We also define a confidence threshold, representing the minimum confidence score that we require in order to accept a detection as a real object:

```
confidence_threshold = 0.5
```

5. The model supports 20 classes of objects, with IDs from 1 to 20 (not 0 to 19). The labels for these classes can be defined as follows:

```
labels = ['airplane', 'bicycle', 'bird', 'boat', 'bottle', 'bus',
    'car', 'cat', 'chair', 'cow', 'dining table', 'dog',
    'horse', 'motorbike', 'person', 'potted plant', 'sheep',
    'sofa', 'train', 'TV or monitor']
```

 Later, when we use class IDs to look up labels in our list, we must remember to subtract 1 from the ID in order to obtain an index in the range 0 to 19 (not 1 to 20).

With the model and parameters at hand, we are ready to start capturing frames.

6. For each frame, we begin by calculating the aspect ratio. Remember that this DNN expects the input to be based on an image that is 300 pixels high; however, the width can vary in order to match the original aspect ratio. The following code snippet shows how we capture a frame and calculate the appropriate input size:

```
cap = cv2.VideoCapture(0)

success, frame = cap.read()
while success:

    h, w = frame.shape[:2]
    aspect_ratio = w/h

    # Detect objects in the frame.

    blob_width = int(blob_height * aspect_ratio)
    blob_size = (blob_width, blob_height)
```

7. At this point, we can simply use the `cv2.dnn.blobFromImage` function, with several of its optional arguments, to perform the necessary preprocessing, including resizing the frame and converting its pixel data into a scale from -1.0 to 1.0:

```
blob = cv2.dnn.blobFromImage(
    frame, scalefactor=color_scale, size=blob_size,
    mean=average_color)
```

8. We feed the resulting blob to the DNN and get the model's output:

```
model.setInput(blob)
results = model.forward()
```

The results are an array, in a format that is specific to the model we are using.

9. For this object detection DNN – and for other DNNs trained with the SSD framework – the results include a subarray of detected objects, each with its own confidence score, rectangle coordinates, and class ID. The following code shows how to access these, as well as how to use an ID to look up a label in the list we defined earlier:

```
# Iterate over the detected objects.
for object in results[0, 0]:
    confidence = object[2]
    if confidence > confidence_threshold:

        # Get the object's coordinates.
```

```
x0, y0, x1, y1 = (object[3:7] * [w, h, w, h]).astype(int)

# Get the classification result.
id = int(object[1])
label = labels[id - 1]
```

10. As we iterate over the detected objects, we draw the detection rectangles, along with the classification labels and confidence scores:

```
# Draw a blue rectangle around the object.
cv2.rectangle(frame, (x0, y0), (x1, y1),
              (255, 0, 0), 2)

# Draw the classification result and confidence.
text = '%s (%.1f%%)' % (label, confidence * 100.0)
cv2.putText(frame, text, (x0, y0 - 20),
    cv2.FONT_HERSHEY_SIMPLEX, 1, (255, 0, 0), 2)
```

11. The last thing we do with the frame is show it. Then, if the user has hit the *Esc* key, we exit; otherwise, we capture another frame and continue to the next iteration of the loop:

```
cv2.imshow('Objects', frame)

k = cv2.waitKey(1)
if k == 27: # Escape
    break

success, frame = cap.read()
```

If you plug in a webcam and run the script, you should see a visualization of detection and classification results, updated in real-time. Here is a screenshot showing Joseph Howse and Sanibel Delphinium Andromeda (a mighty, great, and righteous cat) in their living room in a Canadian fishing village:

The DNN has correctly detected and classified a human *person* (with 99.4% confidence), a *cat* (85.4%), a decorative *bottle* (72.1%), part of a *sofa* (61.2%), and a woven picture of a *boat* (52.0%). Evidently, this DNN is well equipped to classify the contents of living rooms in nautical settings!

This is only a first taste of the things that DNNs can do – and do in real time! Next, let's see what we can achieve by combining three DNNs in one application.

Detecting and classifying faces with third-party DNNs

For this demonstration, we are going to use one DNN to detect faces and two other DNNs to classify the age and gender of each detected face. Specifically, we will use pre-trained Caffe models that are stored in the following files in the `chapter10/faces_data` folder of this book's GitHub repository.

Here is an inventory of the files in this folder, and of the files' origins:

- `detection/res10_300x300_ssd_iter_140000.caffemodel`: This is the DNN for face detection. The OpenCV team has provided this file at `https://github.com/opencv/opencv_3rdparty/blob/dnn_samples_face_detector_20170830/res10_300x300_ssd_iter_140000.caffemodel`. This Caffe model was trained with the SSD framework (`https://github.com/weiliu89/caffe/tree/ssd/`). Thus, its topology is similar to the MobileNet-SSD model that we used in the previous section's example.

- `detection/deploy.prototxt`: This is the text file that describes the parameters of the preceding DNN for face detection. The OpenCV team provides this file at `https://github.com/opencv/opencv/blob/master/samples/dnn/face_detector/deploy.prototxt`.

The `chapter10/faces_data/age_gender_classification` folder contains the following files, which are all provided by Gil Levi and Tal Hassner in their GitHub repository (`https://github.com/GilLevi/AgeGenderDeepLearning/`) and on their project page (`https://talhassner.github.io/home/publication/2015_CVPR`) for their work on age and gender classification:

- `age_net.caffemodel`: This is the DNN for age classification.
- `age_net_deploy.protext`: This is the text file that describes the parameters of the preceding DNN for age classification.
- `gender_net.caffemodel`: This is the DNN for gender classification.
- `gender_net_deploy.protext`: This is the text file that describes the parameters of the preceding DNN for age classification.
- `average_face.npy` and `average_face.png`: These files represent the average faces in the classifiers' training dataset. The original file from Levi and Hassner is called `mean.binaryproto`, but we have converted it into a NumPy-readable format and a standard image format, which are more convenient for our purposes.

Let's see how we can use all these files in our code:

1. To begin the sample program, we load the face detection DNN, define its parameters, and define a confidence threshold. We do this in much the same way as we did for the object detection DNN in the previous section's sample:

```
import cv2
import numpy as np
```

```
face_model = cv2.dnn.readNetFromCaffe(
    'faces_data/detection/deploy.prototxt',
 'faces_data/detection/res10_300x300_ssd_iter_140000.caffemodel')
face_blob_height = 300
face_average_color = (104, 177, 123)
face_confidence_threshold = 0.995
```

We do not need to define labels for this DNN because it does not perform any classification; it just predicts the coordinates of face rectangles.

2. Now, let's load the age classifier and define its class labels:

```
age_model = cv2.dnn.readNetFromCaffe(
    'faces_data/age_gender_classification/age_net_deploy.prototxt',
    'faces_data/age_gender_classification/age_net.caffemodel')
age_labels = ['0-2', '4-6', '8-12', '15-20',
              '25-32', '38-43', '48-53', '60+']
```

Note that in this model, the age labels have gaps between them. For example, '0-2' is followed by '4-6'. Thus, if a person is actually 3 years old, the classifier has no proper label for this case; at best, it can pick either of the neighboring ranges, '0-2' or '4-6'. Presumably, the model's authors deliberately chose disconnected ranges, in an effort to ensure that the classes are **separable** with respect to the inputs. Let's consider the alternative. Based on data from facial images, is it possible to separate a group of people who are 4 years old from a group of people who are 4-years-less-a-day? Surely it isn't; they look the same. Thus, it would be wrong to formulate a classification problem based on contiguous age ranges. A DNN could be trained to predict age as a continuous variable (such as a floating-point number of years), but this would be altogether different than a classifier, which predicts confidence scores for various classes.

3. Now, let's load the gender classifier and define its labels:

```
gender_model = cv2.dnn.readNetFromCaffe(
 'faces_data/age_gender_classification/gender_net_deploy.prototxt',
    'faces_data/age_gender_classification/gender_net.caffemodel')
gender_labels = ['male', 'female']
```

4. The age and gender classifiers use the same blob size and the same average. Rather than using a single color as the average, they use an average facial image, which we will load (as a NumPy array in floating-point format) from an NPY file. Later, we will subtract this average facial image from an actual facial image before we perform classification. Here are the definitions of the blob size and average image:

```
age_gender_blob_size = (256, 256)
age_gender_average_image = np.load(
    'faces_data/age_gender_classification/average_face.npy')
```

If you want to see what the average face looks like, open the file at `chapter10/faces_data/age_gender_classification/average_face.png`, which contains the same data in a standard image format. Here it is:

Of course, this is only the average face for a particular training dataset; it is not necessarily representative of the true average face in the world population, or in any particular nation or community. Even so, here, we can see a face that is a blurry composite of many faces, and it contains no obvious clues about age or gender. Note that the image is square, it is centered around the tip of the nose, and it extends vertically from the top of the forehead to the base of the neck. To obtain accurate classification results, we should take care to apply this classifier to facial images that are cropped in the same manner.

5. Having set up our models and their parameters, let's proceed to capture and process frames from a camera. With each frame, we begin by creating a blob that is the same aspect ratio as the frame, and we feed this blob to the face detection DNN:

```
cap = cv2.VideoCapture(0)

success, frame = cap.read()
while success:
```

```
    h, w = frame.shape[:2]
    aspect_ratio = w/h

    # Detect faces in the frame.

    face_blob_width = int(face_blob_height * aspect_ratio)
    face_blob_size = (face_blob_width, face_blob_height)

    face_blob = cv2.dnn.blobFromImage(
        frame, size=face_blob_size, mean=face_average_color)

    face_model.setInput(face_blob)
    face_results = face_model.forward()
```

6. Like the object detector that we used in the previous section's sample, the face detector provides confidence scores and rectangle coordinates as part of its results. For each detected face, we need to check whether the confidence score is acceptably high, and, if it is, we'll get the coordinates of the face rectangle:

```
    # Iterate over the detected faces.
    for face in face_results[0, 0]:
        face_confidence = face[2]
        if face_confidence > face_confidence_threshold:

            # Get the face coordinates.
            x0, y0, x1, y1 = (face[3:7] * [w, h, w, h]).astype(int)
```

7. This face detection DNN produces rectangles that are taller than they are wide. However, the age and gender classification DNNs expect square faces. Let's widen the detected face rectangle to make it a square:

```
            # Classify the age and gender of the face based on a
            # square region of interest that includes the neck.

            y1_roi = y0 + int(1.2*(y1-y0))
            x_margin = ((y1_roi-y0) - (x1-x0)) // 2
            x0_roi = x0 - x_margin
            x1_roi = x1 + x_margin
            if x0_roi < 0 or x1_roi > w or y0 < 0 or y1_roi > h:
                # The region of interest is partly outside the
                # frame. Skip this face.
                continue
```

Note that if part of the square falls outside the bounds of the image, we skip this detection result and continue to the next one.

8. At this point, we can select the square **region of interest** (**ROI**), which contains the image data that we will use for age and gender classification. We proceed by scaling the ROI to the classifiers' blob size, converting it into floating-point format, and subtracting the average face. From the resulting scaled and normalized face, we create the blob:

```
age_gender_roi = frame[y0:y1_roi, x0_roi:x1_roi]
scaled_age_gender_roi = cv2.resize(
    age_gender_roi, age_gender_blob_size,
    interpolation=cv2.INTER_LINEAR).astype(np.float32)
scaled_age_gender_roi[:] -= age_gender_average_image
age_gender_blob = cv2.dnn.blobFromImage(
    scaled_age_gender_roi, size=age_gender_blob_size)
```

9. We feed the blob to the age classifier, pick the class ID with the highest confidence score, and then take note of the label and confidence score for this ID:

```
age_model.setInput(age_gender_blob)
age_results = age_model.forward()
age_id = np.argmax(age_results)
age_label = age_labels[age_id]
age_confidence = age_results[0, age_id]
```

10. Similarly, we classify the gender:

```
gender_model.setInput(age_gender_blob)
gender_results = gender_model.forward()
gender_id = np.argmax(gender_results)
gender_label = gender_labels[gender_id]
gender_confidence = gender_results[0, gender_id]
```

11. We draw a visualization of the detected face rectangle, the expanded square ROI, and the classification results:

```
# Draw a blue rectangle around the face.
cv2.rectangle(frame, (x0, y0), (x1, y1),
              (255, 0, 0), 2)

# Draw a yellow square around the region of interest
# for age and gender classification.
cv2.rectangle(frame, (x0_roi, y0), (x1_roi, y1_roi),
              (0, 255, 255), 2)

# Draw the age and gender classification results.
text = '%s years (%.1f%%), %s (%.1f%%)' % (
    age_label, age_confidence * 100.0,
    gender_label, gender_confidence * 100.0)
```

```
cv2.putText(frame, text, (x0_roi, y0 - 20),
        cv2.FONT_HERSHEY_SIMPLEX, 1, (0, 255, 255), 2)
```

12. To conclude, we show the annotated frame, and we keep capturing more frames
    until the user hits the *Esc* key:

```
cv2.imshow('Faces, age, and gender', frame)

k = cv2.waitKey(1)
if k == 27: # Escape
    break

success, frame = cap.read()
```

What does this program report about Joseph Howse? Let's take a look:

Without vanity, Joseph Howse is going to write a couple of paragraphs about this result.

First, let's consider the detection of the face and the selection of the ROI. The face has been accurately detected. The ROI has been correctly expanded to a square region that includes the neck – or, in this case, the full beard, which could be an important region for the purposes of classifying age and gender.

Second, let's consider the classification. The truth is that Joseph Howse is male and is approximately 35.8 years old at the time of this picture. Other human beings who see Joseph Howse's face are able to judge with perfect confidence that he is male; however, their estimates of his age vary widely. The gender classification DNN says with perfect confidence (100.0%) that Joseph Howse is male. The age classification DNN says with high confidence (96.6%) that he is 25-32 years old. Perhaps it is tempting to take the midpoint of this range, 28.5, and say that the prediction has an error of -7.3 years, which is subjectively a big underestimate, being -20.4% of the true age. However, this type of assessment is a stretch of the prediction's meaning.

Remember that this DNN is an age classifier, not a predictor of continuous age values, and that the DNN's age classes are labeled as disconnected ranges; the next one after `'25-32'` is `'38-43'`. Thus, the model has a gap around Joseph Howse's true age, but at least it managed to choose one of the two classes that border this gap.

This demonstration concludes our introductory tour of ANNs and DNNs. Let's review what we have learned and done.

Summary

This chapter scratched the surface of the vast and fascinating world of ANNs. We learned about the structure of ANNs, and how to design a network topology based on application requirements. Then, we focused on OpenCV's implementation of MLP ANNs, as well as on OpenCV's support for diverse DNNs that have been trained in other frameworks.

We applied neural networks to real-world problems: notably, handwritten digit recognition; object detection and classification; and a combination of face detection, age classification, and gender classification in real time. We saw that even in these introductory demos, neural networks show a lot of promise in terms of versatility, accuracy, and speed. Hopefully, this encourages you to try out pre-trained models from various authors, and to learn to train advanced models of your own in various frameworks.

With this thought, and with good wishes, we shall part for now.

This book's authors hope that you have enjoyed our journey together through the Python bindings of OpenCV 4. Although covering all of OpenCV 4's functionality and all its bindings would take a series of books, we have explored a broad selection of fascinating and futuristic concepts, and we encourage you to get in touch with us, and with the OpenCV community, to let us know about your next groundbreaking project in the field of computer vision!

Appendix A: Bending Color Space with the Curves Filter

Starting in Chapter 3, *Processing Images with OpenCV*, our Cameo demo application incorporated an image processing effect called **curves**, which it uses to emulate the color bias of certain photo films. This Appendix describes the concept of curves and their implementation using SciPy.

Curves are a technique for remapping colors. With curves, a channel's value at a destination pixel is a function of (only) the same channel's value at the source pixel. Moreover, we do not define functions directly; instead, for each function, we define a set of control points that the function must fit by means of interpolation. In pseudocode, for a BGR image, we have the following:

```
dst.b = funcB(src.b) where funcB interpolates pointsB
dst.g = funcG(src.g) where funcG interpolates pointsG
dst.r = funcR(src.r) where funcR interpolates pointsR
```

This type of interpolation may vary between implementations, though it should avoid discontinuous slopes at control points and, instead, produce curves. We will use cubic spline interpolation whenever the number of control points is sufficient.

Let's start by taking a look at how interpolation can be implemented.

Formulating a curve

Our first step toward curve-based filters is to convert control points into a function. Most of this work is done for us by a SciPy function called `scipy.interp1d`, which takes two arrays (*x* and *y* coordinates) and returns a function that interpolates the points. As an optional argument to `scipy.interp1d`, we may specify the `kind` interpolation; supported options include `'linear'`, `'nearest'`, `'zero'`, `'slinear'` (spherical linear), `'quadratic'`, and `'cubic'`. Another optional argument, `bounds_error`, may be set to `False` to permit extrapolation as well as interpolation.

Let's edit the `utils.py` script that we use with our Cameo demo and add a function that wraps `scipy.interp1d` with a slightly simpler interface:

```python
def createCurveFunc(points):
    """Return a function derived from control points."""
    if points is None:
        return None
    numPoints = len(points)
    if numPoints < 2:
        return None
    xs, ys = zip(*points)
    if numPoints < 3:
        kind = 'linear'
    elif numPoints < 4:
        kind = 'quadratic'
    else:
        kind = 'cubic'
    return scipy.interpolate.interp1d(xs, ys, kind,
                                      bounds_error = False)
```

Rather than two separate arrays of coordinates, our function takes an array of (*x*, *y*) pairs, which is probably a more readable way of specifying control points. The array must be ordered so that *x* increases from one index to the next. Typically, for natural-looking effects, the *y* values should increase too, and the first and last control points should be (0, 0) and (255, 255) in order to preserve black and white. Note that we will treat *x* as a channel's input value and *y* as the corresponding output value. For example, (128, 160), would brighten a channel's midtones.

Note that cubic interpolation requires at least four control points. If there are only three control points, we fall back on quadratic interpolation, and if there are only two, we fall back on linear interpolation. For natural-looking effects, these fallback cases should be avoided.

Throughout the remainder of this chapter, we seek to use the curves generated by our `createCurveFunc` function in an efficient and well-organized way.

Caching and applying a curve

By now, we can get the function of a curve that interpolates arbitrary control points. However, this function might be expensive. We don't want to run it once-per-channel, per - pixel (for example, 921,600 times per frame if applied to three channels of 640 x 480 video). Fortunately, we are typically dealing with just 256 possible input values (in 8 bits per channel) and we can cheaply precompute and store that many output values. Then, our per-channel, per-pixel cost is just a lookup of the cached output value.

Let's edit the `utils.py` file and add a function that will create a lookup array for a given function:

```python
def createLookupArray(func, length=256):
    """Return a lookup for whole-number inputs to a function.

    The lookup values are clamped to [0, length - 1].

    """
    if func is None:
        return None
    lookupArray = numpy.empty(length)
    i = 0
    while i < length:
        func_i = func(i)
        lookupArray[i] = min(max(0, func_i), length - 1)
        i += 1
    return lookupArray
```

Let's also add a function that will apply a lookup array (such as the result of the preceding function) to another array (such as an image):

```python
def applyLookupArray(lookupArray, src, dst):
    """Map a source to a destination using a lookup."""
    if lookupArray is None:
        return
    dst[:] = lookupArray[src]
```

Note that the approach in createLookupArray is limited to input values that are whole numbers (non-negative integers) since the input value is used as an index into an array. The applyLookupArray function works by using a source array's values as indices into the lookup array. Python's slice notation ([:]) is used to copy looked-up values into a destination array.

Let's consider another optimization. What if we want to apply two or more curves in succession? Performing multiple lookups is inefficient and may cause a loss in precision. We can avoid these problems by combining two curve functions into one function before creating a lookup array. Let's edit utils.py again and add the following function, which returns a composite of two given functions:

```
def createCompositeFunc(func0, func1):
    """Return a composite of two functions."""
    if func0 is None:
        return func1
    if func1 is None:
        return func0
    return lambda x: func0(func1(x))
```

The approach in createCompositeFunc is limited to input functions that take a single argument. The arguments must be of compatible types. Note the use of Python's lambda keyword to create an anonymous function.

The following is a final optimization issue. What if we want to apply the same curve to all the channels of an image? In this case, splitting and remerging channels is wasteful because we don't need to distinguish between channels. We just need one-dimensional indexing, as used by applyLookupArray. For this, we can use the numpy.ravel function, which returns a one-dimensional interface to a preexisting, given array that may be multi-dimensional. The return type is numpy.view, which has much the same interface as numpy.array, except numpy.view only owns a reference to the data, not a copy.

 NumPy arrays have a flatten method, but this returns a copy.

`numpy.ravel` works for images with any number of channels. Thus, it allows us to abstract the difference between grayscale and color images in cases when we wish to treat all channels the same.

Now that we have addressed several important optimization issues concerning the use of curves, let's consider how to organize our code to provide a simple and reusable interface to applications such as Cameo.

Designing object-oriented curve filters

Since we cache a lookup array for each curve, our curve-based filters have data associated with them. Thus, we will implement them as classes, not just functions. Let's make a pair of curve filter classes, along with some corresponding higher-level classes that can apply any function, not just a curve function:

- `VFuncFilter`: This is a class that is instantiated with a function, which it can then apply to an image using `apply`. The function is applied to the V (value) channel of a grayscale image or to all the channels of a color image.
- `VCurveFilter`: This is a subclass of `VFuncFilter`. Instead of being instantiated with a function, it is instantiated with a set of control points, which it uses internally to create a curve function.
- `BGRFuncFilter`: This is a class that is instantiated with up to four functions, which it can then apply to a BGR image using `apply`. One of these functions is applied to all the channels, while the other three functions are each applied to a single channel. The overall function is applied first and then the per-channel functions.
- `BGRCurveFilter`: This is a subclass of `BGRFuncFilter`. Instead of being instantiated with four functions, it is instantiated with four sets of control points, which it uses internally to create curve functions.

Additionally, all these classes accept a constructor argument that is a numeric type, such as `numpy.uint8` for 8 bits per channel. This type is used to determine how many entries should be in the lookup array. The numeric type should be an integer type, and the lookup array will cover the range from 0 to the type's maximum value (inclusive).

First, let's look at the implementations of VFuncFilter and VCurveFilter, which can both be added to filters.py:

```
class VFuncFilter(object):
    """A filter that applies a function to V (or all of BGR)."""

    def __init__(self, vFunc=None, dtype=numpy.uint8):
        length = numpy.iinfo(dtype).max + 1
        self._vLookupArray = utils.createLookupArray(vFunc, length)

    def apply(self, src, dst):
        """Apply the filter with a BGR or gray source/destination."""
        srcFlatView = numpy.ravel(src)
        dstFlatView = numpy.ravel(dst)
        utils.applyLookupArray(self._vLookupArray, srcFlatView,
                               dstFlatView)

class VCurveFilter(VFuncFilter):
    """A filter that applies a curve to V (or all of BGR)."""

    def __init__(self, vPoints, dtype=numpy.uint8):
        VFuncFilter.__init__(self, utils.createCurveFunc(vPoints),
                             dtype)
```

Here, we are internalizing the use of several of our previous functions: utils.createCurveFunc, utils.createLookupArray, and utils.applyLookupArray. We are also using numpy.iinfo to determine the relevant range of lookup values, based on the given numeric type.

Now, let's look at the implementations of BGRFuncFilter and BGRCurveFilter, which can both be added to filters.py as well:

```
class BGRFuncFilter(object):
    """A filter that applies different functions to each of BGR."""

    def __init__(self, vFunc=None, bFunc=None, gFunc=None,
                 rFunc=None, dtype=numpy.uint8):
        length = numpy.iinfo(dtype).max + 1
        self._bLookupArray = utils.createLookupArray(
            utils.createCompositeFunc(bFunc, vFunc), length)
        self._gLookupArray = utils.createLookupArray(
            utils.createCompositeFunc(gFunc, vFunc), length)
        self._rLookupArray = utils.createLookupArray(
            utils.createCompositeFunc(rFunc, vFunc), length)

    def apply(self, src, dst):
        """Apply the filter with a BGR source/destination."""
```

```
        b, g, r = cv2.split(src)
        utils.applyLookupArray(self._bLookupArray, b, b)
        utils.applyLookupArray(self._gLookupArray, g, g)
        utils.applyLookupArray(self._rLookupArray, r, r)
        cv2.merge([b, g, r], dst)

class BGRCurveFilter(BGRFuncFilter):
    """A filter that applies different curves to each of BGR."""

    def __init__(self, vPoints=None, bPoints=None,
                 gPoints=None, rPoints=None, dtype=numpy.uint8):
        BGRFuncFilter.__init__(self,
                               utils.createCurveFunc(vPoints),
                               utils.createCurveFunc(bPoints),
                               utils.createCurveFunc(gPoints),
                               utils.createCurveFunc(rPoints), dtype)
```

Again, we are internalizing the use of several of our previous functions: `utils.createCurvFunc`, `utils.createCompositeFunc`, `utils.createLookupArray`, and `utils.applyLookupArray`. We are also using `numpy.iinfo`, `cv2.split`, and `cv2.merge`.

These four classes can be used as-is, with custom functions or control points being passed as arguments at instantiation. Alternatively, we can make further subclasses that hard-code certain functions or control points. Such subclasses can be instantiated without any arguments.

Now, let's look at some examples of subclasses.

Emulating photo films

A common use of curves is to emulate palettes that were common in pre-digital photography. Every type of photo film has its own unique rendition of color (or gray), but we can generalize some of the differences from digital sensors. Film tends to suffer a loss of detail and saturation in shadows, whereas digital tends to suffer these failings in highlights. Also, film tends to have uneven saturation across different parts of the spectrum, so each film has certain colors that pop or jump out.

Thus, when we think of good-looking film photos, we might think of scenes (or renditions) that are bright and that have certain dominant colors. At the other extreme, maybe we remember the murky look of an underexposed roll of film that couldn't be improved much by the efforts of the lab technician.

In this section, we are going to create four different film-like filters using curves. They are inspired by three kinds of film and a processing technique:

- Kodak Portra, a family of films that is optimized for portraits and weddings.
- Fuji Provia, a family of general-purpose films.
- Fuji Velvia, a family of films that is optimized for landscapes.
- Cross-processing, a nonstandard film processing technique, sometimes used to produce a grungy look in fashion and band photography.

Each film emulation effect is implemented as a very simple subclass of `BGRCurveFilter`. Here, we simply override the constructor to specify a set of control points for each channel. The choice of control points is based on recommendations by photographer Petteri Sulonen. See his article on film-like curves at `http://www.prime-junta.net/pont/How_to/100_Curves_and_Films/_Curves_and_films.html` for more information.

The Portra, Provia, and Velvia effects should produce normal-looking images. These effects should not be obvious except in before-and-after comparisons.

Let's examine the implementation of each of the four film emulation filters, starting with the Portra filter.

Emulating Kodak Portra

Portra has a broad highlight range that tends toward warm (amber) colors, while shadows are cooler (blue). As a portrait film, it tends to make people's complexions fairer. Also, it exaggerates certain common clothing colors, such as milky white (for example, a wedding dress) and dark blue (for example, a suit or jeans). Let's add this implementation of a Portra filter to `filters.py`:

```
class BGRPortraCurveFilter(BGRCurveFilter):
    """A filter that applies Portra-like curves to BGR."""

    def __init__(self, dtype=numpy.uint8):
        BGRCurveFilter.__init__(
            self,
            vPoints = [(0,0),(23,20),(157,173),(255,255)],
            bPoints = [(0,0),(41,46),(231,228),(255,255)],
            gPoints = [(0,0),(52,47),(189,196),(255,255)],
            rPoints = [(0,0),(69,69),(213,218),(255,255)],
            dtype = dtype)
```

Moving from Kodak to Fuji, we'll emulate Provia next.

Emulating Fuji Provia

Provia has a strong contrast and is slightly cool (blue) throughout most tones. Sky, water, and shade are enhanced more than the sun. Let's add this implementation of a Provia filter to `filters.py`:

```python
class BGRProviaCurveFilter(BGRCurveFilter):
    """A filter that applies Provia-like curves to BGR."""

    def __init__(self, dtype=numpy.uint8):
        BGRCurveFilter.__init__(
            self,
            bPoints = [(0,0),(35,25),(205,227),(255,255)],
            gPoints = [(0,0),(27,21),(196,207),(255,255)],
            rPoints = [(0,0),(59,54),(202,210),(255,255)],
            dtype = dtype)
```

Next up is our Fuji Velvia filter.

Emulating Fuji Velvia

Velvia has deep shadows and vivid colors. It can often produce azure skies in daytime and crimson clouds at sunset. This effect is difficult to emulate, but here is an attempt that we can add to `filters.py`:

```python
class BGRVelviaCurveFilter(BGRCurveFilter):
    """A filter that applies Velvia-like curves to BGR."""

    def __init__(self, dtype=numpy.uint8):
        BGRCurveFilter.__init__(
            self,
            vPoints = [(0,0),(128,118),(221,215),(255,255)],
            bPoints = [(0,0),(25,21),(122,153),(165,206),(255,255)],
            gPoints = [(0,0),(25,21),(95,102),(181,208),(255,255)],
            rPoints = [(0,0),(41,28),(183,209),(255,255)],
            dtype = dtype)
```

Now, let's go for the cross-processed look!

Emulating cross-processing

Cross-processing produces a strong blue or greenish-blue tint in shadows and a strong yellow or greenish-yellow in highlights. Black and white are not necessarily preserved. Also, the contrast is very high. Cross-processed photos take on a sickly appearance. People look jaundiced, while inanimate objects look stained. Let's edit `filters.py` and add the following implementation of a cross-processing filter:

```python
class BGRCrossProcessCurveFilter(BGRCurveFilter):
    """A filter that applies cross-process-like curves to BGR."""

    def __init__(self, dtype=numpy.uint8):
        BGRCurveFilter.__init__(
            self,
            bPoints = [(0,20),(255,235)],
            gPoints = [(0,0),(56,39),(208,226),(255,255)],
            rPoints = [(0,0),(56,22),(211,255),(255,255)],
            dtype = dtype)
```

Now that we have looked at a few examples of how to implement film emulation filters, we'll wrap up this Appendix so that you can return to the main implementation of the Cameo application in Chapter 3, *Processing Images with OpenCV*.

Summary

Building on the `scipy.interp1d` function, we have implemented a collection of curve filters that are efficient (due to the use of lookup arrays) and easily extensible (due to an object-oriented design). Our work has included special-purpose curve filters that can make digital images look more like film shots. These filters can be readily integrated into an application such as Cameo, as demonstrated by the use of our Portra film emulation filter in Chapter 3, *Processing Images with OpenCV*.

Other Book You May Enjoy

If you enjoyed this book, you may be interested in this other book by Packt:

Hands-On Computer Vision with TensorFlow 2
Benjamin Planche, Eliot Andres

ISBN: 978-1-78883-064-5

- Create your own neural networks from scratch
- Classify images with modern architectures including Inception and ResNet
- Detect and segment objects in images with YOLO, Mask R-CNN, and U-Net
- Tackle problems faced when developing self-driving cars and facial emotion recognition systems
- Boost your application's performance with transfer learning, GANs, and domain adaptation
- Use **recurrent neural networks (RNNs)** for video analysis
- Optimize and deploy your networks on mobile devices and in the browser

Leave a review - let other readers know what you think

Please share your thoughts on this book with others by leaving a review on the site that you bought it from. If you purchased the book from Amazon, please leave us an honest review on this book's Amazon page. This is vital so that other potential readers can see and use your unbiased opinion to make purchasing decisions, we can understand what our customers think about our products, and our authors can see your feedback on the title that they have worked with Packt to create. It will only take a few minutes of your time, but is valuable to other potential customers, our authors, and Packt. Thank you!

Index

1

10-bit images
  converting, to 8-bit 86, 87, 88

3

3D image tracking 250, 252, 253
3D tracking 250
3D tracking algorithm
  about 292
  approaches 291
  improving 291
3D translation 250

6

6 degrees of freedom (6DOF) tracking 250

A

additive models 55
ANN classifier
  training, in multiple epochs 303, 304, 306
ANN's training
  improving 321, 323
ANN-related parameters
  reference link 322
application
  modifying 64, 65, 66, 89, 92
array slicing 33
artificial neural networks (ANNs)
  about 293, 295
  module implementation, for training 310, 312,
    313, 314
  training, in OpenCV 300, 301, 302, 303
  used, for recognizing handwritten digits 308
ASCII keycodes
  reference link 39
augmented reality (AR) 250, 252, 253

B

background subtraction
  about 206
  GMG background subtractor, using 218, 220
  implementing 208, 209, 210, 211
  KNN background subtractor, using 216, 217,
    218
  limitations 206
  MOG background subtractor, using 212, 213,
    214, 215, 216
  other background subtractor 218
  used, for detecting moving objects 206, 207
bag of visual words (BoVW) 182
bag-of-words (BoW)
  about 182, 183
  applying, to computer vision 183, 184
barrel distortion 257
Binary Robust Independent Elementary Features
    (BRIEF) 147
blob 137
blue-green-red (BGR) 27, 54, 223
bounding box 69, 70, 71, 72
BRIEF keypoint descriptor
  ORB, using 145, 146
brute-force 148
brute-force matching 147, 148

C

Caffe
  reference link 324
cameo.Cameo
  applying with 49, 51
Cameo
  about 42
  cameo.Cameo, used for applying 49, 51
  used, for face tracking 41

used, for image manipulation 41
video stream, abstracting with
  managers.CaptureManager 42, 43, 45, 48
window and keyboard, abstracting with
  managers.WindowManager 48, 49
Camera Calibration
  reference link 258
camera frames
  capturing 36, 37, 38
  displaying, in windows 39, 40, 41
camera matrix 255
camera parameters 253, 255, 256, 257, 258
Canny
  used, for edge detection 66, 67, 68
car detector
  training 184, 185, 186, 187, 188, 189, 190,
    191, 192
Carl Vondrick's MIT
  reference link 173
circles
  detecting 75, 77, 78
clustering 184
CMake configuration flags, OpenCV
  reference link 17
codebook 182
color histogram
  about 221
  back-projecting 223, 224, 226
  calculating 223, 224, 226
  cv2.calcBackProject, parameters 227
  cv2.calcHist, parameters 226
color models
  images, converting between 54
colorful objects
  tracking, with CamShift 221, 222
  tracking, with MeanShift 221, 222
confidence score 120
Continuously Adaptive MeanShift (CamShift)
  about 230
  used, for tracking colorful objects 221, 222
  using 231, 232
contour detection
  about 68, 69
  bounding box 69, 70, 71, 72
  convex contours 73

Douglas-Peucker algorithm 73, 74
  minimum area rectangle 69, 70, 71, 72
  minimum enclosing circle 69, 70, 71, 72
convergence 222
convex contours 73, 74
convolution matrix 62
corners 137
count criterion 229
custom kernels 62, 63, 64
cv2.calcBackProject
  parameters 227
cv2.calcHist
  parameters 226
cv2.solvePnPRansac function
  about 258, 261
  arguments 260
  return values 259

D

Darknet
  reference link 324
Debian
  Python, installing on 17, 18
Deep Learning Deployment Toolkit (DLDT)
  reference link 324
deep neural networks (DNNs)
  about 293, 298, 323
  using, from other frameworks in OpenCV 324
demo application
  2D-to-3D spatial conversions, performing 263,
    264, 265
  executing 286, 288, 289, 290
  grayscale conversion, performing 262, 263
  ImageTrackingDemo class, implementing 265
  implementing 261
  modules, importing 261
  testing 286, 288, 289, 290
depth camera
  about 92
  frames, capturing from 83, 85
depth estimation
  with normal camera 92, 93, 94, 96, 97, 98
depth map 83
Difference of Gaussian (DoG) 141, 188
discrete Fourier transform (DFT) 55

discriminant 297
disparity map
  about 83
  mask, crating 88
  mask, creating 89
Distinctive Image Features, from Scale-Invariant
  Keypoints
  reference link 153
distortion coefficients
  about 257
  radical distortion 257
  tangential distortion 257
DoG features
  detecting 140, 141, 142
Douglas-Peucker algorithm 73, 74
DPEx
  about 224
  reference link 224

E

edge detection
  about 60, 61, 62
  with Canny 66, 67, 68
Eigenfaces
  about 119
  used, for performing face recognition 122, 123,
  124
epipolar geometry 93
epsilon criterion 229
error 297

F

face detection, on still image
  performing, with OpenCV 111, 112
face detection, on video
  performing, with OpenCV 113, 115, 116
face detection
  performing, with OpenCV 110
face recognition, algorithms
  Eigenfaces 119
  Fisherfaces 119
  Local Binary Pattern 119
  Principal Component Analysis (PCA) 119
face recognition
  about 119, 120

data, generating 117, 118, 119
  performing 117
  performing, with Eigenfaces 122, 123, 124
  performing, with Fisherfaces 124
  results based, discarding based on confidence
    score 125, 126
  training data, loading 120, 121, 122
  with LBPH 125
faces swapping
  application's loop, modifying 127, 128, 129, 130
  copy operation, masking 130, 131, 132
  in Near-Infrared (NIR) camera 126
faces, with third-party DNNs
  classifying 329, 330, 332, 334, 336
  detecting 329, 330, 332, 334, 336
fast Fourier transform (FFT) package 55
Fast Hessian features
  detecting 143, 144
FAST keypoint detector
  ORB, using 145, 146
Fast Library for Approximate Nearest Neighbors
  (FLANN) 155
  about 155, 157, 158, 159, 160, 186
  reference link 155
feature detection
  defining 137
  types 136
feature matching, methods
  Brute-force matching 137
  FLANN-based matching 137
feature matching
  types 136
features 108
Features from Accelerated Segment Test (FAST)
  146, 147
field of view (FOV) 254
Fisherfaces
  about 119
  used, for performing face recognition 124
FLANN-based matches
  used, for performing homography 160, 161,
  162, 163
focal distance 253
focal length 253
focal plane 253

foreground detection
   GrabCut algorithm, using 99, 100, 101, 103
Fourier Transform
   exploring 55, 56
   high-pass filter (HPF) 56, 57, 58, 59, 60
   low-pass filter (LPF) 56, 57, 58, 59, 60
frames per second (FPS) 266

G

Gaussian Mixture Model (GMM) 99
generator function
   reference link 197
get() method
   reference link 37
Global Minimum with a Guarantee (GMG) 220
GMG background subtractor
   using 218, 220
GrabCut 99
GrabCut algorithm
   used, for foreground detection 99, 100, 101, 103
grayscale 54

H

Haar cascade data
   obtaining 109, 110
Haar cascades
   conceptualizing 108, 109
handwritten digits
   MNIST database 308
   recognizing, with ANN 308
Harris corner detection algorithm 137, 138, 139
high-pass filter (HPF) 56, 57, 58, 59, 60
histogram back-projection 223
HOG descriptors
   about 172, 173
   used, for detecting people 178, 179, 181
   used, to describe image 175
   visualizing 173, 174, 175
HOGgles (HOG goggles) 173
Homebrew
   using, with custom packages 17
   using, with ready-made packages 15, 16
homography
   performing, with FLANN-based matches 160,
161, 162, 163
hue-saturation-value (HSV) 54, 223

I

I/O scripts 26
IEEE
   reference link 222
image data
   accessing, with numpy.array 32, 33, 34
image file
   reading 26, 27, 28, 29
   writing 26, 27, 28, 29
image plane 253
image pyramid 109
image sensor 254
image
   and raw bytes, converting between 29, 30, 31, 32
   converting, between different color models 54
   displaying, in window 38
   segmenting, with Watershed algorithm 103, 104, 105, 106
ImageTrackingDemo class, methods
   __init__ method 266, 268, 269, 270, 271, 273
   _apply_kalman method 283, 284, 285
   _init_kalman_transition_matrix method 279, 280
   run method 274
   track_object method 275, 276, 278
ImageTrackingDemo class
   implementing 265
infrared (IR) 84

J

Jacobian matrix 284

K

k-means clustering 184
k-nearest neighbors (KNN)
   about 152
   used, for filtering matches 151, 153, 154, 155
Kalman filter
   mouse cursor, tracking 234, 235, 237
   post-correction state matrices 279
   pre-correction state matrices 279
   predict phases 233

transition matrix 279
update phases 233
used, for finding trends in motion 232, 233
kernel 56
kernel density tree (kd-tree) 158
keyboard
  abstracting, with managers.WindowManager 48,
  49
keypoint
  anatomy 143
  properties 143
KNN background subtractor
  using 216, 217, 218

L

lens 253
lens parameters 253, 255, 256, 257, 258
lines
  detecting 76, 77
Linux Mint
  Python, installing on 17, 18
Local Binary Pattern 119
local binary pattern histogram (LBPH)
  about 119, 173
  used, for performing face recognition 125
logo
  matching, in images 148, 150, 151
low-pass filter (LPF) 56, 57, 58, 59, 60

M

macOS
  Python, installing on 15
MacPorts 15
magnitude spectrum
  exploring 56
main module
  implementing 315, 317, 318, 319, 320, 321
managers.CaptureManager
  used, for abstracting video 42, 44, 46, 48
managers.WindowManager
  used, for abstracting window and keyboard 48
mask
  creating, from disparity map 88, 89
MeanShift
  example, implementing 228, 229, 230

sample, planning 222, 223
  used, for tracking colorful objects 221, 222
minimal test module
  implementing 315
minimum area rectangle 69, 70, 71, 72
minimum enclosing circle 69, 70, 71, 72
MNIST database
  of handwritten digits 308
  training parameters, selecting 310
MobileNet 325
Modified National Institute of Standards and
    Technology (MNIST)
  reference link 308, 309
modules
  creating 60, 82
MOG background subtractor
  using 212, 213, 214, 215, 216
mouse cursor
  tracking 234, 235, 237
moving objects
  detecting, with background subtraction 206, 207
multi-layer perceptron (MLP) 294, 297, 300
multihead camera 38
mustache distortion 257

N

name mangling 45
near infrared (NIR) 84
Near-Infrared (NIR) camera
  faces swapping 126
neural network
  about 298
  hidden layer 298
  hidden layer size, selecting 299
  input layer 298
  input layer size, selecting 299
  layers 298
  output layer 298
  output layer size, selecting 299
neurons 296, 297
nodes 296
non-maximum suppression (NMS)
  about 67, 176
  approach 176
normal camera

used, for depth estimation 92, 93, 94, 96, 97, 98
NummSquared 2006a0
    reference link 238
NummSquared, formal methods
    reference link 238
NumPy 7
numpy.array
    used, for accessing image data 32, 33

O

object detector
    bag-of-words (BoW) 182, 183
    BoW, applying to computer vision 183, 184
    creating 181
    training 181
object-oriented
    versus functional paradigms 238, 239
objects, with third-party DNNs
    classifying 325, 326, 327
    detecting 325, 326, 327
Ogg Vorbis option 36
ONNX
    reference link 324
Open Model Zoo
    reference link 324
Open Source Computer Vision (OpenCV)
    about 7
    ANN, training 300, 301, 302, 303
    building, from source 11, 12, 14, 19, 20
    DNNs, using from other frameworks 324
    parameters 98
    URL 8, 23
    used, for performing face detection 110
    used, for performing face detection on still image
        111, 112
    used, for performing face detection on video 113
OpenCV 4
    enhancements 9
OpenCV's documentation
    finding 23, 24
OpenCV's help
    finding 23, 24
OpenCV's updates
    finding 23, 24
OpenCV

used, for performing face detection on video
    115, 116
OpenNI 2
    about 7
    URL 11
optical center 253
optical character recognition (OCR) 323
Oriented FAST and Rotated BRIEF (ORB)
    about 136, 172
    used, with BRIEF keypoint descriptor 145, 146
    used, with FAST keypoint detector 145, 146
overfitting 300

P

pedestrian
    application flow, planning 237
    class, implementing 240, 241, 242
    examples 246
    main function, implementing 242, 243, 244,
        245, 246
    object-oriented, versus functional paradigms
        238, 239
    tracking 237
perceptron 297
Perspective-n-Point (PnP) 258
pincushion distortion 257
pip 10
pixel-equivalent units 255
point cloud map 83
preceding
    convex contours 74
predict phases 233
Principal Component Analysis (PCA) 119
priori 296
Python
    about 23
    installing, on Debian 17, 18
    installing, on Linux Mint 17, 18
    installing, on macOS 15
    installing, on Ubuntu 17, 18
    installing, on Unix-like systems 21
    installing, on Windows 10
    setup tools, selecting 9, 10
    setup tools, using 9, 10
    URL 10

R

radial distortion 257
ratio test
  about 153
  used, for filtering matches 151, 153, 154, 155
raw bytes
  and image, converting between 29, 30, 31, 32
ready-made OpenCV package
  using 11, 18
red-green-blue (RGB) 28, 54
region of interest (ROI) 33, 68, 130, 197, 334
regional handwriting variation
  reference link 322
reinforcement learning 296
reprojection error 259
ridge 137
Rodrigues rotation vector 251

S

samples scripts
  executing 22, 23
scale-invariant 109
scale-invariant feature transform (SIFT) 141, 172
SciPy 7
semiglobal block matching 94
shapes
  detecting 75, 78
SIFT descriptors
  extracting 140, 141, 142
Single Shot Detector (SSD) MultiBox 325
speeded-up robust features (SURF) 172
Stanford Cars Dataset
  reference link 185
statistical model 295
stereo imaging 81
stereo vision 93
structure from motion (SfM) 81
subclass 89
subject 253
supervised learning 295
support vector machine (SVM) 177, 178, 246
SURF descriptors
  extracting 143, 144
SVM classifier

car detection, training 194, 195, 196, 197, 199,
  200, 201, 202
combining, with sliding window 193
loading 202
saving 202

T

tangential distortion 257
tattoo forensics
  about 164
  image descriptors, saving to file 164, 165, 166
  matches, scanning 166, 167
TensorFlow
  reference link 324
Torch
  reference link 324

U

Ubuntu
  Python, installing on 17, 18
UIUC dataset
  download link 185
UIUC Image Database, for Car Detection
  reference link 185
units 296
Unix-like systems
  Python, installing on 21
unsupervised learning 296
update phases 233

V

valid depth mask 83
Variante Ascari chicane 141
venv
  reference link 10
video file
  reading 34, 36
  writing 34, 36
Video for Linux (V4L) 19
video stream
  abstracting, with managers.CaptureManager 42,
  43, 45, 47

W

Watershed algorithm
  about 103
  used, for image segmentation 103, 104, 105,
    106
window size 109
window
  abstracting, with managers.WindowManager 48,
    49
  camera frames, displaying 39, 40, 41
  image, displaying 38
Windows
  Python, installing on 10

Z

zoom lens 255

Made in the USA
Middletown, DE
13 July 2023